The Origin of the Right of Fishery in Territorial Waters

LONDON : HUMPHREY MILFORD
OXFORD UNIVERSITY PRESS

THE ORIGIN OF
THE RIGHT OF FISHERY
IN TERRITORIAL WATERS

BY

PERCY THOMAS FENN, JR.

ASSISTANT PROFESSOR OF POLITICAL SCIENCE IN
WASHINGTON UNIVERSITY, ST. LOUIS

CAMBRIDGE
HARVARD UNIVERSITY PRESS
1926

PRINTED AT THE HARVARD UNIVERSITY PRESS
CAMBRIDGE, MASS., U. S. A.

To

MY MOTHER AND FATHER

PREFACE

LEGAL theories concerning maritime jurisdiction of fisheries exist in abundance. They may be found in treaties, in conventions, in diplomacy, in the records of arbitration cases, in the annals of legislation, in the works of the publicists, and in the writings of propagandists. There are books of history and books of law which are the product of a study of this material. But of books dealing with the origins of these theories, there is not one which attempts to cover the whole field. The nearest approach to such a book is the scholarly work of Thomas Wemyss Fulton on *The Sovereignty of the Sea*, published in 1911. But Mr. Fulton is concerned with history and diplomacy. He deals sparingly with legal theory. Those parts of his work which touch this subject are necessarily limited by his major interest, which leads him to give most attention to the controversies on the freedom of the sea which broke out in the opening years of the seventeenth century.

The fundamental ideas expressed in this controversy were not created to meet the exigencies of the moment. They were the result of a long and complex development which had its origin in the life of the ancient world. They are so much the product of their past that they cannot be fully apprehended without a knowledge of their intellectual forebears.

The ideas expressed in this controversy represent the maturity of legal theory on the subject. Continental writers on the same subject, who were relatively aloof from the dispute, show a similar ripeness, and a more sober wisdom, in their theories. It may be fairly said that after 1648 nothing new is added. The year 1648 marks the end of the growth of legal theory on the legal status of the sea. After 1648, controversy became reiteration. Constructive theory became concerned with the work of sifting existing notions, with the work of modification, of correction, and of adjustment.

The period of origins, then, is from the earliest expression of a theory of the legal status of the sea — or a little time before — to

1648, the year of the Treaty of Westphalia, when all the theories concerned with this subject and with maritime jurisdiction of fisheries had reached their maturity, or, at least, their point of extreme development.

Since these all are theories of law, and not of politics, the sources from which the ideas contained therein flow are the law and lawyers, or, more strictly, law books and legal books. It has been necessary to go outside of these sources in the chapter on Germanic Law in order to find any theory at all. In that chapter reliance is placed upon documents which are either royal or imperial grants of privileges which involve marine subjects, or which, in allotting boundaries to grants of territory, involve the sea in one way or another. These documents may be supposed to reflect the customs of the time, and therefore to reflect customary law; for the German tribes were governed chiefly by their customary law until after the Reception. It is only towards the end of the period covered by this study that it is possible to use such sources as diplomatic documents, royal proclamations, and ordinances. These sources are not used because they are not, properly considered, sources of legal theory. They are not doctrinaire statements; they do not set forth the theory of anything. They may reflect law; they may create law; but they are not theoretical expositions of what is or at least ought to be true. The law is one thing. The theory of the law is another. To include them in a study of pure theory — a study which at times enters the field of jurisprudence — would be to adulterate the sources in a manner dangerously to obscure a clear vision of the very theory which is supposed to be illuminated. Much damage can be done to the elucidation of a subject by including in the study of it extraneous matter, the primary significance of which is in other fields, under the mistaken idea that they are sources. The material alluded to finds its place in studies of the political and historical development of that subject the theory of which is investigated here.

Since the present work is a study in a field which has been almost untouched, the present writer has felt it necessary to emphasize, perhaps to overemphasize, his conception of the subject.

The classification of the sources is largely the result of natural grouping. In the two chapters on the Jurisconsults and the Acquisition of Rights of Property in Maritime Fisheries the sources have been consciously arranged in a certain relation to each other. The conclusions reached are necessarily of a tentative character. If they have no other merit than that of providing a starting-point for future investigators in this very interesting field, they will have justified their formulation. These conclusions have been epitomized at the end of Chapter VII, that on maritime fisheries. It may seem strange to find them there instead of at the end of the final chapter; but it is hoped that the logic of their location will make itself apparent.

Most of the writers considered have at least one peculiarity — besides their bad Latin — in common: they state their theories in a remarkably brief and fragmentary form in volumes which are packed with expositions of a great variety of subjects. This is particularly true of the jurisconsults. It does not apply, of course, to the seventeenth-century controversialists. Any one who has views on fisheries or on the freedom of the sea has, by his statement of them, contributed to the formulation of a theory. By sorting them out, and putting together those which approximate with sufficient exactness the same idea, it is possible to obtain a tolerably clear understanding of the various lines of thought which appear. This process is made reasonably sure because an occasional writer will be found who states a particular theory with some detail, and thus exposes the elements of which it is composed.

The attempt has been made to provide both the books and the men with enough of a background to make them intelligible and to give a clue as to the motives influencing them, at the same time avoiding historical disquisitions. Everything has been sacrificed which does not throw into relief the ideas which are the subject of this study.

The manipulation of the footnotes has proved something of a problem. It may be that the method followed has overburdened the text. It was selected as being the least of several evils. The reasons governing this method are two. The first one is that the language of the vast majority of the sources is not only Latin, which is serious enough, but Latin of all shades of quality. It has seemed advisable on this account to provide the reader with the original words of the theorist. The second reason is that nearly all the sources cited are not to be found outside of a few of the great libraries. For this reason they have been quoted with a greater fullness than would have been necessary were they readily available. Translations have not been added (for the most part), not only out of deference to the desire of a reader to see for himself what a given passage actually is, but also because there seemed to be no place to put them, without making the treatment of the subject too cumbersome, burdened as it is with much quotation.

One omission has been made (to the writer's knowledge) concerning which there may be a difference of opinion. Reference is made to the bulls of Alexander VI granting to their Most Catholic Majesties Ferdinand and Isabella of Spain exclusive possession of lands discovered by them in the new world, excepting those which are occupied by some other monarch. These bulls (involving a division of lands between Spain and Portugal) necessitated the drawing of a line of demarcation at sea. They are also one of the bases of the claims put forward by Philip II in his dispute with the States-General at the opening of the seventeenth century, that which called forth Grotius's booklet, *Mare liberum*. The most important reason for not including them is that they do not profess to state a theory, but a fact. Aside from this consideration, they are concerned with the partition of land, and not with the sea. The fact that the line of demarcation was drawn over the sea is of negligible importance. The purpose of the bulls was to partition land with reference to this line. A satisfactory account of the affair may be found in Harisse's *Diplomatic History of America*. Solorzano gives three bulls which seem to be those quoted by Harisse. Cherubini gives the first one only, the bull *Inter cetera*. Solorzano and Cherubini will be found in the bibliography.

The attempt has been made to make that part of the bibliography which is composed of source material exhaustive, although it is realized that this goal has probably not been reached. In order to make the roll as nearly complete as possible, those writers have been included who reached their prime before 1648, even though a given work may have been published in, say, the fifties. On the other hand, those writers who, it was estimated, or known to be a fact, were too young to be productive, have been omitted. Of these there are but two or three. Of the former there are about the same number, or possibly, half a dozen. The secondary works included in the bibliography are those which have played an important part in the make-up of the whole study. Not all of the works cited in the footnotes have been included. Those omitted have been excluded because reference to them in the text, while necessary in the judgment of the present writer, can hardly be said to be indispensable.

ACKNOWLEDGMENTS

The following work was written as a thesis in partial fulfilment of the requirements for the degree of Doctor of Philosophy in Harvard University. I am happy to take this opportunity to acknowledge my debt to Professor Wilson of Harvard University, to whom I am under obligation for the subject, and under whose direction the study was undertaken, for his sympathetic guidance and advice at various stages of the work. Professor McIlwain of Harvard introduced me to the sources of Roman law; suggested to me much essential material; and read for me the chapter on the jurisconsults, in the absence of Professor Wilson. I am more than grateful for his generous coöperation. I am indebted to Dean Pound of the Harvard Law School for tracing for me an obscure reference of critical importance to a passage in Bartolus. I wish also to acknowledge the aid of my friend, Warren Crocker Herrick, in checking and verifying with me the bibliography. The courteous assistance of the staffs of the University libraries has smoothed the labor of procuring desired material throughout the course of this work.

PERCY THOMAS FENN, JR.

CAMBRIDGE, MASS.
AUGUST, 1925

CONTENTS

CHAPTER I

The Period before Justinian

CHAPTER II

The Institutes and the Digest of Justinian

CHAPTER III

The Glossators

CHAPTER IV

Germanic Law

CHAPTER V

The Feudal Law

CHAPTER VI

The Jurisconsults

CHAPTER VII

Acquisition of Rights of Property in Maritime Fisheries

CHAPTER VIII

Mare liberum vs. *Mare clausum*

CHAPTER IX

ABBREVIATIONS

The following abbreviations are used in the text:

G. I. = Institutes of Gaius. G., alone, has the same meaning. The book is cited first, and then the law. Thus, G. 2. 1. signifies the first law of the second book of the Institutes of Gaius.

The same principle is followed in citing from the Corpus Iuris. I. = Institutes; D. = Digest; C. = Code. The figures mean in order, book, title, fragment, section. Thus:

D. 1. 8. 3. = Digest, first book, 8th title, 3rd law or fragment. The fragments are the chief subdivisions of a title. D. 41. 2. 14. 7. = Digest, 41st book, 2nd title, 7th section of the 14th fragment.

The abbreviation, pr., designates the unnumbered portion of a title immediately preceding the first fragment, e.g., D. 1. 8. pr.

I. 2. 1. 5. = the 5th section of the first fragment of the 2nd book of the Institutes of Justinian.

The books of the jurists of the period are usually numbered by page and section; a section may or may not be a paragraph. Thus, Alciatus, ***, p. 251. 44 = page 251, section 44. ii. 251. 44 = book two, etc. If a chapter is given instead of a page, then the figures will read, book II., chapter 251, section 44. An occasional jurist numbers his pages on one side only. If a given section does not appear on the "front" side, it will be at the back, on the obverse side.

In general, the rule governing the arrangement of these figures is from the largest division down to the smallest.

Frequently, more than one book is bound in a volume. If the books are paged consecutively, this is not noted. If they are paged separately, the book is noted.

The Origin of the Right of Fishery in Territorial Waters

CHAPTER I

THE PERIOD BEFORE JUSTINIAN

I. Popular Belief. Non-Roman Practice. Greek Law

The text of the jurist Marcianus, preserved in the Digest of Justinian,[1] is the first formal pronouncement in recorded legal theory on the legal status of the sea and on the right of men to use the sea and its products. It is stated that the sea and its shores are in common to all men. Since Marcianus lived in the early years of the second century of the Christian era, it follows that this doctrine was known in a written form at least as early as the beginning of the second century. Furthermore, since Marcianus belonged to that class of jurisconsults whose official pronouncements were recognized (in general) as being statements of the law and as being binding on the judges calling for them, it follows that the doctrine of the common right of all men to a free use of the sea was a law of the Roman Empire at the beginning of the second century, even though this law was not put in a codified form until the sixth century.

That the statement of this doctrine in the form of law did not mark a break with the theory of the past — in so far as any theory on the subject may be said to have existed — may be gathered by inference from a number of sources. In the first place, there are historical evidences not only that fish was a food staple among the Mediterranean peoples from early times, but also that fish were an important article of commerce with them.[2]

[1] See D. 1. 8. pr. and 1. 8. 1.

[2] Strabo, *Geography*, translated by H. C. Hamilton and W. Falconer, 3 vols., London, 1857; iii, 14 (Strabo, lib. xiv. cap. I. sec. 26, p. 642). He writes: "Next to the mouth of the Cäyster is a lake called Selinusia, formed by the overflowing of the sea. It is succeeded by another, which communicates with this. They afford a large revenue, of which the kings, although it was sacred, deprived the goddess, but the Romans restored it; then the tax-gatherers seized upon the tribute by force, and converted it to their own use. Artemidorous, who was sent on an embassy to

The Athenian and the Roman states derived income from their fisheries.[1]

It does not necessarily follow, however, that because the exploitation of sea fisheries was a profitable industry and form of

Rome, as he says, recovered possession of the lakes for the goddess. . . ." Strabo mentions two cities with establishments for salting fish (iii. 1. 6–9). He makes reference to the "goodly products of the sea" (iii. 2. 6–8), and includes oysters among the edible fish. For these references, see *Strabo*, translated by H. L. Jones, 8 vols., London and New York, 1923, ii, 15; 35–38; 183; 191. In speaking of Libya Strabo says that its coastline affords only a moderate sustenance to the inhabitants; he refers to "Gedrosia where the Fish-Eaters live" (ii. 5. 33) Jones, *ibid.*, i, 501.

A. Böckh, *Die Staatshaltung der Athener*, 2d ed., 4 vols., Berlin, 1851, dealing with the interval between the Persian War and the time of Alexander, while considering the food of the Athenians, says (i, 145), "Eingesalzenes, besonders Fische, wurde aus dem Pontus, Phrygien, Agyptien, Sardinien und Cadix weit verführt, und war zu Athen in Menge vorhanden, aber von verschiedener Güter."

[1] See the references in Strabo cited above.

Plutarch's *Lives*, The Translation called Dryden's, corrected from the Greek and revised by A. H. Clough, 5 vols., London, 1859: *Poplicola*, in i, 214. Plutarch records that Publius Valerius designated the Temple of Saturn for the public treasury, and granted to the people the liberty of choosing two young men to act as quaestors or treasurers.

Livy, ii. 9. 30 writes of "portoriis . . . et tributo plebes liberata (by the senate), ut divites conferrent, qui oneri ferendo essent."

Ulpian, D. 50. 16. 17. 1, makes an oblique reference to this: " 'Publica' vectigalia intellegere debemus, ut quibus vectigal fiscus capit: quale est vectigal portus vel venalium rerum, item salinarum et metallorum et piscariarum."

Böckh, *op. cit.*, i, 414, states that part of the property of the Athenian state consisted of Meeresgewasser, and, in Note c, says, "Die Attische Tempelbehörde von Delos verpachtet Meeresgewasser, seies in Rücksicht des Salzgewinnes oder der Fischerei," and adds that both in Asia (citing Strabo xiv. 642) and Byzantium the state owned salt (or sea) water.

Charles Maynz, *Cours de Droit Romain*, 4th ed., 3 vols. (Bruxelles, 1876), i, 145, says that "Le république recevait en outres les amendes encourues par . . . le produit des droits de port et douane, des salines, des pêcheries publiques et des mines." He is writing of the Roman Republic. He adds, in Note 13, "Les droits de ports, *portoria*, abolis la seconde année de la republique, furent rétablis vers le milieu du sixième siècle; abolis de nouveau par une loi Caecilia, en 692; enfin, de nouveau rétablis par Jules César." He proceeds, in Note 14, as follows: "L'Etat prit d'abord le monopole des salines pour que le peuple pût se procurer le sel à bon marché; mais on ne tarda pas à en faire surtout une source de bénéfices, qui cependant disparut vers la fin de la république. Dans les provinces, la république exercait souvent aussi ce monopole."

Dionysii Halicarnassensis, *Operum volumen quintum*, curavit Io. Iac. Reiske, Lipsiae, 1774–1777, vol. v, *De Lysia Iudicium*, p. 522: "Scitis autem, imperium esse eorum, qui mari dominantur pecuniarum dispensatorem esse Regem; Grae-

commerce, and that the Mediterranean states derived income therefrom, that the sea was held to be free to the common use of all men. That such was the general opinion is rendered probable partly from the fact that no records have been preserved of any legal doctrine of a *mare clausum;* or of a claim to dominion over the sea or a part thereof on the ground that the waters are adjacent to the territory of the state or government setting up the claim,[1] or for any other reason; and finally, that there were claims to the right to exercise jurisdiction over some part of the sea, or to possess the *imperium;* yet this claim was not expanded into a claim involving any sort of property right in the sea itself; the claim to *imperium* was not developed into a claim to *dominium*. Beyond this, positive evidence exists that, in the opinion of men generally, at least during the period of Roman greatness — in other words, when Rome was in a position to assert effectively the opposite position — the sea, and the fish in it, were open or common to all men, for their use, as to the sea, or for their appropriation, as to the fish. The works of Cicero,[2] Seneca,[3]

corum vero corpora eorum, qui consumi et deleri possunt. Naves ipse multas possidet, multas etiam Siciliae tyrannus." Naval dominance in the Mediterranean undoubtedly carried *imperium* with it; this point will receive consideration below. After making due allowance for the political theory of the eighteenth century, the observation of d'Halicarnasse remains sound.

Aristotle, *Oeconomica*, translated by E. S. Forster (Oxford, 1920), ii. 2. 1346b, is writing of "the Byzantines being in need of money." He says, "To the associations they sold other lands, *viz.*, the public lands around the gynmasium, or the market-place, or the harbour . . . and they gave the rights over the sea-fisheries and the sale of salt. . . ."

[1] Polybius, *The Histories*, translated by W. R. Paton, 6 vols. (London and New York), 1922, i, 9, in referring to Rome, writes of the "enterprise which has made them (the Romans) lords over our land and our seas." After the overthrow of Carthage, the Romans were, of course, the dominant naval power in the Mediterranean. It would, we think, be erroneous to read into this phrase of Polybius any right of property or right of sovereignty.

[2] *Pro Sex. Roscio Amerino*, 26. 11. "Etenim quid tam est commune quam spiritus vivis, terra mortuis, mare fluctuantibus, litus eiectis?" Note also, *De Officiis*, i. 7. 21.

[3] *De Beneficiis*, 4. 28. 4. "Deus quoque quaedam munera in universum humani generi dedit, a quibus excluditur nemo. Nec enim poterat fieri, ut ventus bonis viris secundus esset, contrarius malis: commune autem bonum erat, patere commercium maris et regnum humani generis relaxari."

Paulus,[1] and Ovid [2] express this belief as being a matter of common opinion shared by all men.

Whether these sea fisheries were located in harbors, or close to the shore-line, or out at sea, is a question without significance, for the reason that there was no *extension* of state jurisdiction seaward. But it seems reasonable to suppose, taking into consideration the character of the thought of the time, that the state-owned fisheries were located only a short distance off shore.

From the beginning there seems to have been exercised extensive jurisdiction by the maritime powers over their seamen, over their sea-borne commerce, over the ships flying the national flag, and over the relations, business and personal, between their merchants and seamen. The maritime laws of Rhodes are the earliest laws of this sort, record of which has been preserved. Both the Greeks and the Latins adopted them for the regulation and control of their navigation and sea-borne commerce.[3] Tiberius ordered them to be codified, and the resulting work received the approval or sanction of several of his successors.[4] The collection which has been preserved is a reconstruction, and is the body of law used by the Romans after Tiberius.[5] It is concerned with

[1] *Rudens*, 4. 3. 33. GR. — "Ecquem esse dices in mari piscem meum? Quos quom capio, siquidem cepi, mei sunt; habeo pro meis. Nec manu adseruntur neque illinc partem quisquam postulat. In foro palam omnis vendo pro meis venalibus. Mare quidem commune certost omnibus."

[2] *Metamorphoseon*, 6. 349. "Quid prohibetis aquis? usus communis aquaram Nec Solem proprium Natura, nec aera fecit. Nec tenues undas."

[3] D'O. Dapper, *Description exacte des Isles de L'Archipel. Traduite du Flamand* (Amsterdam, 1703), p. 146. Changes in the Rhodian laws were made from time to time by both the Athenian and Roman states to meet particular requirements.

[4] M. L. Lacroix, *Isles de la Grèce*, (Paris, 1881), p. 139: "On retrouve en grande partie ces réglements sur le commerce et la navigation dans les compilations des jurisconsultes romains et dans les édits et ordonnances des empereurs. . . . C'est en puisant à ces sources que le savant Leunclavius est parvenu à reconstruire le code commercial et maritime des Rhodiens, dont il a donne un recueil divisé en cinquante et un chapitres, la plupart extraits des onze livres du Digeste." For Leunclavius, or Löwenklau, himself, see R. Stintzing, *Geschichte der Deutschen Rechtswissenschaft*, 2 vols. (München & Leipzig, 1880–1884), i, 239 and Note 1.

[5] Leunclavius has incorporated his reconstruction of these laws in two works. The first one is entitled *Ioan. Leunclavium, LX Librorum*, Basilikon [Greek lettering], *id est, Universi iuris Romani*, Basileae, 1575. The other, *Iohannes Leunclavii Iuris Graeco-Romani*, Francofurti, 1596. At end of each volume.

matters of the kind specified above; there is no fishery legislation contained in it.

In Telfy's *Corpus Iuris Attici*[1] there are two laws dealing directly with fish, but neither one is of more than domestic interest. The first forbids fishing for certain kinds of sea fish which are sacred to Ceres and Proserpine, save by the priests of those goddesses. The other deals with fish which are on sale in the market place, and is aimed against misrepresentation by the merchant of the quality of the fish. Two sections are given to marine affairs, one outlining the duties of the governmental authorities, and the other, *de mercatoribus*.

Thus the maritime legislation of the Greeks, as it has been preserved in the works of Leunclavius and Telfy, show an absence of a legal doctrine as to the status of the sea or as to the right of men to appropriate the products thereof. The exercise of maritime jurisdiction carried with it no implication of a right by a state to appropriate the sea, or to restrict the right of access to it. In other words, a claim to jurisdiction did not and could not involve a claim to ownership. The status of ports and navigable rivers differed from the status of the sea; these seem to have been considered as the property of the state; yet they remained open to all men. Greek jurisprudence had no place in it for a thoroughgoing division of things such as was made by the fully developed Roman law. There was no classification of *res* into all possible kinds; nor were there analogues to the Roman *res communes*,[2] in which class was placed the sea. The Greek jurist studied things solely in their relationships to men, with the purpose of determining the rights of which they could be the objects.[3] The term, thing, comprehended both animate and inanimate objects, including those of juridical creation, as did the word in Roman law. But the Greek did not possess a complete system.

[1] I. B. Telfy, *Corpus Iuris Attici, Graece et Latine, e fontibus composuit* (Pestini et Lipsiae, 1868), p. 98. Cap. V. *De Sacris*, 396. "Solis sacerdotibus licet pisces capere ex alveis, qui Rhiti appellantur, quique Cereri ac Proserpinae sacra sunt." Page 397: "Piscium venditoribus ne liceat amplius aridos pisces rigare." On marine affairs, p. 78, sec. V., and p. 301, Part X.

[2] On this whole subject see L. Beauchet, *Histoire du Droit Privé de la République Athénienne*, 4 vols. (Paris, 1897), iii, *passim*.

[3] Beauchet, *op. cit.*, p. 3.

That the Greek and Roman systems should be able to start from an almost identical conception of a thing, of *Res*, and yet develop along lines which, so far as their treatment of the sea and of sea fishing are concerned (with other differences this study is not concerned) are not the same, is explainable by the lack in Greek jurisprudence of an expression equivalent to that of the right of property. There is an absence, that is to say, of words equivalent to the Roman *dominium* and *proprietas*.[1] There was not, of course, an absence of the right of private property, or of state, community, or corporate property. What was missing was the legal content, so to say, of the Roman *dominium* and *proprietas*.

Like the Romans, the Greeks knew of a "natural" method of acquiring property. Aristotle writes that it is Nature's part "to supply her offspring with food"; and that the "natural riches of all men arise from fruits and animals."[2] Among the natural means of acquiring food are hunting and fishing.[3] It would be also natural for men to look upon the sea as a source of food, and to regard it as incapable, by its nature, of appropriation by any man or body of men. The fish or animals thus captured (by hunting or fishing) would be regarded as belonging to the captor. If they escaped, they would become free, and could be recaptured. They were, in fact, *res nullius*,[4] even if the law provided no niche to contain them.

[1] Beauchet, *op. cit.*, pp. 52, 53. "(L)a langue grecque ne paraît pas avoir d'expression juridique pour désigner ce droit (de propriété). Il vaut donc mieux reconnaître l'absence dans le droit hellénique d'expressions analogues au dominium ou a la proprietas des Romans. . . ."

[2] *A Treatise on Government*, translated from the Greek of Aristotle by W. Ellis, No. 605, Everyman's Library (New York, 1919), p. 19. (*Politics*.)

[3] *Politics*, p. 13. Beauchet, *op cit.*, p. 109. "Quant à la pêche, elle ne peut être au mode légal d'acquisition par voie d'occupation que dans la mer, les fleuves et les rivières, mais non dans les eaux appartenant à des particuliers, comme les étangs."

[4] Beauchet, *op. cit.*, pp. 108, 109 for the acquisition of private property. "Il est vrai que les anciens n'ont pas été portés à croire, comme les modernes, que les droits de propriété derivé de l'occupation et du travail . . . ce fut la religion qui, en Grèce, servit de principal fondement à la propriété foncière. . . . Neanmoins il y avait toujours des choses nullius, ne fut-ce que le gibier et le poisson, et dès lors l'occupation restait le mode normal d'acquerir cette espèce de choses." Thus, though the Greek jurisconsults make no allusion to this manner of acquisition, it

II. Roman Law before Gaius. The Theodosian Code

The earliest Roman laws of which records have been preserved, those of the Twelve Tables, are silent on the status of the sea; nor is reference made to any sort of fishery.[1] With due consideration for the character and purpose of the Twelve Tables as furnishing a cause for this silence, it remains, we think, unlikely that there was a legal theory on the subject at the time of the promulgation of this body of law, the middle of the fifth century before Christ.

The next great body of law which has come down to the present day is likewise silent on this subject. The compilation of the *Edictum Perpetuum* as it is known to-day, was made by an eminent jurisconsult of the time of Hadrian, 117–138, named Salvius Julianus, who possessed the rank of praetor.[2] His collection seems to have been ordered by the Emperor and to have received the sanction of a *senatusconsultum*.[3] It contains edicts relating to maritime commerce and to navigation,[4] of the usual sort, though nothing bearing on the maritime jurisdiction of fisheries. It may be observed that the body of law included in this compilation has grown in fullness and detail since the promulgation of the Twelve Tables. *Res publicae, res religiosae, sanctae,* and *sacrae* are provided for.[5]

A source of law outside the stream of edicts and codes attained importance from the second century on. The work of the great lawyers or jurisconsults was regarded as a part of the law of the

existed, and the silence is explainable, in the domain of legal theory with which we are concerned.

[1] Table X has a number of provisions "de iure sacro." IX treats "de iure publico." They were promulgated in the 303d year of Rome. For an account of their formation, with a reconstruction of the text, see Ortolan, *Explication historique des Instituts de l'Empereur Justinien*, 8th ed., 3 vols. (Paris, 1870), i, 102.

[2] Ortolan, *ibid.*, p. 304.

[3] *Ibid.*, p. 305.

[4] Provisions respecting sailors are to be found in Title XI, sec. 49; XV, 78; XXIII, 136. See O. Lenel, *Das Edictum Perpetuum*, Zweite Auflage, Leipzig, 1907 pp. 126 and 322.

[5] Title XVI, secs. 91, 92, 93, 94; XLIII, 235, 236, 237, 238, 239, 240 (Lenel, *op. cit.*, pp. 442, 443), 241, 242, 243, 244. XLIV, 273, deals with prescription. Of this, Lenel says, p. 485 "Der praescriptio longi temporis begegnen wir in den Ediktkommentaren nicht. Ihre frühesten Spuren gehen nicht über die Zeit der Severe zurück. Sie ist ohne Zweifel postediktal."

empire. Justinian's Digest, as is well known, is a compilation of fragments from the works of men of this class. A portion of the writings of Paul, Gaius and Ulpian, in addition to that which appears in the Digest, has been preserved. The work of Gaius will be considered in detail below, in another connection. In none of that portion of their work that has not been incorporated in the Digest is there a treatment of the status of the sea in law, or of the maritime jurisdiction of fisheries.[1] Paul and Ulpian lived under the Emperor Caracalla at the end of the first century; Gaius's work was done early in the second century.[2]

After the *Edictum Perpetuum*, the next great body of codified law is the Theodosian Code, which was promulgated in the East and in the West in 438. The Code of Justinian was promulgated in 529. Neither code contains a direct pronouncement upon the subject of a common right of fishing, or upon the sea as open to the free use of every man. Both codes contain edicts relating to maritime commerce and navigation. Nearly every edict which appears in the Theodosian Code upon these subjects reappears either in substance or verbatim in the Code of Justinian.[3] It would

[1] The *Sententia* of Paul and the *Fragments* of Ulpian are to be found in *Ulpiani Liber Singularis Regularum, Pauli Libri Quinque Sententiarum. Fragmenta Minora Saeculorum* P. Chr. N. Secundi et Tertii, edidit Paulus Krueger, Berolini, 1878; also in Ph. Eduardus Huschke, *Iurisprudentiae Anteiustinianae Quae Supersunt*, 4th ed., Lipsiae, 1879. Paul has a sentence on the *lex Rhodia*, ii. 7, and two on fishing apparatus, iii. 6. 41 and iii. 6. 66. Paul has something to say concerning the boundary of the seashore, a subject which will receive further consideration. He writes, Huschke, *op. cit.*, p. 18: "Solebat igitur Aquillius, collega et familiaris meus, quum de litoribus ageretur, quae omnia publica esse vultis, quarentibus iis, ad quos id pertinebat, quid esset litus, ita definire: 'qua fluctus eluderet.'"

[2] Ortolan, *op. cit.*, i, 690–691; 341.

[3] For the Theodosian Code see Krueger and Mommsen, *Theodosiani Libri XVI cum constitutionibus Sirmondianis*, 2 vols., *Berolini*, 1905. For the Code of Justinian, see Paulus Krueger, *Codex Iustinianus, Berolini*, 1877. The former will be cited here as T. C., the latter as J. C. The edicts referred to in the text are as follows: T. C. vii. 16; vii. 16. 2; vii. 16. 3, which reappears in J. C. xii. 44. T. C. xiii. 6 and and J. C. xi. 3. T. C. xiii. 7. 1; xiii. 7. 2, and J. C. xi. 4. 1. J. C. xi. 4. 2. T. C. xiv. 20. T. C. xiv. 21. 1 and J. C. xi. 27. T. C. xiii. 6. 1–10 and J. C. xi. 3. 1–3. In vol. ii of Krueger and Mommsen, entitled, *Leges Novellae ad Theodosianum pertinentes*, is vii. 4. 8. All of these edicts are dated in the 4th and 5th centuries. T. C. v. 20. 1. concerns the value of custom as a source of law. Edicts to the same effect, J. C. viii. 52.

seem reasonable to conclude that this class of law had become settled through the action of experience and practice.

Thus the Roman law outside of the Digest, before the work of compilation undertaken by the order of the Emperor Justinian, is as silent as the Greek law upon the subject of the status of the sea and upon that of the maritime jurisdiction of fisheries. But unlike the situation in respect to Greek jurisprudence, we know that there were statements of the law in regard to these points, for they have been preserved in the Digest; and it is known that they date from the second century.

While the result of the foregoing investigation is perhaps on the whole negative, certain conclusions may be drawn without doing violence to the evidence. There is no trace of a break in the continuity of juristic thought regarding the sea and sea fisheries. Consequently, when a second century statement occurs that the sea is common to all by the law of nature, the presumption would seem to be that this statement is one of a recognized fact. This presumption is strengthened by the evidence of such a belief in public opinion. It is noteworthy that this belief finds expression in the writings of Cicero, for, if he was not a creative thinker, he was a great advocate with a gift for stating clearly what common belief held to be true.

The ownership of sea fisheries by a state does not necessarily conflict with this position, nor does the ownership of *Meeresgewasser*, whether the purpose of such ownership was the exploitation of a fishery or for the procuring of salt. The only case mentioned by name is that of the Temple at Delos. This should, we think, be taken in connection with the ownership by the state of its harbors or ports and of its navigable rivers.

The jurisdiction of a state over its harbors and rivers was based upon ownership of them; yet they remained *res publicae*, and open as of right to all men. Jurisdiction over the sea by one power alone seems to have been based upon naval supremacy, with no implication of ownership or of a right potential or actual of appropriation. There is nothing to indicate an exercise of jurisdiction beyond the enforcement of police measures.

Finally it may be noted that Greek jurisprudence was acquainted with *res nullius*, and that fish in their natural state belonged in this class.

III. The Institutes of Gaius

The similarity between the Greek and Roman concepts of *res* has been observed. The word is used in Roman law to designate that which is capable of becoming the object of rights. In general, all those things which man feels to be required either for his pleasure or for his needs are placed within the meaning or scope of this term.[1] While this definition may not be given by the Roman jurists, it is apparent that the concept thus expressed was present to their minds;

> leur esprit s'est d'abord porté sous le nom des choses (res), sur les objets corporels qui, pouvant etre d'une utilité quelconque à l'homme, peuvent faire pour lui l'objet d'un droit.

In practice, the jurists did not confine themselves strictly to this classification, for they extended the meaning to cover abstractions — to things which were juridical creations.[2]

It will have been observed that reference has been made to certain primitive and not inclusive divisions of things in the ancient law. The classification of things adopted by Gaius in his *Institutes* is the most detailed up to his time, and is of course the direct forerunner of the classification which appears in the law books of Justinian, a classification which is at once intricate, elaborate, and confused.

The divisions stated by Gaius are broadly sketched and are given in summary fashion. Not all of the terms used in the law books of Justinian are known to him. He first states that things are divided into two classes, that is, into *res in nostro patrimonio*, and into *res extra nostrum patrimonium*.[3] The next great division is likewise divided into two classes, *res divini iuris* and *res humani iuris*. This second great division is independent of the first; the two are disparate, and on a parity. Gaius is using concepts which were not accurately defined in his day. Consequently his terminology is confused. He is unable strictly to maintain this sys-

1 Ortolan, *op. cit.*, i, p. 595.

2 *Ibid.*, p. 596.

3 Gaius, *Institutes*, 2. 1. (G. 2. 1.)

tem of independent classification. *Res sanctae*, for example, which naturally fall in the class of *res extra patrimonium*, may also be *res in patrimonio* if the state acts as trustee. *Res publicae*, while generally *res extra patrimonium*, may include *res in patrimonio*.

The tabulation of the second great division follows:[1]

I. *Res divini iuris.*

1. *Res sacrae.* Belonging to the gods above.
2. *Res religiosae.* Belonging to the gods below.
3. *Res sanctae.* Under divine law to a certain extent.

The *res* of Class I are all *nullius in bonis.*

II. *Res humani iuris.*

1. *Res publicae.* *Nullius in bonis* so far as individuals are concerned, but belonging to the corporate body considered as a unit.
2. *Res privatae.* Belonging to individuals. *Res singulorum.*

The *res* of this class are *res alicuius in bonis.*

[1] Abdy and Walker, *Commentaries of Gaius and Rules of Ulpian* (Cambridge, 1874), p. 71, Note 1, give the following table as the scheme of Gaius's classification:

<table>
<tr><td>A. In Patrimonio—res singulorum. Inapplicable to this subject.
B. Extra Patrimonium.—(1) Res communes. Of which the use is common to all the world; the proprietas belongs to none.
(2) Res publicae. Of which the use is common to all the members of a unit, e. g., state. The proprietas is in the unit. (A. & W. say "state," not, "unit."
(3) Res Universitatis. The use of which may or may not be in the members of the corporations; but no non-member may use. The proprietas is in the corporation.</td><td>HUMANI</td><td rowspan="2">IURIS</td></tr>
<tr><td>(4) Things consecrated.
(a) Res Santae.
(b) Res religiosae
(c) Res sacrae.</td><td>DIVINI</td></tr>
</table>

By the time of Justinian, the distinction between *res corporales* and *res incorporales* had lost its importance. See Bonjean, *Explication Methodique des Instituts de Justinien*, 2 vols. (Paris, 1878–1880), i, 413. The classification of *res mancipi* and *res nec mancipi* had been suppressed. *Ibid.*, p. 409. The pagan institutions behind the distinction between *res iuris divini* and *res iuris humani* had disappeared. *Ibid.*, p. 404.

According to this classification, there are but two kinds of things *humani iuris*, namely, things public, and things private. *Res communes* do not appear.

Gaius names other classes of things, which do not touch the problem of the status of the sea, as, *res corporales* and their opposites, *res incorporales; res mancipi* and *res nec mancipi*.

Gaius's point of view seems sufficiently clear from this partial analysis. Of the grand division of things into those *in patrimonio* and those *extra patrimonium*, little need be said. The first class eliminates itself.[1] *Res communes* would properly belong in the second. *Res publicae* occur in both. Under *res publicae extra patrimonium* are included all things belonging to the community and used by the members thereof, as, for example, public rivers.

Things, says Gaius in the second book of his *Institutes*,[2] are either subject to private dominion, or are incapable of being so subjected. The division of things which he makes is one of *ius:* some things are *divini iuris*, some, *humani iuris*.[3] The wording of the *Institutes* of Justinian parallels that of Gaius up to the point where he makes this division of things according to their relationship to divine or human law. Instead of this division, the *Institutes* of Justinian has a passage beginning, *quaedam enim naturali iure communia sunt omnium, quaedam publica, quaedam universitatis*, and the nature of *res communes* is developed.[4] Then, according to Gaius, those things which are of human law

[1] The principal headings are (as to modes of acquisition):

- I. Natural modes.
  - 1. Occupation.
  - 2. Accession.
    - (*a*) Natural.
    - (*b*) Industrial.
    - (*c*) Mixed.
  - 3. Tradition.
- II. Civil modes.
  - 1. Universal.
  - 2. Singular.

This table is given in full by Abdy and Walker, *Institutes of Justinian* (Cambridge, 1874), pp. 438, 439.

[2] E. Poste, *Gaii Institutionum Iuris Civilis Commentarii quattuor*, 3d ed. (Oxford, 1890), p. 153. G. 2. 1.

[3] G. 2. 2.

[4] J. 2. 1. pr.

are either public or private.[1] Those which are public are not owned by any individual, but by the body politic; those which are private are those owned by individuals.[2,3] *Res communes* can not appear in this classification, for they have no owner, either public or private.

All things within the territory of a state are subject to its dominion in a general sense, and are, in a sense equally loose, *res publicae*.[4] Those things which are properly *res publicae* fall into two classes: first, things affected with a public character by reason of a public use, such as navigable rivers, roads, and ports; secondly, things (or goods) belonging to the state, such as slaves, houses, territory, which have been conquered from the enemy. Things of the first class can not be alienated. Things of the second class may be. Things of the first class are *extra patrimonium;* things of the second class are in *patrimonio*.[5]

In both cases, however, ownership is vested in the state. It is this characteristic which makes of these things *res publicae*. Conversely, things the ownership of which is vested in individuals are properly *res privatae*.

Res communes are present in Gaius in an undeveloped form.[6] These things are incapable of becoming the object of private property, by natural law. They may be used by everyone under the *ius gentium*.

Gaius also seems to know of a class of *res nullius humani iuris*, of things which may be appropriated, but which are for the time

[1] G. 2. 10.

[2] G. 2. 11.

[3] Before the investigations of Studemund, the passage, G. 2. 11, was reproduced in the editions as a conjectural reading. Since and as the result of his work, the passage has been verified. J. B. E. Boulet (1827), C. A. C. Klenze and E. Boecking (1829), J. F. L. Groeschen and C. Lachmann (1842), E. Boecking (1866), G. Studemund (1874), Abdy and Walker (1874), Krueger and Studemund (1877, 1899, 1905), E. Huschke (4th ed., 1879), J. Muirhead (1880), Poste (3d ed., 1890) may be consulted.

[4] Poste, *op. cit.*, p. 153.

[5] Bonjean, *op. cit.*, i, 411; Ortolan, *op. cit.*, i, 608. Poste, p. 153, points out the fact that the kind of dominion exercised by the state is not known to the civil law, because the state has no political superior, and is not restrained by the positive law of any superior. It may perhaps be noted that dominion is not used as the English equivalent of *dominium*.

[6] See Poste, *op. cit.*, pp. 162, 163.

being without an owner.[1] Whether these things belong *in nostro patrimonio*, since they come under private ownership if and when they are possessed and appropriated, or whether they belong in the class of things *extra nostrum patrimonium*, since, like the *res communiae omnium*, they have, in their original state, no owner, is open to conjecture. Wild beasts, birds and fish are within this class. They are *res nullius*. If and when they are captured, they are understood to be the property of the captor while they are within his power of control. Release, or escape from the power of the captor, brings with it a return to natural liberty unless and until they are either recaptured at once or captured again at some other time.

[1] G. 2. 66. This passage is, unfortunately, partly illegible. For reconstructions of it, see J. Muirhead, *Institutes of Gaius and Rules of Ulpian*, Edinburgh, 1880, p. 94. E. Böcking, *Gaii Institutionum*, Ph. E. Huschke, *Beiträge*, Krüger and Studemund, *Gaii Institutiones*, may be compared. Compare also 2. 9.

CHAPTER II

THE INSTITUTES AND THE DIGEST OF JUSTINIAN

I. Method of Approach

The scheme of classification laid down by Gaius, who, of course, in his time had been building on already existing foundations, was taken over by Justinian's jurists. These men modified it and amplified it — in short, they brought it up to date, brought it, that is, up to the middle of the sixth century. The chief grand division of things is that composed of the two classes, *res in nostro patrimonio*, and *res extra nostrum patrimonium*. Concern here is with the latter of the two classes.

One of the subdivisions of this class is comprised of the *res nullius*. *Res nullius* may be either *divini iuris* or *humani iuris;* it is the latter only, *res humani iuris*, which need be considered. Within the *res nullius humani iuris* is a class of things which are *res communes*. And one of the things composing this class is *mare*, the sea.

The class of things called *res communes* is endowed with its own proper rights and obligations. The sea, as a member of this class, shares in them. For example, the sea is open to the use of all men *iure naturale*, and is owned by none. The *ius piscandi* is derived from the status of the sea, and has its own rights and obligations. Thus the sea and sea fisheries are expressly given a definite place in the Roman law of the Institutes and the Digest. And this expression is but the recognition of a prevailing belief, the roots of which are sunk in the distant past.

The place occupied by *res communes* in the fabric of the law is one of distinctly minor importance, compared to those which present opportunities for litigation by reason of their involving questions in one form or another relating to property. *Res com-*

munes fill but a niche in the highly complicated[1] organization of the legal system.

It would be possible to pluck the class of *res communes* out of its place in the structure which contains it, and then to study it *in vacuo*, so nicely is the whole fabric articulated. By using this method one could substantiate the statements made in the two preceding paragraphs of this section. There would be lost, however, that information which a study of the whole system is able to give to a study of any part of it. A second method which could be used is the tabulation of the entire division of *res extra patrimonium*. This method would indeed orientate the class of *res communes* in which the sea falls. Yet it seems to be over-elaborate for the use to be made of it. It does not seem necessary to construct so huge a skeleton in order to discover the function and meaning of this particular joint. This method also suffers from the disadvantage which inheres in the construction of any skeleton without the accompanying tissue. To add this tissue would mean the writing of a treatise on Roman law. The remaining method, and the one which is applied here, is to start with the most inclusive classification, and then to work down through those subdivisions which lead ultimately to the *res communes*, omitting a consideration of those subdivisions which lead elsewhere, although this may involve certain preliminary remarks of a general character which traverse familiar ground.

II. The Significance of Res Communes in the Legal Structure

Rights *in rem* are those which are correlative to that class of duties which bind all men generally.[2] This class of duties is negative in character; that is to say, the duties of which it is composed enjoin forbearance. Duties to forbear bind all men generally. Therefore, rights *in rem* are correlative to negative duties. These

[1] It is not difficult to make complex divisions of *res*. The latent possibilities of classification in the mature Roman law are visible in a table compiled by Ortolan, *op. cit.*, pp. 595–609.

[2] W. A. Hunter, *A Systematic and Historical Exposition of Roman Law in the Order of a Code* (London, 1876), p. ix. The statement is, of course, of rights and duties in Roman law.

rights fall into three classes. The first class is composed of those rights which a freeman has in respect of his personality. The second class is made up of rights which he has over persons belonging to him. In the third class are the rights which he has in respect to things and animals.[1]

This third class contains a group of property rights in the widest sense of the term.[2] It is divided into two subclasses: first, that of independent rights, that is, rights created for their own sake; secondly, dependent rights, that is, rights created to give security for debts.[3]

The class of independent rights is the significant class for the purpose of arriving at the position occupied by the sea in the general scheme of classification. This class has several subdivisions. A single division is composed of the rights of absolute ownership.[4] Within this class is the Roman *dominium*. This word, *dominium*, "taken with its strict sense, . . . denotes a right, indefinite in point of user — unrestricted in point of disposition — and unlimited in point of duration — over a determinate thing." [5]

There are two classes of things over which one may have rights of ownership such as have been defined, namely, things moveable and things immoveable. These rights of ownership are, briefly, two: the right to the exclusive use of the thing, and the right to alienate it.[6] And these two are generally combined in Roman law.[7] Further, and in regard to immovables (which are, naturally, such things as land and objects permanently affixed thereto), the rights of the owner have a twofold character: they are made up of his rights against all men generally, and his rights against an adjoining proprietor or proprietors.[8] There may be, therefore, a conflict arising from the interaction of the rights of owners of conterminous immoveables.[9]

[1] W. A. Hunter, *op. cit.*, p. xi. [2] *Ibid.*, p. xii. [3] *Ibid.*, p. xx. [4] *Ibid.*

[5] Austin, *Lectures on Jurisprudence*, ed. by R. Campbell, 3d ed., 2 vols. (London, 1869), ii, pp. 817, 818.

[6] Hunter, *op. cit.*, p. 85, [7] *Ibid.* [8] *Ibid.*, pp. xx, 103.

[9] *Ibid.*, p. 107. See also, pp. 103, 105, 108, 109.

It will be observed that I am indebted to Hunter for the whole of the above exposition, just as I am indebted to Ortolan for my definition of the concept of *Res* in Roman jurisprudence.

In contrast to the immovable things which have owners are the immovable things which have no owners. The first thing which is evident is, that a *res* which has no owner may or may not be capable of having one; that is, the *res* may or may not be capable of appropriation. If a thing is incapable of appropriation, that is, if it is incapable of becoming the object of private property, then its free condition is permanent. There are certain things which, by their nature, are so incapable, and are therefore in a permanently free condition. It is their nature or character which has caused this condition. The law may be said to recognize this character, when it lays down the doctrine of which mention has been made, namely, that the sea is common to all by the law of nature. There are other things which are also without an owner, but the nature of which is such that the condition of being without an owner is temporary. These things are capable of becoming the object of private property.

From this point on, the Justinian terminology lacks precision.[1] *Any* thing which is without an owner is classed as a *res nullius*. In this general sense, then, the term must be coextensive in its meaning with that division of things which is called *extra nostrum patrimonium*. It follows that all those things of which the free condition is permanent are *res nullius*. Therefore *res communes* are *res nullius*, for they are owned by no one. In like manner, those things of which the free condition is temporary are *res nullius*. Fish, then, are *res nullius* if they have no owner; sea fish are *res nullius*. In this same class are things which have been abandoned by their owner, and things which have not yet been taken possession of by their owner, as, for example, a heritage. Since by property, private property is meant, and by owner, private owner, it follows that *res divini iuris*, *res universitatis*, and *res publicae* are *res nullius*. The term *res nullius* is, then, used in a general sense and in a narrow, technical sense. It means, when used generally, a thing which is without a private owner, whether that condition is due to the nature of the thing or not. It means, when used technically, a thing which, being susceptible of private

[1] Bonjean, *op. cit.*, i, 412, 413.

ownership, is without an owner. It is in this sense that Gaius uses the phrase.[1]

The distinctive difference between *res communes*, *res publicae*, and *res privatae*, is evidently one of ownership and not of use.[2] This is true with the addition of *res universitatis* and *res nullius*. After this fact has been stated, it may be added that the element of use did actually prove an influential factor in the methods of classification adopted by the Roman jurists. The division of *res* by their physical differences did play an important part in Roman jurisprudence. Yet it played a subordinate part. Ultimately the division of things had to be made by proprietorship in order truly to determine the character of the rights and obligations attaching to them.

The foregoing discussion has been designed to furnish the background for the texts of Justinian on the status of the sea. Those texts will now be examined.

III. Justinian on the Freedom of the Sea

When the texts of the Institutes and Digest which state the Roman law doctrine regarding the sea and the right of fishery therein have been collected and placed together, they form a concise little body of law which states in unambiguous terms the position of Roman jurisprudence. Nor does the lack of precision in the use of some of the phrases mar the general consistency of this presentation. The law is as follows:

> Et quidem naturali iure communia sunt omnium haec: aer et aqua profluens et mare et per hoc litora maris.[3] Est autem litus maris, quatenus hibernus fluctus maximus excurrit.[4]

[1] Of this laxity Hunter, *op. cit.*, p. 110, says that the phrase, "thing belonging to nobody," "should be restricted to things capable by appropriation of becoming the objects of private property. If the terms employed in the Institutes were correct, the maxim of Roman Law that what belongs to no one (*res nullius*) becomes the property of the first one that takes possession of it, would no longer be true."

[2] Poste, *op. cit.*, p. 152. Compare Ortolan, *op. cit.*, i, 608; L. Thézard, *Répétitions Écrites sur le Droit Romain*, 2d ed. (Paris, 1873), p. 118; T. E. Sandars, *Institutes of Justinian* (London, 1853), p. 177.

[3] J. 2. 1. 1.

[4] J. 2. 1. 3.

This is the statement of the Institutes.[1] The Digest goes into the same position more fully; a certain amount of repetition is unavoidable, because of the widely scattered sources from which the Digest was compiled.

The theory of Marcianus is that

quaedam naturali iure communia sunt omnium, quaedam universitatis, quaedam nullius, pleraque singulorum, quae variis causis cuique adquiruntur.[2] Et quidem naturali iure omnium communia sunt illa: aer, aqua profluens, et mare, et per hoc litora maris.[3]

Celsus lays down the doctrine that

Maris communem usum omnibus hominibus, ut aeris. . . .[4]

Ulpian is in agreement:

et quidem mare commune omnium est et litora, sicuti aer. . . .[5]

Paulus groups *litora* with *loca publica*, though he does not call the shore either public or common:

. . . nullius sunt, sed iure gentium omnibus vacant . . . litora et loca publica in modum cedant.[6] Neratius agrees with Paulus that the seashore is res nullius: . . . litora publica . . . ita sunt . . . ut ea, quae . . . in nullius adhuc dominium pervenerunt.[7]

Litorum quoque usus publicus iruis gentium est, sicut ipsius maris . . . proprietas autem eorum potest intellegi nullius esse, sed eiusdem iuris esse, cuius et mare et quae subiacent mari, terra vel harena.[8]

[1] L. Thézard, *op. cit.*, p. 118: "Cette règle (referring to the rule defining the shore-line) a été faite pour la Mediterranée."

T. E. Sandars, *op. cit.*, p. 177: "Celsus ascribes this definition to Cicero, who apparently borrowed it from Aquilius." The reference to Celsus is to D. 50. 16. 96; to Cicero, Top. 7.

[2] D. 1. 8. 2. pr.

[3] D. 1. 8. 2. 1.

[4] D. 43. 8. 3. 1.

[5] D. 47. 10. 13. 7.

[6] D. 18. 1. 51.

[7] D. 41. 1. 14.

[8] J. 2. 1. 5. Having just said that the sea is common to all by the *ius naturale*, Justinian now says that the use of the shore of the sea is public by the *ius gentium*, just as is that of the sea. And yet, when he said that the sea was common to all *iure naturali*, he said also, et *per hoc*, the shore. Marcianus and Celsus both say, *per hoc*.

Justinian has made *publicus* a synonym for *communis*, in this place, though elsewhere he differentiates the two.

He has used interchangeably the two terms, *ius naturale* and *ius gentium*.

Taking everything into consideration, it seems that the meaning is, that the sea is common to all men by the law of nature, while the shore is common by the *ius gentium*. There is a difference in wording in the two passages in the Institutes, 2. 1. 1 and 2. 1. 5, which seem to distinguish between proprietorship and use, in regard to the sea and the shore. Both are *nullius*.

Thus the sea is common to all, both as to ownership and as to use. It is owned by no one; it is incapable of appropriation, just as is the air. And its use is open freely to all men. The same is true of the shore, which derives its character from the sea. The shore extends as far as the winter tides can reach. The shore is measured from the sea inland, and not from the land seaward. The land which is the territory of the state does not reach to low-water mark; but the shore, which is the boundary of the sea, extends to the high-water mark of the winter tides. The sea extends as far as the great storms can drive it. The Roman jurists taught that the coast line of the states bordering the sea was not the *property* of the particular state whose territory was bounded by it, but, on the contrary, was open by the *ius gentium* to the use of all men.[1]

No one might be forbidden to fish in the sea from the shore.[2] The right to fish in the sea was derived from the status of the sea. The right included that of drying nets on the shore, and of building shelters.[3] When a fisherman erected a hut, he acquired a right of ownership in it which lasted as long as the building remained standing. When the building fell, the right was extinguished, the place became common once again, and some one else might build a structure there and in his turn possess a property right in it.[4]

[1] Compare Paulus, D. 18. 1. 51. "Litora, quae fundo vendito coniuncta sunt, in modum non computantur, quia nullius sunt, sed iure gentium omnibus vacant. nec viae publicae aut loca religiosa vel sacra. itaque ut proficiant venditori caveri solet, ut viae, item litora et loca publica in modum cedant."

[2] Ulpian, D. 47. 10. 13. 7. "Et quidem mare commune omnium est et litora, sicut aer, et est saepissime rescriptum non posse quem piscari prohiberi."

Marcianus, D. 1. 8. 4. pr. "Nemo igitur ad litus maris accedere prohibeatur piscandi causa."

[3] J. 2. 1. 5. "Et ob id quibuslibet liberum est casam ibi imponere, in qua se recipiant, sicut retia siccare et ex mare deducere."

Gaius, D. I. 8. 5. 1. "In mare piscantibus liberum est casam in litore ponere, in qua se recipiant."

[4] Marcianus, D. 1. 8. 6. "In tantum, ut et soli domini constituantur qui ibi aedificant, sed quamdiu aedificium manet: alioquin aedificio dilapso quasi iure postliminii revertitur locus in pristinam causam, et si alius in eodem loco aedificaverit, eius fiet."

Pomponius, D. 1. 8. 10. pr. "Aristo ait, sicut id, quod in mare aedificatum sit, fieret privatum, ita quod mari occupatum sit, fieri publicum."

Neratius, D. 41. 1. 14. "Quod in litore quis aedificaverit, eius erit: nam litora

It will be perceived that these principles involve the exercise of jurisdiction over the seashore. A dictum of Celsus clothes this authority with the sanction of the law and at the same time indicates its nature. He says,[1]

Litora, in quae populus Romanus imperium habet, populi Romani esse arbitror.

In commenting on this text, Moyle[2] expresses the opinion that "if we are to bring this opinion of Celsus into harmony with the opinions of other jurists, we must understand 'populi Romani esse' to mean 'are subject to the guardianship of the Roman people.'" This would seem to be a reasonable interpretation. To read into the text any modern notions of sovereignty would be an extremely hazardous proceeding.

The question of the origin of this jurisdiction raises an interesting problem. Certainly its source is difficult to locate. It cannot flow from any sovereignty of the Roman people over the sea or the shore, for the existence of such sovereignty has been expressly denied. The conclusion would seem to be that the Roman jurists, postulating a legal person which is created in agreement with the most recent juristic philosophy, regarded their coasts as being protected and guarded by the Roman people as "a sacred trust of civilization."[3] This conclusion is strengthened by Celsus's selec-

publica non ita sunt; ut ea, quae in patrimonio sunt populi, sed ut ea, quae primum a natura prodita sunt et in nullius adhuc dominium pervenerunt: nec dissimilio condicio eorum est atque piscium et ferarum, quae simul atque adprehensae sunt, sine dubio eius, in cuius potestatem pervenerunt, dominii fiunt."

[1] D. 43. 8. 3. "The modern doctrine that the seashore between high and low tide belongs to the state is derived from Celsus 43. 8. 3." J. B. Moyle, *Imperatoris Iustiniani Institutionum*, 2 vols. (Oxford, 1883), i, 177. Note on sec. 1.

[2] *Ibid.*, ed. 1853, p. 177. For further provisions for the exercise of this jurisdiction, see D. 47. 10. 13. 7, 43. 8. 2. 8, 9.

[3] *Treaty of Peace with Germany*, June 28, 1919, Art. 22. "To those colonies . . . which are inhabited by peoples not yet able to stand by themselves under the strenuous conditions of the modern world, there should be applied the principle that the well-being and development of such peoples form a sacred trust of civilization."

Vol. 38, p. 424, Congressional Record, 58th Congress, 2d Session: President Roosevelt, in his special message to Congress of Jan. 4, 1904, said, "In the third place, I confidently maintain that the recognition of the Republic of Panama was an act justified by the collective interests of civilization. If ever a government could be said to have received a mandate from civilization to effect an object the accom-

tion of the word, "arbitror." It is noteworthy, further, that the exercise of this jurisdiction was directed to assuring the public welfare, as may be clearly seen from the provisions that huts and fishing paraphernalia used by a fisherman must not interfere with the public use of the place,[1] or with the rights of other fishermen.[2]

Harbors are differentiated from the sea; they fall within the class of *res publicae*.[1] There is no definition to settle the question where the sea ends and the harbor begins. Consequently there is no indication of the point where the shore of the sea becomes the shore of the harbor. Navigable rivers are also within the class of *res publicae*.[3] This means, as has been noted, that the *proprietas* is lodged in the state. It is the use of the harbor or river which is public; over this use the state has jurisdiction, but not ownership.[4] The Institutes state that in rivers and harbors the *ius piscandi* is common to all men.[5] Modern commentators limit the

plishment of which was demanded by the interest of mankind, the United States holds that position with regard to the inter-oceanic canal."

[1] Celsus, D. 43. 8. 3. 1. "Maris communem usum omnibus hominibus, ut aeris, iactisque in id pilas eius esse qui iecerit: sed id concedendum non esse, si deterior litoris marisve usus eo modo futurus sit."

Scaevola, D. 43. 8. 4. "Respondit in litore iure gentium aedificare licere, nisi usus publicus impediretur."

[2] See note 4 above. Also, D. 43. 8. 5. D. 41. 1. 50. Bonjean, *op. cit.*, p. 410.

[3] J. 2. 1. 2. "Flumina autem omnia et portus publica sunt: ideoque ius piscandi omnibus commune est in portubus fluminibusque. And, D. 1. 8. 4. pr. Sed flumina paene omnia et portus publica sunt."

[4] "The better view is perhaps that also stated in the Institutes, *i. e.*, that only the use was public, as is clearly the case with the banks of rivers." W. W. Buckland, *A Text-Book of Roman Law from Augustus to Justinian* (Cambridge, 1921), p. 186 and notes, especially Note 5. Hunter, *op. cit.*, pp. 165–166, agrees with him that the state's authority over fishing rights was one of jurisdiction and not of ownership.

[5] See Note 1. J. 2. 1. 2. It was an offense known to the law as an *injuria*, intentionally to prevent a person from fishing in the sea, according to Paulus, D. 47. 10. 14

Ulpian, D. 43. 8. 2. 9: "Si quis in mari piscari aut navigare prohibeatur, non habebit interdictum . . . sed . . . iniuriarum actione utendum est." And again, in D. 47. 10. 13. 7, the jurisconsult writes, "Si quis me prohibeat in mari piscari vel everriculum . . . ducere, an iniuriarum me possum me possi agere: et ita Pomponius et plerique esse huic similem eum, qui in publicum lavare vel in cavea publica sedea vel in quo alio loco agere sedere conversari non patiatur, aut si quis re mea uti me non permittat: nam et hic iniuriarum conveniri potest. conductori autem veteres interdictum dederunt, si forte publice hoc conduxit: nam vis ei prohibenda est, que minus conductione sua fruatur. si quem tamen ante aedes meas vel ante praetorium meum piscari prohibeam, & quod dicendum est? me iniuriarum iudicio

exercise of this right to those which are to-day termed nationals of the state possessing the rivers and harbors; whether this interpretation expresses the thought of the Roman lawyers of the sixth century is a matter for speculation; in the opinion of the present writer, such limitation was not intended.[1] It is true that the *proprietas* of the harbors was lodged in the state, while there was no *proprietas* of the sea to be lodged anywhere. On the other hand, the right of fishing in both sea and harbors was common to all, without restriction. Furthermore, the authority of the state over fishing rights in its harbors was one of jurisdiction and not of sovereignty. With all due respect for eminent opinion, the present writer ventures to suggest that the interpretation disapproved of is due to a confusion of thought in respect to the characteristics of jurisdiction and sovereignty.

The application of the word, public, to the use of harbors and rivers, seems to indicate that it is used as being synonymous (here) with the word, common.[2]

The Institutes assert that all rivers are public. It is perhaps worth noting that Marcianus restricts the statement to rivers that flow the year round, thus excluding torrents.[3]

teneri an non? et quidem mare commune omnium est et litora, sicuti aer, et est saepissime rescriptum non posse quem piscari prohiberi: sed nec aucupari, nisi quod ingredi quis agrum alienum prohiberi potest. usurpatum tamen et hoc est, tametsi nullo iure, ut quis prohiberi possit ante aedes meas vel praetorium meum piscari: quare si quis prohibeatur, adhuc iniuriarum agi potest." . . . See also, D. 8. 4. 13; 44. 3. 7; 47. 10. 14; 41. 1. 58.

[1] Sandars, *op. cit.*, p. 177, holds the view contended for above.

[2] That the antithesis is common versus private use, is shown in the case of rivers in J. 2. 1. 4. "Riparum quoque usus publicus est iuris gentium, sicut ipsius fluminis . . . sed proprietas earum illorum est quorum praediis haerent." Gaius, in the Digest, 1. 8. 5, is of the same opinion: "Riparum usus publicus est iure gentium sicut ipsius fluminis . . . sed proprietas illorum est, quorum praediis haerent." A repetition nearly verbatim.

[3] D. 1. 8. 4. pr. See Note 1 on the preceding page. Ulpian, D. 41. 12. 1. 2, says, "Item fluminum quaedum sunt perennia, quaedum torrentia. perenne est, quod semper fluat." And in 41. 12. 1. 3, he says, "Fluminum quaedum publica sunt, quaedum non. publicum flumen esse Cassius definit, quod perenne sit. haec sententia Cassii, quum et Celsus probat, videtur esse probabilis."

Further definitions of the word, *publicus*, are given in the chapter *De verborum significatione*, D. 50. 16. 15–17. Ulpian says, "Bona civitatis abusive 'publica' dicta sunt: sola enim ea publica sunt, quae populi Romani sunt. Inter 'publica'

IV. Conclusions

In considering the doctrine of the Roman jurists on the freedom of the sea, the first thing of importance which appears is the small amount of space their treatment of the subject occupies in Roman jurisprudence. The facts from which they seem to have drawn their ideas offered, apparently, no serious problems of state. The peoples living on the shores of the Mediterranean used the sea in common. The precarious internal condition of the Roman Empire of the West in the sixth century, and the situation beyond its frontiers in the heart of western and central Europe, did not influence the fact that at the time the Institutes and Digest of Justinian were promulgated, there was no rival power on the shores of the Mediterranean which could dispute the Roman supremacy. As will be observed in another connection, the failure of the barbarian invaders to extinguish the practice of Roman law in Italy supported the continuity of Roman jurisprudence, and was another factor in stabilizing this situation. Had there been a France or a Holland on one side of the Mediterranean at this time, with Rome corresponding to England, it is possible that the Roman law might have evolved a different doctrine, and one to which a fuller treatment would have been given.

Confusion in the use of certain terms is a pronounced characteristic of the juristic writings. This confusion attends the use of the term *res nullius*, where it is used sometimes to denote any thing without an owner, whatever be the cause of the condition, and sometimes to denote only a thing which, being susceptible of becoming the object of private property, is for the time being without an owner. There is a lack of precision in the use of the

habemus non sacra nec religiosa nec quae publicis usibus destinata sunt; sed si qua sunt civitatium velut bona. . . . Publica vectigalia intellegere debemus, ex quibus vectigal fiscus capit: quale est vectigal portus vel venalium rerum, item salinarum et metallorum et picarum."

Gaius: "Enim qui vectigal populi Romani conductum habet, 'publicanum' appellamus. nam 'publica' appellatio in compluribus causis ad populum Romanum respicit: civitates enim privatorum loco habentur."

The extent to which rivers are public is sharply defined. See J. 2. 1. 4. It will be noticed that there is no similarity of treatment regarding the banks of a river and the seacoast.

word *publicus*. It is used in the technical sense which appears in the phrase *res publica*, as denoting something the *proprietas* of which is lodged in the *populus Romanus* considered as a unit; it is used also as a synonym for *communis*. This laxity of use is carried to a high point by the Glossators.

It is important to note that this lack of consistency in the use of terminology has not resulted in producing a hazy statement of the law concerning the sea. The doctrine of the lawyers seems unambiguous and clear. The theory of the second century was that the sea is *res communis*, incapable of appropriation, open freely to the use of all men. Marcianus, living at the beginning of this century, and Ulpian, living at the end, are in accord on this point. Ulpian adds that the right of fishing may not be prohibited to any one. This doctrine, having now been stated in terms of law, does not disappear, but becomes an integral part of the contents of the law books. Even Gaius, who says nothing about the sea, has a place in his analysis of the law for *res communes*, and expressly refers to fish as *res nullius*. Paulus, a contemporary of Ulpian, Scaevola, who lived early in the third century, and Neratius, a jurist of the time of Trajan, agree in holding the position that the use of the shore of the sea is common to all by the *ius gentium*. There is nothing antagonistic to this doctrine in the position of Gaius, Marcianus, Ulpian, and Celsus; on the contrary it would seem to be a logical development from the teaching of those jurists. If there was no need for precise definitions, if the jurisconsults were engaged merely in rounding out the fabric of the law, if they were only putting into formal statement (on some appropriate occasion) a belief which was shared by men generally, when they elucidated their theory of the freedom of the sea, if their statements of the law had no immediate and pressing practical importance and effect, then the phraseology which clothes their theories is just the phraseology which it would be natural to expect from such men under such circumstances. Where careful statement was needed, there careful statement was given. The restrictions which governed the construction of buildings on the shore were formulated with precision. It is worth noticing that there is preserved in D. 1. 8. 4. pr. a statement of the fact that the

Emperor, the Divine Pius, sent a rescript on this subject to the fishermen of Formianus and Capenatus.

An analysis of the theory of the Roman jurists concerning the *ius naturale* and the *ius gentium* would lead far from their theory in regard to the sea and the right of fishing therein. It seems desirable, however, to observe certain facts in respect to it.[1] Gaius, in his Institutes, uses the terms interchangeably. For Ulpian, on the other hand, they mean two different things. The *ius gentium* is not, for Gaius, much different from the *ius naturale* understood as an eternal law in its relation to the world.[2] It is for him a universal, rational and just principle of life to which human laws must conform. It is learned by men from their reason. Paulus[3] and Marcianus[4] seem to share this view. But for Ulpian, the opposition between the terms is complete.[5] Natural law is discovered by the instincts; it is implanted in all animals. The *ius gentium* is, on the other hand, the law of the nations of the world. All animals obey the *ius naturale.* Mankind alone obeys the *ius gentium.* Ulpian, whose life carried him into the third century, is supported so far as the point that there is a distinction (whatever it may be) between the *ius naturale* and the *ius gentium* is concerned, by two third-century jurists, Tryphoninus[6] and Florentinus.[7] It may perhaps be suggested that for these men the law of nature was a law lying behind the *ius gentium*, performing the double function of serving as the ultimate source and sanction for the law of nations; Ulpian's view of the law of nature does not seem to have commanded acceptance. Hermogenianus, a jurist of the third century, under Constantine, gives a list of things which come under the *ius gentium:* [8] no one of them could be placed under the *ius naturale.* Though he does not state the contrast, he clearly sides with those who make the distinction between the two laws.

[1] This subject is exhaustively treated in Carlyle, *A History of Mediaeval Political Theory in the West*, 4 vols., New York, 1903 and after. See i, 1903, *passim*, especially chaps. 3 and 7; ii, 1909, *passim*, especially chap. 3. In each volume, the chapters are in Part I.

[2] G. 1. 1; D. 1. 1. 9; D. 41. 1. 1.

[3] D. 1. 1. 11.

[4] D. 1. 8. 2. and 4.

[5] D. 1. 1. 1. 2–4.

[6] D. 12. 6. 64.

[7] D. 1. 5. 4.

[8] D. 1. 1. 5.

V. The Basilicus

While the *Basilicus*, promulgated probably in the period of Leo the Philosopher, 906–911, is of an age later than that of the law books of Justinian, it is a work of general compilation and revision, and recalls the work of Justinian. It may therefore properly be included in a chapter which is concerned with the maturity of the Roman law, as an integral part of that system, although of eastern and not western origin.

> Les textes compilés sont censés ceux de Justinien, combinés avec les dispositions ou les règles de jurisprudence postérieures formant le droit en vigeur. En realité, ce sont les ouvrages grecs des jurisconsultes du sixième siécle qui sont mis à contribution: les Basiliques sont formées d'extraits puisés dans les traductions, paraphrases, commentaires ou abrégés de ces auteurs sur les Instituts, en petit quantité, sur le Digeste, sur le Code et sur les Nouvelles, dans le texte même de ces Nouvelles pour celles qui avaient été promulguées en grec, et dans le Prochiron de Basile le Macédonien.[1]

The text is printed with *scoliae* in a manner which recalls the editions of the Corpus Iuris Civilis with the notes of the Glossators. These *scoliae* contain interpretations and illustrations of the text. Occasionally they are in flat opposition to the law which they profess to elucidate. For there is one striking distinction between them, which divides them into two classes;

> les unes sont des extraits puisés dans les ouvrages des jurisconsultes du sixième siécle, les autres sont des annotations qui ont été ajoutées aux Basiliques par des jurisconsultes postérieurs à ce Code.[2]

The latter class are perhaps the *scoliae* proper. This body of law was not promulgated with the purpose of abrogating all law existing anterior to, and outside of itself. The laws of Justinian continued to remain at least in name the source of law, and hence superior to the *Basilicus*. By the end of the eleventh century, however, the *Basilicus* had definitely superseded the law of Justinian.[3]

The doctrine of the *Basilicus*[4] on the subject of the sea and of

[1] Ortolan, *op. cit.*, i, 407. [2] *Ibid.*, p. 488. [3] *Ibid.*, and p. 489.

[4] *Basilicorum Libri LX.* "Post Annibalis Fabroti Curas. Ope Codd. MSS. . . . Translationem Latinam et Adnotationem Criticam, adiecit D. Carolus Guilielmus Ernestus Heimbach," 5 vols., Lipsiae, 1836–1850.

maritime fisheries is in accord with that of the Institutes and Digest of Justinian. The whole subject is treated with greater brevity, though in terms which are unmistakably familiar. The following passages are noteworthy:

> Litora in omnium potestate sunt: unde et dominus sum eorum, quae in iis a me aedificantur, sicut et eorum, quae a me capiuntur.
> Sed si ceciderit aedificium, litus rursum commune fit.[1]
> Marcianus. Quaedam sunt omnium, quaedam universitatis, quaedam nullius, quaedam singulorum. Omnium sunt aer, aqua profluens, mare, et litus maris.[2]
> 1. (quaedam sunt omnium.) Hinc Marcianus aliam facit rerum differentiam, et ita ait: . . . Et naturali iure communes omnium sunt aer et aqua perennis, et mare, et propter hoc et litora maris. . . . Nemo igitur ad litus accedere prohibetur piscandi causa, dum tamen abstineat a villis et aedificiis. . . . Sed et flumina paene omnia et portus publica sunt, seu eius civitatis, sub qua sunt.
> . . . Et flumina paene, et portus publica sunt.
> 1. (et flumina paene.) Innominati. Illud paene dictum est propter torrentes.[3]

The law in regard to the use of river banks, and in regard to the use of the seashore, both as to the erection of buildings and as to the accommodation of the apparatus of fishermen is that of the Digest. The law regarding fishing off-shore in front of a private residence is the same as that in the law of Justinian.[4]

[1] 50. 1. 13.
[2] 46. 3. 2.
[3] 46. 3. 3.
[4] These laws are as follows:

50. 3. 43. "Nemo locum publicum per longi temporis praescriptionem acquirit. Itaque si collapsum sit, quod in litore aedificavi, aut ego illud reliquero, et alius postea aedificaverit, praescriptionem loci nomine non habeo."

53. 6. 5. "Licet mos obtineat, ut quidam contra leges alios ante domicilia sua piscari prohibeant, tenetur tamen prohibens iniuriarum actione."

43. 3. 4. "Usus ripae fluminis publicum est, et licet cuilibet ad eam navem applicare, et onera in ripa reponere, et retia siccare, et in fluminibus navigare, et funes in arboribus in ripa natis religare. Sed dominium ripae et arborum, quae in ea sunt, est dominorum fundorum, in quibus positae sunt." In the long *scolia* following, particular attention is paid to river banks.

46. 3. 8. "Et quod in mari aedificatum est, privatum sit: et quod mare occupaverit, sit publicum."

As a comment on the law which provides an action at law for the injured party against one who forbids him to fish off shore in front of his house, may be noted numbers 56, 102–104 of the *Novellae Leonis.* See Gothofredus, D., *Corpus Iuris Civilis,* 2 vols. (Amstelodami, 1663), vol. ii.

The following texts will also show the close connection between the theory of the Basilicus and that of Justinian; they are all taken from vol. 5, lib. LX. 1.

ii. "Omnia igitur animalia terrestria, marina, aërea capientum fiunt, una cum iis, quae apud nos pariunt."

iii. "Nam quod nullius est, occupantis sit, etiamsi quis in alieno agro ceperit."

xiii. "Litora in omnium potestate sunt: une et dominus sum eorum, quae in iis a me aedificantur, sicut et eorum, quae a me capiuntur."

"Sed si ceciderit aedificium, litus rursum commune sit."

xxix. "Si pilae in mare iactae superstruxero, aut in marina insula aedificavero utrumque meum erit: quod enim nullius est, occupantis est."

CHAPTER III

THE GLOSSATORS

I. From the Sixth to the Twelfth Century

Dès que l'Italie, à la suite des victoires de Belisaire et de Narsès, lui été soumise, Justinien se hâta d'y faire publier et mettre en vigeur au sein des populations, devant les juges et dans l'école de Rome, ses recueils de droit. Julien, dans son abrégé des Nouvelles, nous a transmis le résumé d'une pragmatique sanction de l'empereur, en date de l'an 554, par laquelle est ordonné cette publication en Italie, y compris celle des Nouvelles. . . .[1]

On sait que Justinien, dans sa constitution portant confirmation du Digeste [section 24] avait ordonné que tous les juges eussent, dans leur jurisdiction, le texte des Instituts et du Digeste: "Omnes itaque judices nostri pro sua jurisdictione easdem leges suscipiant, et tam in suis judices quam in hac regia urbe habeant et proponant." [2]

[1] Ortolan, *op. cit.*, i, 498, sec. 596. "Pragmatica sanctio (vers la fin du *Corpus juris*, apres les *Nouvelles* de Tibère) ch. iii: Jura insuper, vel Leges Codicibus nostris insertis, quas jam sub edictali programmate in Italiam dudum misimus, obtinere sancimus: sed et eas, quas postea promulgavimus Constitutiones, jubes sub edictali propositione vulgari ex eo tempore, quo sub edictali programmate evulgatae fuerint, etiam per partes Italiae obtinere, ut una, Deo volente, facta Republica, Legum etiam nostrarum ubique prolatetur auctoritas." *Ibid.*, Note 1.

The *Corpus Iuris Civilis*, edited by the Fratres Kriegelii, by D. A. Hermann and D. E. Osenbruegen, *editio stereotypa*, 15th impression, 3 vols., Lipsiae, 1875, gives the above as follows: "Aliae Aliquot Constitutiones Imperatoris Iustiniani, Iustini et Tibirii A. Ex diversis fontibus collectae. Constitutio I. cap. xi (iii, 736). Ut Leges imperatorem per provincias ipsorum dilatentur. (The preceding is the title. The text then follows:) Iura insuper vel leges Codicibus nostris insertas, quas iam sub edictali programmate in Italiam dudum misimus, obtinere sancimus. Sed et eas, quas postea promulgavimus constitutiones, iubemus sub edictali propositione vulgari, et ex eo tempore, quo sub edictali programmate evulgatae fuerint etiam per partes Italiae obtinere, ut iura deo volente facta republica, legum etiam nostrarum ubique prolatetur auctoritas."

[2] Ortolan, *ibid.*, i, 499, Note 2. The *Corpus Iuris* above cited gives section 24 as follows: "De Confirmatione Digestorum: Universi igitur laudatissimi nostri imperii magistratus sacram hanc nostram accipientes Constitutionem, ut utantur praedictis nostris legibus, unusquisque in sui ipsorum tribunali se accingat" etc., without giving the above passage.

Ce droit, en tant que droit civil privé, ne fut modifié que par les nouveaux usages ou par les dispositions spéciales des statuts qui purent survenir, surtout après l'affranchissement des villes; mais les lois Justinien en restèrent le fondement.[1]

[In Gaul] le droit romain consistait dans les monuments même du droit anté-justinien et plus encore, pour l'application pratique, dans les lois romain colligées et publiées par ordre des rois germains.[2] . . . [He quotes Laferrière, "Histoire du droit français," *tom.* 4, p. 285 et 286] . . . tous les emprunts, . . . toutes les citations qui se rapportent au droit de Justinien, dans les documents privés ou publics de la France du moyen âge jusqu'a fin du onzième siécle, se réfèrent uniquement aux Nouvelles de Justinien comprises dans la collection de Julien.[2]

A fact which will be noted later may be stated here, namely, that the *Novellae* contain no reference to the status of the sea or to the maritime jurisdiction of fisheries.

Ortolan [3] and Savigny [4] agree that the Roman law continued to be applied in certain courts from the fall of the Western Empire to the twelfth century. The years of obscurity and confusion in the middle ages were, however, years of obscurity and confusion for the law as well as for the arts and sciences. The law was practised, "mais sans culture." [5] At the end of the eleventh century the Roman law flamed up suddenly with a new and fresh brilliance.[6] The new schools, and especially that at the University of Bologna, gathered students from all over Europe. These in turn spread the law wherever they went.

Since the time of Charlemagne the attempt had been made to bind the diverse states and peoples of western and central Europe into a permanent union. To this fabric, the bonds of which were the Church, the Emperor, a common *Geistlichkeit*, and a common commercial language, was now to be added the Roman law.[7]

1 Ortolan, *op. cit.*, pp. 500, 501.

2 *Ibid.*, p. 508. M. F. Laferrière, 6 vols. (Paris, 1852–1853), iv, 286, 287.

3 *Op. cit.*, i, 512, 513.

4 F. C. von Savigny, *Geschichte des Römischen Rechts im Mittelalter*, 6 vols., 2d ed. (Heidelberg, 1834–1851), iii, 83.

5 Ortolan, *op. cit.*, i, 512.

6 Savigny, *op. cit.*, iii, 83, and Ortolan, *op. cit.*, pp. 512, 513.

7 Savigny, *op. cit.*, iii, 87.

As is known, the law school at the University of Bologna was founded by Irnerius at the beginning of the twelfth century. He was the first of that long line of commentators or glossators which closed with Accursius in the middle of the thirteenth century. At the time of his death the work of this school had degenerated into a lifeless series of dry and fairly obvious comments on the great texts of the Roman law.

II. The Petri Exceptiones and the Brachylogus

Two documents may be mentioned which are not the product of the school of Bologna, according to Ortolan and Savigny. One is known as the "Petri Exceptiones Legum Romanorum," and is of French origin.[1] It is silent on the status of the sea, and says nothing of the maritime jurisdiction of fisheries.[1] Savigny places the date of its appearance between 878 and the eleventh century, that is, before the founding of the school at Bologna.[2] Ortolan, on the other hand, dates it later than the founding of the school.[3] The other work is known to-day as the "Brachylogus." Ortolan thinks that it appeared certainly at the end of the eleventh century or at the beginning of the twelfth,[4] and Savigny is of the same opinion.[5] Both agree that it was composed in Italy. Whether it appeared before the founding of the Bolognese school, or whether its appearance was due to that event, cannot be told. Savigny thinks it not impossible that Irnerius himself wrote it; but Savigny admits that he has no ground for thinking so.[6] Ortolan notes his guess, but is not warmed by it.[7]

[1] Savigny has published the text in the appendix to ii. The identity of Petrus is unknown (Savigny, *op. cit.*, p. 148). It originated in Valence, in the Dauphiné (Savigny, *op. cit.*, p. 141).

[2] *Ibid.*, p. 142.

[3] *Op. cit.*, i, 520, 521.

[4] *Op. cit.*, i, 519.

[5] *Op. cit.*, ii, 259, 263.

[6] *Ibid.*, ii, 263: "Ja ich würde es nicht für unmöglich halten, dass dieser der Verfasser wäre, obgleich ich auch gar keinen besondern Grund dafür habe."

[7] *Ibid.*, p. 520. The text of the work used here is entitled: *Brachylogus: Iuris Civilis sive Corpus Legum*, etc., edited by D. H. C. Senckenberg, Francofurti et Lipsiae, 1743. Savigny says that this text is unreliable, ii, p. 259. Use has also been made of the critical work of Böcking, to correct Senckenberg.

The "Brachylogus" refers to *res publicae, res universitatis, res singulorum* and *res nullius* as being *humani juris*.[1] It states, further, that the sea is *res publica*, with the shores thereof, and rivers; and that the use of the seashore and of the river banks is public. Then it proceeds to state that the common use of the shore must not be impeded.[2] It is obvious that this doctrine is either a corruption of the Roman law, or else it represents a complete identification of the meaning of *publicus* with *communis*. The writer has a note on *publicae;* in this class belong those things "quae vel natura communes sunt, ut aer, mare, aqua profluens: vel populi Romani quasi propriae, et populicae, ut flumina et portus." [2] According to this explanation, *publicae* may be used to denote things which are placed in different classes in the law books of Justinian. The law of Justinian might call the use of the seacoast public when common was meant; but it never calls the sea public. Furthermore, when the writer says, as he does,[2] *Publicae, ut mare, flu(mina), . . . littora (sic) maris*, he is using both meanings at the same time, for he has linked the sea with rivers, things which even he proceeds to differentiate at once in the note on *publicae* just quoted. His exposition comes down to this: *res communes* are *publicae; res publicae* are *publicae. Res communes* and *res publicae* are *publicae*. Or, it may be stated this way: The sea is *publica*, because it is *communis* by nature. Rivers and harbors are *publicae*, because they are *populi Romani quasi propriae*. Therefore one may say that the sea and rivers are *res publicae*. Whether or not the use of *quasi* to describe the property right of the state is significant in the writer's mind, it is impossible to judge from the text.

[1] 2. 1. 6. (9). "Res autem humani juris, aliae sunt publicae, aliae universitatis, aliae singulorum, aliae nullius in bonis." Words or numbers in parenthesis are from Böcking, p. 44.

[2] 2. 1. 7. (10). "Publicae, ut mare, flu(mina) . . . littora maris: usus quoque riparum publicus est. Itaque per ea navigare, naves arboribus ibi natis ligare, retia siccare, pisces capere; et caetera facere (et cuncta facere), quae communi usui impedimento non sint, cuilibet liberum est. Proprietas autem riparum, eorum est, qui propre ripam praedia possident." The note on *publicae* is annexed hereto.

Nullius in bonis sunt [he says] ut bestiae, volucres, pisces: quae in naturali libertate retenta a nullo possessa sunt.[1]

The note on *nullius*, which follows at once, reads: "Haec nullius esse dicuntur quae neque sunt communia, neque publica, neque universitatis, neque singulorum, sed quae divini iuris sunt, ex hominum dispositione. Etsi igitur communia et publica interdum nullius dicuntur . . . hoc tamen a sacris et religiosis differunt, quod haec sunt in usu Dei, alia vero in usu hominum."

For brilliant clarity of thought, this note on *nullius* is equalled only by the note on *publicae*.

Böcking, in his work on the "Brachylogus," omits these notes and thus restores reason to the text. The sea and the rivers still remain together as *res publicae*,[2] however, and bear witness to a change of thought. But whether it is a change in the doctrine concerning *flumina*, *mare*, or *publicae*, is not apparent from the text. Probably it is most reasonable to presume a laxity in the use of the word *publica*.

III. The Doctrine of the Glosses

The glosses on the texts of the Roman law, which have already been referred to, fall within the period 1100–1260, or the period from the founding of the school of law at the University of Bologna to the death of Accursius, the last of the Glossators. The texts which deal with the status of the sea and with sea fisheries are located in the Institutes and in the Digest, the majority of them being in the latter. The doctrine of the Glossators is expressed in their comments on these texts.[3] By combining these glosses, it is possible to arrive at a small body of theory in the

[1] 2. 1. 9. (13).

[2] See note 2 on the preceding page.

[3] To be found in the *Corpus Iuris Civilis; Digestum vetus, seu Pandectarum Iuris Civilis . . . Commentariis Accursii, & multorum insuper aliorum doctorum virorum scholiis atque observationibus illustratus.* In 5 vols., Paris, 1559. The texts in question are in tome I. The remarks above are not meant to imply that the work of the Glossators was confined to the marginal notes which have been preserved in the *Corpus Iuris Civilis*, though it is from those notes that their theory of the sea will be found to have been drawn. A source outside the body of the *Corpus*, for example, is the *Summa* of the Instiutes, the work of Azo, which is noted in the proper place.

same way in which it was done in connection with a study of the texts themselves.[1]

D. 1. 8. 2. has a gloss on *naturali iure*. The *ius naturale* is defined as the *ius gentium*, "quod est instinctu naturae inductum." This definition follows that school headed by Gaius which makes no distinction between the two laws. The gloss on *littora:* [2] "Communia sunt quo ad usum, & dominium: ut hic. sed quo ad protectionem sunt populi Romani." Here, *communis* is used for *publicus*, thus reversing the usual method. But there seems to be no change in doctrine. The statement that the Roman people have the right to protect the shore comes of course from D. 43. 8. 3., where the doctrine is credited to Celsus.

> Mare est cummune, quo ad usum: sed proprietas [3] est nullius: sicut aër est communis usu: proprietas tamen est nullius [4] . . . sed iurisdictio est Caesaris. . . .

[1] Following is a *divisio rerum* of the period. Published by Savigny, *op. cit.*, ii, 435, Anhang, I. B., who says that it is the "Turiner Glosse zu den Institutionen:

res una
- al. constans ex rebus plurimum
  - al. discreta
  - al. continua
    - ex unabus principalibus
      - al.
      - al. non
        - al. ex valentibus separari, quae non est communis nisi in consensu ut argento et plambo
        - al. ex non valentibus
          - al. eiusdem generis, quae semper communis est
          - al. diversi quae similiter ut ex aere et auro"
    - al. ex principali et accessione ut solo et aedificio, carta et litteris
    - alii ex quasi principali et quasi accessione ut vestimenta et purpura, vehiculo et rata, candelabro et gemma
- al. non, quae potest aliquando peti ab utroque ut grex tota ab uno, licet non singulae oves; et singula ovis ab altero, licet non tota grex

[2] *Litora* is always spelled *littora* by the glossators.

[3] This word appears in the Roman texts as *pprietas* or *pptas*. In this and in all other cases the Latin abbreviation has been expanded into the complete form of the word.

[4] The glosses on D. 43. 8. 2. 9. and D. 41. 1. 14. are in accord.

The statement that the sea is common so far as the use thereof is concerned, and that the *proprietas* thereof is *nullius*, is obviously in full accord with the doctrine of the Digest. But the statement that Caesar — no doubt the Emperor is meant by this title — exercises jurisdiction over it represents the development of a new theory. It does not represent, of course, the development of a new *fact*. After the fall of Carthage, for example, Rome was without a question "lord" of the Mediterranean. This situation was met in connection with the ante-Justinianian jurisprudence. What is new is the appearance of the theory after the codification of the law of Justinian with its foundation resting on the Digest itself. There is no clue here as to the scope of this jurisdiction. So far as the theory or doctrine itself is concerned, it should be read in connection with statements to the effect that the sea is incapable of appropriation.

There are two important glosses on D. 1. 8. 3. and D. 41. 1. 3. The gloss on D. 1. 8. 3. is on *Item lapillae & gemmae*.

Ea demum dicuntur communia, quae cum sint in communia animantium, occupanti conceduntur. Publica autem sunt communia, vel in communi usu: sed non conceduntur occupanti: quod est contra Placentinum qui dicebat omnia publica esse communia: & econtra communia dicebat esse publica, ex eo quod omnibus animantibus permittitur publice his uti sicut communibus: ut lavando, bibendo, & similia faciendo. communia dicebat esse publica quo ad quosdam usus, qui tantum hominibus competunt: ut navigare, piscari.

Here, the glossator gives the accepted view, and the view of Placentinus, and controverts the latter. Placentinus, according to his reporter, makes the distinction between *res communes* and *res publicae* turn not on the question of *proprietas*, but on the question whether these *res* are used by all animals, or whether their use is common to men alone. By this test, those things which in the accepted view are termed common, are in reality public, such as sailing and fishing.

D. 41. 1. 3. pr. begins as follows:

Quod enim nullius est, id ratione naturali occupanti conceditur. Nullius is used here in its technical signification. [The gloss reads:] Neque dei, neque hominis, re vel spe, hominum censura, quod sit occupabile: & sic non recipit instantiam.

Referring to these two glosses, those, namely, on D. 1. 8. 3. and on D. 41. 1. 3. pr., E. Landsberg writes in his book, *Die Glosse der Accursius*,"[1]

Nicht verstanden unter den *res nullius*, welche der an die Spitze gesetzte Satz behandelt, sind die *res nullius, quae nunquam ullius esse possunt;* also doch die eigentlichen *res nullius*. Dagegen gehören ganz besonders hierher die *res communes*, denn dieser sind solche *quae cum sint in communem usum omnium animantium, occupanti conceduntur;* eine besondere Lehre mit weiterer Unterscheidung, welche Placentinus aufgestellt hat, wird ausdrücklich verworfen. Occupirbar sind demnach:

(1) alle *res communes;* und

(2) diejenigen *res privatae*, welche momentan gerade keinen Eigenthümer haben.

(*a*) Alle Producte des Meeres sind occupirbar.[2]

Azo, one of the great Glossators, devotes some space in his Summa of the Institutes to this teaching of Placentinus. Azo died not earlier than 1230, according to Savigny.[3] He was a native of Bologna, and taught in the university.[4] "Early in the thirteenth century he stood at the head of the Bolognese school of law which was accomplishing that grand feat, the resuscitation

[1] Leipzig, 1883, p. 213.

[2] *Ibid.*, p. 214.

Landsberg states that D. 41. 1. 3. pr. begins, "Quod nullius est, occupanti fieri videntur." I am unable to locate this phrase in that fragment, or in D. 1. 8. 3. Nor can I find it in either of the glosses on these two passages. He must have used an edition of the *Corpus* which I have not at hand. At any rate, the difference is verbal only, for the meaning remains unchanged. It is noteworthy that in his sentence just quoted, *est* is not in agreement with *videntur*, the one being singular and the other plural.

The significant sentence in D. 41. 1. 3. pr. is given in the text. D. 1. 8. 3. reads: "Item lapilli & gemmae, & caetera quae in littore invenimus, iure naturali nostra statim fiunt." There is no *quod nullius est.* Part of the gloss on this passage (D. 41. 1. 3.) is quoted in the text. The remainder is as follows: "fallit in libero homine: & est ratio, quae haec regula loquitur de his quae possunt subiici nostro dominio; quod in libero homine non est: ut institu. de inuti. stipu. in princip. & ※. j. Item fallit in servo aegrotante eiecto a dominio. qui fit liber: ut C. de Laty. liber. tol. l. unica. ※ sed scimus. & quia in multis aliis videntur fallere haec regula: ideo dic quot modis dicitur res in bonis nullius: ut not. supra de re. divi. l. j. Item not. quod que aliasdicuntur communia in divisione: ut instit. eo. in prin. hic sub genere nullius appellatur, sed occupando officiuntur alicuius."

[3] *Op. cit.*, v, 8.

[4] *Ibid.*, p. 4.

of the classical Roman jurisprudence."[1] During the remainder of the Middle Ages his treatises were held in high repute.[2]

Azo opens his discussion of *res communes* with a statement of the things which are *res communes*.[3]

Naturali autem iure communia sunt omnia haec, aer, aqua profluens, mare, & per hoc littora maris. Nemo igitur ad littus maris accedere prohibetur, dum tamen villis & monumentis & aedificijs abstineat, quia non sunt iuris gentium (communia) sicut est (or et) mare.[4] [This is a repetition verbatim of J. 2. 1. 1.]

Immo aedificia in mari vel in littore posita, aedificantium sunt & ita in hoc casu solum cedit aedificio, licet aliud sit secundum regulum ut inf. e. § & quidem naturali. & § cum in suo, ut ff. e. l. in tantum.[4] [This is a summary or paraphrase, and not a quotation. The reference is to J. 2. 1. 29. and D. 1. 8. 6.]

Est autem littus maris, quatenus hybernus fluctus maxim(us) excurrit, & in eo licet retia siccare, & ex mari deducere, ut inf. e. § est autem littus & § littorum.[4] [This paragraph is based on J. 2. 1. 3–5.]

Publica autem sunt omnia flumina & portus, ideoque ius piscandi omnibus est commune in portu fluminibusq(ue). Riparum quoq(ue): usus publicus est iure gentium, sicut & ipsius fluminis. Itaque naves ad eas applicare funes arboribus ibi natis religare, onus aliquod in his reponere, cuilibet liberum est, sicuti p(er) ipsum flumine navigare. Sed proprietas earum est illorum quorum praedijs adhaerent, qua de causa arbores in ijsdem natae eorundem sunt, ut inf. e. § flumina.[4] [This is a repetition of J. 2. 1. 2.]

quare (sic) autem littora non cedant, sicut & ripae, his qui prope possident praedia, potest quaeri. (This is Azo's own reflection.) Sunt autem haec intelligenda de fluminibus pereuntibus (perennibus, according to Maitland), temporalia enim possunt esse privata, ut ff. de flumi. l. j. § itê. & § fluminñ.[5] [He is referring to the classification of rivers made in D. 43. 12. 1. 2., where rivers which flow all the year are called public, and distinguished from torrents.]

Up to the reflection noted above, Azo has stated the law in the terms of Justinian Institutes, that is, in the terms of the classical Roman jurisprudence, and without embellishment. He finds the Roman doctrine of the sea to be what he has stated. In J. 2. 1. 1. he has noted that *litora maris* are *communia naturali iure.*

[1] F. W. Maitland, *Selected Passages from Bracton and Azo*, edited for the Selden Society, London, 1895, p. ix.

[2] *Ibid.*, p. x. Savigny, *op. cit.*, v, 33–38, lists thirty-one editions of his treatises printed between 1582 and 1610. Maitland calls attention to this fact.

[3] *Summa Azonis sive Locuples Iuris Civilis Thesaurus*, Venetiis, 1610. I have availed myself of the editing done by Maitland in his reproduction of the pertinent passages of the *Summa* in his *Bracton and Azo*.

[4] II. 1061. 4 *et seq.*

[5] See note 4 *supra*.

But in J. 2. 1. 5. he observes *litorum quoque usus publicus iure gentium est.* He does not approve of this lax use of the word *publicus.* No *res communes* can be *res publicae,* for they are in different classes of things; thus a *res communis* cannot be endowed with a public use. His remedy is the effective one of substituting *communis* for *publicus* wherever the latter word is misused. But while he could use his own remedy, he could not persuade his colleagues to do so.

This subject leads him on to attack the doctrine of Placentinus that *res communes* and *res publicae* are really distinguished by their capacity for use — the former being used by all animals, the latter, by men alone. Azo holds that the two classes are essentially different, the distinction being the right to appropriate by *occupatio.* The *res communis* may be appropriated; the *res publica,* not.[1] He continues as follows:

Liquet igitur secundum praedictas divisiones (quod) nulla communia sunt publica, vel e converso, cum sub hoc genere res assignent(ur) velut species pares et coaequae. Et ideo mirum est quod dicitur usus littorum publicus, ut inf. eo. § littorum. (J. 2. 1. 5.) Debuit enim dicere communis, sicut & littus commune est, ut supra dictum est. Ita, publicum dicitur ipsum mare, ut ff. eo. l. sicut. (D. 1. 8. 10.)

Ad hoc respondit Placentinus (quod) omnia communia sunt publica & e converso, sed ratione quorundam usuum, quae sunt publica non sunt communia, & e converso. ut ecce aer, mare, & littora maris, flumina etiam communia, et eorundem ripae communia sunt omnium animalium, quia omnia animalia rationalia & irrationalia his vescuntur & utuntur, abluendo, bibendo, & in eis commorando, & similia, quae natura exigit, faciendo. Eadem etiam ista omnia possunt dici publica ratione quorundam usnum qui solis hominibus competunt, puta piscandi (et) navigandi & retia siccandi & onera reponendi.[2] Portus tamen ait Placentinus esse publicos non communes. Publica autem ita accipiuntur quae sunt omnium populorum. (id est quod spectat) ad usum hominum tantum. Alias publicum apellatur quod est in patrimonio huius vel illius populi tantum, ut C. de sacrosan. eccle. l. ut inter divinum (C. 1. 2. 23.), ut ager et vinea. Eiusdem populi dicitur publicum[3] quantum ad usum, ut ecce via publica, campus Martius. Domino autem meo visum est quod nulla publica sunt communia, nec (vel) e converso. Nam ea demum dicuntur communia quae, cum sint usu omnium animantium, conceduntur tamen occupanti, sicut patet in littore maris, & lapillis & gemmis & caeteris quae in littore inveniuntur, ut ff. eo. l. item lapilli. (D. 1. 8. 3.)

[1] Cf. Maitland, *op. cit.*, p. 95.

[2] Maitland has after *siccandi, et involucra reponendi et similia.*

[3] Maitland has no new sentence: *et eiusdem,* etc.

Non dicat aliquis hac ratione pro derelicto habita communia esse, quia licet concedantur occupanti non tamen sunt in usu omnium animantium. Publica autem nedum non conceduntur occupanti, sed etiam interdicta proponuntur contra eum qui aliquid fecit in eis in laesionem publicam, ut ff. ne quid in loco publico & de flumi. & ne quid in flumi. publi. (D. 43. 8. and D. 43. 12.) Nec obstant his quae dicta sunt (quia),[1] quod alias dicuntur littora populi Romani esse, ut ff. ne quid in loco publico l. littora. (D. 43. 8. 3.) Sunt enim populi Romani quantum ad iurisdictionem, vere tamen sunt communia sunt enim omnium animalium, ut hic dictum est. Non tamen licet in littore aedificare si usus publicus impediatur ex eo, ut ff. ne quid in lo. pu. l. respondendi. (D. 43. 8. 4.)

This exposition may be taken as the classical position on the subject.

Not all of the texts which have been cited as presenting the classical position of the Roman law attracted glosses. Of those that remain, there are several which serve to illuminate the theory of the Glossators.

The gloss on *alioquin*, D. 48. 9. 9., offers a definition of the sea.

Mare comprehendere etiam amnem & flumen, cum mare sit congregatio aquatum multarum.

Bartolus, the great founder of the school of the Post-Glossators, took over this definition with the addition of one word and the substitution of a synonym for *congregatio:*

Mare est collectio aquarum multarum salsarum.[2]

The doctrine of Paulus in D. 47. 10. 14. was to become disputed ground between those who contended that the sea was capable of becoming the object of private property, or, at least, that a state might acquire rights of ownership in the sea, and those who denied it absolutely. The text begins as follows:

Sane si maris proprium ius ad aliquem pertineat: uti possidetis interdictum ei competit, si prohibeatur ius suum exercere.

Azo has left this gloss on *Sane:*

Pertineat: per privilegium, vel per longam consuetudinem.

During the feudal age, in which, of course, Azo lived, the grant of a privilege by the king or emperor was generally recognized as

[1] Instead of *quod*, according to Maitland's version.

[2] Bartolus de Saxoferrato, *Tractatus de Fluminibus* (Bononiae, 1576), p. 54.

conveying valid rights in a thing which was by law *res communis*. In this way a right of fishery might be granted in a public river, or even, in the opinion of the majority of jurists, in the sea. The efficacy of *longa consuetudo* was disputed by the strict classicists, who advocated a custom that reached beyond the memory of man for its inception. This divergence from the doctrine of a Glossator is a brilliant exception to the rule which gave these teachers an authority equal in practice with the texts which they expounded. It may be observed that the doctrine was abandoned only for one more strict.

Another gloss which reflects the influence of the period in which it was written is that on D. 8. 4. 13. The text reads,

> quamvis mari, quod natura omnibus patet, servitus imponi privata lege non potest.

The gloss on *privata*,

> sed princeps potest. . . .

To the position indicated here should be added that which is implicit in a gloss on D. 1. 8. 10. pr.

> Aristo] Casus. Hic dicit . . . sicut quando quis aedificat in maris efficitur aedificium privatum: ita si mare aliquid occupet, sit commune & publicum id quod occupatur.

Classical Roman lawyers found the problem presented by Venice peculiarly annoying. The Glossators' position is stated here unequivocally with a flat disregard of the existence of any such problem. Venice might be within the law in building in the sea. It could be said that the property rights of the Venetians were no more than those of fishermen who erected shelter or docks in the sea. The Venetians, however, claimed certain exclusive rights which were incompatible with the law as here stated. Thus arose the problem.

Four glosses remain to be noted.

D. 18. 1. 51. *Littora:* "quae si sint maris, communia sunt: si fluminis, tunc publica." The gloss on *publica:* "scilicet alia: alias autem non cedunt." These two glosses bear the great name of Accursius.

D. 43. 8. 3. *Littora:* "maris scilicet." *Arbitror:* "quo ad jurisdictionem." These glosses are from the hand of Accursius.[1] He might have added, *et protectionem*. He has also a gloss on J. 2.1.1., in which he identifies the *ius naturale* with the *ius gentium*, but qualifies it by describing it as primeval. All things were common under primeval natural law, or, the *ius gentium*.[2]

IV. Conclusions

The resuscitation of the Roman law was the resuscitation of the law promulgated by Justinian, the Roman law in effect in the sixth century, and contained in the law books written or compiled by his orders. The Glossators used these original texts, and the Roman law was in danger of becoming ossified under the rigidity of interpretation which had become the standard method of study and exposition. The departure of Placentinus from the accepted terminology of his school brought repudiation from his colleagues.

In their observations on the jurisdiction of the Roman people, or of "Caesar" over the sea, it seems impossible that any modern idea of sovereignty could have entered.[3] The middle age missed the conception of the personality of the state. The location of the sovereign power proved a moot question until the modern period. There were conflicting theories not only as to the source of the power and authority of the Prince, but also as to the scope thereof, and as to his responsibility for the exercise thereof. Always he was restricted by the *ius divina* (transformed into terms of ecclesiastical law), and probably in general by the *ius naturale*. In the later middle age there were difficulties over the question whether the princely authority lodged in the office of monarch or in the man. Furthermore, the attitude of jurisprudence towards the law was unlike the modern position. Legislation in the sense of law-*making* was a concept foreign to the mediaeval spirit. Ex-

[1] The probable dates of Accursius, the last and greatest of the Glossators, are 1182–1260. He was a pupil of Azo. Savigny, *op. cit.*, v, 268–270.

[2] *Institutiones, . . . cum Accursiana Interpretatione* (Lugduni, 1542), p. 25.

[3] Otto Gierke, *Political Theories of the Middle Age*, translated by F. W. Maitland, Cambridge, 1922, *passim*. The statements following are also based upon my understanding of this book. It is perhaps well to add that I have used the word "state" throughout for the sake of its brevity, and not as implying the modern concept.

isting law was interpreted, was stated, was even suspended; but it seems that law was not *made*. When the sea was declared to be by the law of nature incapable of becoming the object of private property, or of any kind of property — for such is the meaning of course of the set terms which have been the subject of this study — the matter was closed. When the shores of the sea were declared free of access to all men for the exercise of the right of fishing, by the *ius gentium*, there was no sovereign power which could override this law and annul it. It is in the light of these considerations that the exercise of jurisdiction over the shore or over the sea should be understood.

The *res publicae* were things of quite a different class. With regard to things of this class, the *proprietas* was lodged in the state, according to the familiar doctrine of the law. A tendency to place the *litora maris* and even the sea itself among the *res publicae* is observed in the "Brachylogus." Some such shifting of base was perhaps necessary before a theory of sovereignty over the sea could be elaborated. It seems plausible in view of the doctrine of the classical Roman law on the subject to presume that a state would develop its claim not directly by an assertion, but more slowly and through the medium of the *res publicae*, by a gradual broadening of that class to include the object proprietorship of which was desired. The development of this theory could, in the nature of the case, be scarcely perceptible in mediaeval thought; but with the break-up of the idea of unity, and with the disintegration of feudalism and the subsequent rise of national selfconsciousness, together with the development of the absolute monarchical form of government, this growth would be accelerated. It is not impossible though it is perhaps not capable of verification, that the theory expressed in the "Brachylogus"—the bracketing of the sea with rivers and harbors as *res publicae* — marks the beginning of that doctrine which culminated with the publication of Selden's work on the *mare clausum*, and found practical expression in the claim of the English Stuarts to the sovereignty of the sea.[1]

[1] For a brilliant account of the diplomatic and political history of the claim of the Stuarts, with its relation to the maritime jurisdiction of fisheries, see T. W. Fulton, *The Sovereignty of the Sea*, Edinburgh and London, 1911.

The confusion of terminology among the Glossators in regard to things which are *nullius*, common, or public is marked. The double use of *res nullius* is retained. On the one hand, the phrase is used in its narrow meaning to denote things which, being susceptible of private appropriation, are without an owner; in this meaning are embraced those things which are open to acquisition by occupation. In its wide connotation the term denotes those things which are incapable of appropriation by a private individual, that is, by single persons, and the class is coterminous with *res extra nostrum patrimonium*. In it are the *res sacrae, religiosae* and *sanctae*, which are the property of God; in it also are the *res publicae* and the *res universitatis*, for they cannot become the objects of private property; in it, finally, are the *res communes*, and for the same reason. *Res communes* are distinguished from *res publicae* by the fact that over them no ownership of any sort may be acquired. But there is to be found another doctrine which is somewhat different. In both classes the right of property is forbidden to individuals. In the case of the *res communes*, the use of them is common to all men; in the case of the *res publicae*, the people of the whole world, all men generally, have a collective property right. That is, all the people in the world, considered as a unity, have this property right. This meaning of the phrase *res publicae* is essentially different from that which is meant when roads, highways, navigable rivers, and ports are being described, for these are state property and not that of the *populus totius mundi*. It is probably in this wider meaning of the phrase that the sea was termed *res publica*. Since it was owned by all men, the use of it was free to all men. If the sea is *res communis*, and as to *proprietas*, *nullius*, then any act of appropriation is contrary to natural law; if the sea is *res publica* in this wide sense of the term, then an act of appropriation is a despoiliation, the violation of a property right.

Azo pointed out that *res communes* are open to occupation. Fishermen who built huts on the seashore, or out in the sea, possessed a certain restricted property right in them. Yet, as to *proprietas*, the shore remained *nullius*. There seems to be involved here no departure from the original doctrine.[1] In such a case, the occupation of a *res communis* would not lead to the acquisition of a property right, by any corporate body.

[1] O. Gierke, *Das Deutsche Genossenschaftsrecht*, 4 vols. (Berlin, 1881), iii, 209, 210 and note 68, p. 210, for the essential points in this summary of the terminology of the Glossators.

"Die keineswegs von Verwirrung freie Terminologie der Quellen, bezüglich der herrenlosen, gemeinen und öffentlichen Sachen bereitete hier den Glossatoren manche Schwierigkeit. Sie helfen sich, indem sie sunächst die römische Kategorie der *res nullius* für mehrdeutig erklären: im engeren Sinn umfasse sie nur die herrenlosen, der Okkupation offenen Sachen, im weiteren Sinn negire sie nur das Eigenthum eines einzelnen Menschen, umfasse daher auch die *res sacrae, religiosae et sanctae*, da deren eigentlicher Eigenthümer Gott sei (*sed sunt in bonis Dei, hominum censura sive dispositione*), sowie die gemeinen, öffentlichen und korporativen Sachen, da diese zwar menschlichen Verbänden, aber keinem Einzelnen gehörten (*quia esse possunt et sunt hominum, licet non humanis singularis; nullius*, i. e., *hominis privati, sed communatis*). Unter den letzteren seien wieder die *res communes* und die eigentlichen *res publicae* von den *res inuversitatis* zu trennen. Die beiden ersteren Kategorien schlössen das Eigenthum nicht nur eines Einzelnen, sondern auch jedes menschlichen Sonderverbandes aus: an ihnen bestehe nur ein Recht des "*populus totius mundi.*" Unter sich seien sie wieder dadurch unterschieden, dass die *res communes* nur dem Gebrauch noch gemein, dem Eigenthum nach herrenlos, die *res publicae* dagegen Eigenthum des Weltvolkes seien," pp. 209, 210.

S. Gl. zu ※. 5 Inst. 2. 1. v. "*publicus:* die *res communes* seien der Okkupation offen, die *res publicae* nicht; heisse das Meerufer hier *publicum*, sonst *commune*, so folge daraus nicht Identität beider Begriffe, da es *quoad usum commune* und insofern also auch *publicum*, aber *quoad proprietatem nullius* sei. Ein späterer Zusatz erklärt, *communia* seien die kraft des *jus naturale* primaevum im ursprünglichen Zustände der Gütergemeinschaft verbliebenen Dinge, welche *propter suam incomprehensibilitatem in solius Dei dominio* stunden; *publica vero veluti comprehensibilior totius populi de mundo per jus gentium fuere applicata dominio. . . .* Andere erklärten dagegen die Begriffe *communia* u. *publica* füridentisch. Und die Gl. zu l. 2 D de R. D. v. "*littora*" sagt, die *littora seien communia quoad usum et dominium, sed quoad protectionem populi Romani*, was dann Baldus dahin deklarirt: *communis* sei nur der *usus*, die *proprietas* sei *nullius*, die *jurisdictio* oder *protectio* sei *Caesaris*." Note 68.

CHAPTER IV

GERMANIC LAW

I. The Codes

In the Roman territory conquered by the Barbarians, each individual was usually judged by the law of his nationality. In the new German kingdoms there were, therefore, in existence at the same time the German laws and the Roman laws promulgated by the order and with the sanction of the German kings.[1]

King Euricus was the principal lawgiver of the Visigoths, though he was not the earliest one. He seems to have collected, supplemented and codified his laws and those of his predecessors. Gundobadus performed a similar work among the Burgundians.[2] According to Zeumer, the date of the Codex of Euricus lies between 469 and 481. It contains the laws in force first among the Goths, and then those in force between Goth and Roman litigants. In causes the parties to which were Roman, Roman law was applied, and thus it remained in force and vigor.

The sources of Roman law were at this time diffused, and accessible with difficulty. Alaric II, son of Euricus, undertook a collection of them and promulgated the resulting *corpus* in 506. This body of laws is known to-day as the "Lex Romana Visigothorum," or the "Code" or the "Breviary of Alaric." Therefore, in general, the Codex of Euricus contains Gothic, and that of Alaric, Roman law.

But the Codex of Euricus was not pure Gothic law. Of its character Zeumer writes:

> Gothi iam pridem, cum in Gallia advenerant, non pauca ex iure Romanorum usu receperant, veteris iuris proprii institutis nonnullis abolitis. Romani autem iureconsulti, qui Eurici decessorumque leges dictabant, for-

[1] Ortolan, *op. cit.*, i, 417.

[2] The Burgundian law contains nothing on the status of the sea and the maritime jurisdiction of sea fisheries.

mabant eas ad exemplum Romanarum legum; itaque iam codex Eurici magis leges Romano-Gothicis quam mere Gothicas continuit.[1]

They were therefore laws for the Visigoths which were formulated under Roman influence.

The next great codification was made almost two centuries later; although there had been made alterations in the existing code from time to time, these had not kept pace with the actual lawgiving. Chindasvindus set himself the task of collecting, digesting, and promulgating the laws ancient and modern common to both Goth and Roman. He succeeded in incorporating many into a *corpus legum*. This work was apparently called the "Liber iudiciorum," which, as completed and promulgated by his son, Recessvindus, is known as the "Liber iudiciorum," or the "Lex Visigothorum Recessvindiana." It seems that the "Liber" was finished and edited by Recessvindus in the second year after the death of his father, or, 654.

Another great renovation of the laws took place by order of King Ervigius in 681. New laws were added, and these were incorporated into the "Liber."

Egica, successor to Ervigius, carried on the process of modernization by adding new laws which were inserted in the corpus. His son, Witizano, seems also to have made additions.[2]

In these bodies of laws, there appears no legal theory regarding the freedom of the sea. A few laws are recorded which touch matters pertaining to maritime commerce or some fishing industry; but it can hardly be said that they indicate any doctrine concerning the status of the sea.

It is perhaps noteworthy that a provision of the *Lex Rhodia* is found in the *Breviary*, although the importance of this fact is limited to its indication of a continuity of maritime jurisdiction, for a similar law, with the same title, appears in nearly every code which has been examined. It appears unconnected with any as-

[1] *Leges Visigothorum*, in the *Monumenta*, cited in full below, p. xiii *et seq.*, for the statements made here, unless otherwise cited.

[2] This résumé is based on Zeumer, *Leges Visigothorum*, in the *Monumenta Germaniae Historica, Legum Sectio* I. Hannoverae et Lipsiae, 1902. See the *Prefatio, cap.* i., especially, pp. xiii–xv.

sertion of wider jurisdiction than that stipulated in its text.[1] Its immediate source is Paulus's *Sententia*.

The "Lex Visigothorum" is likewise silent upon this subject. There are laws of the same general character as those referred to above, all of which are in the tenor of similar laws in the Theodosian Code, though of course there is a difference in detail. The laws of the Visigoths seem to be the only Barbarian laws which even approach the subject. The laws of the Burgundians [2] and those of the Allamanni [3] yield nothing. The laws of the Franks, as contained in the *Breviary of Alaric*, present almost nothing.

[1] M. Conrat, *Breviarum Alaricianum. Romisches Recht im Fränkischen Reich*, Leipzig, 1903. Paul. 11.7. "Obligationes quae consensu contrahuntur," p. 282. On p. 680 is a provision for a tax on transportation to or from ship, of goods. *Cf.* T. C. 4.11.1.

[2] L. R. de Salis, *Leges Burgundionum*, in the *Monumenta*, Hannoverae, 1892.

[3] K. Lehmann, *Leges Alamannorum*, in the *Monumenta*, *Leges Sectio* I. v. i. (Sectio I. Tomus V. Pars I.)

From the *Leges Visigothorum*, *op. cit.*, XXVIIII. *Antiqua*. (VIII. 4.29.) "De discretione concludendorum fluminum: — Flumina maiora, id est, per que isoces aut alii pisces maritimi subricuntur forsitam retia aut quecumque conmercia veniunt navium, nullus ad integrum contra multorum conmune commodum sue tantumodo utilitati consulturus excludat; sed usque ad medium alveum, ubi maximus fluminis ipsius concursus est, sepem ducere non vetetur, ut alia medietas diversorum usibus libera relinquatur. Si quis contra hoc fecerit, exclusa ipsius a comite civitatis vel a iudice sine aliqua excusatione rumpatur, et si honestioris loci persona est, X solidos det illis, quibus inpedire conatus est; si vero inferior persona fuerit, V solidos det et L flagella suscipiat. Quod si ab utraque parte huius flumenis duo manserint, non liceat ad integrum excludere, ut dicat unusquisque eorum, quod medietatem sue partis excluserit; sed alter superios, alter inferius clusuram facere ex medietatem fluminis non proibeatur. Si vero locus non fuerit nisi tantumodo in uno transitu, sic excludatur, ut et naves et retia per medium discurrere possint. Quod si comes civitatis aut aliquis cuiuscumque clusura contra hanc ordinationem nostram evertere presumat, X solidos domino clusure dare debeat. Certe si minor persona hoc fecerit, V solidos clusure domino cogatur exolvere et L flagella a iudice eius loci accipiat. Si servus hoc fecerit, C verberibus subiacebit." Although this law does not apply the term, these *flumina maiora* correspond to the *flumina publica* of Roman law, if one may be guided by the character of the jurisdiction of the exercise of which the above is evidence, in drawing such a conclusion.

Zeumer includes in his work a *Collectionis Iuris Romano-Visigothici, Capita* VII.-XX. (Fragmenta Gaudenziana), which was promulgated about 506. P. 469. It is called variously the *Lex Romana Visigothorum* or the *Codex* or the *Breviarium Alarici*. It is, then, a fragment of the *Breviary of Alaric*, of which Conrat has reconstructed the whole in the work cited above, so far perhaps as it is possible to do so.

II. Practice of the Emperors

The practice of the great emperors, as revealed in the mass of acts, constitutions, capitularies, and treaties which have come down to the present day, show a development from the strict position of the classical Roman law. It is not remarkable that this should be so during the period preceding the resuscitation of the law at the University of Bologna. It is significant that this development should have continued after that event had taken place, and during the period of the activity of the glossators.

The growth alluded to took the following general forms: the grants of river fisheries to private persons or bodies; the grant of sea fisheries to similar persons or bodies; the use of the sea to mark a boundary to a domain or to an estate; the exemption of specified persons or people from the payment of port or harbor dues; and the grant of freedom of commerce or of travel or of both to specified parties. Such acts as these indicate a personal freedom of the monarch to dispose at will of the use of public property. This freedom did not, apparently, extend to the right to alienate the title to public property, which remained vested in the people, or in the state, or in the monarch as the personification or representative of the nation, according to the theory of the times.

It will be observed that the actual practice along the lines indicated does not break with the usage of the past, nor does it mark a rupture in legal or juristic thought. The sea, for example, had been used as a boundary to the land from time immemorial. The states of the ancient world had owned fisheries. Favored cities had been granted especial rights in connection with trade. The development referred to is evidenced rather in the increasing frequency with which private persons are given exclusive rights in the public domains. It was accelerated by the steady concentration of power in the monarch, in spite of theories as to the source and scope of this power, and in particular, by the growth of feudalism. The rivalry between the Emperors and the Popes affected this development by causing the former to emphasize his prerogatives, and by causing him to use every means at his disposal to increase, as well as to preserve, his authority. The results of this development proved to be far-reaching. The uninterrupted practice of granting to loyal subjects or vassals portions of the lands of the state or of the empire, together with the frequent grants of exclusive rights of use in public property eventually became endowed with the sanction of long-established custom. The minds of the people became habituated to a new idea of the relation of the state or of its personal embodiment, the sovereign, to public property. The idea of the nature of public property underwent a corresponding change. It became possible to include within its range things which had hitherto been excluded.

The acceptance of these new relationships as fact created in due time theories to justify and to explain them — theories of politics and theories of law. While the break-up of feudalism and the rise of intensely national states destroyed much, both of fact and theory, much also was preserved; this remainder of a former system took fresh root in the municipal law of the young nations, and in the new science of international law, or, more strictly, of the law of nations. The idea of the possibility of acquiring ownership of, or sovereignty over the sea, though it had heretofore existed in a very primitive form, so far as it was active at all, was one of the ideas which was projected into the modern era, there to take concrete form under the powerful interaction of conflicting practice and opposing theories.[1]

The earliest instance of the practice of granting to subjects the right to the exclusive use of certain public properties which has been preserved in the original record is contained in a royal grant dated January, 777.[2] At this time Charlemagne made to a monastery a grant in perpetuity of exclusive rights to a fishery in the Rhine.[3] There is recorded a gift by Otto II in 975 to a Church in

[1] For a detailed discussion of this subject see the following chapter on feudal law.

[2] *Die Urkunden Otto des III.*, in the *Monumenta Germaniae Historica, Diplomatum Regum et Imperatorum Germaniae, Ottonis II. et III. Diplomata*, ii, 2 (Hannover, 1888–93), p. 592.

[3] E. Mühlbacher, *Die Urkunden Pippins, Karlmanns und Karls des Grossen*, in the *Monumenta, Diplomatum Karolinorum; Pippini, Carlomanni, et Caroli Magni Diplomata* (Hannover, 1906), i, 161.

Utrecht of certain properties, including the grant of a fishery in the Zuidersee.[1] These are merely illustrations of what was a settled practice.[2]

In February, 1022, a royal court sitting under the presidency of Henry II restored to a certain monastery land which had been appropriated by a certain two counts. Appertaining to the land

[1] *Die Urkunden Otto des II.*, in the *Monumenta, Diplomatum, Ottonis II. et III. Diplomata* (Hannover, 1888–93), ii. i, 120. " . . . omnem vero piscationem quam in Almere ad nostram regalitatem habuimus pertinentem, iure perenni illuc relaxavimus."

[2] Otto III. grants to a chapel in Frankfort the yield of a certain fishery in the Main for every Friday. "9 May, 994 . . . dedimus omnem piscationem quae ad nostrum regium ius pertinet in flumine Moynus vocato — a quibuscumque piscatoribus nostris sive aliis in sexta feria, hoc est die Veneris, per totam noctem et diem illum aliqui pisces aliqua arte sive retibus sive hamio seu neste . . . capi possunt." *Die Urkunden Otto des III.*, *op. cit.*, p. 554. For full citation see under Otto II, above.

There is a record of a grant by Otto III. to a monastery of a fishery in the river Flubio or Fibbio, 11 Nov. 995. See *Die Urkunden Otto des III.*, *op. cit.*, p. 592.

Otto III grants to the Cathedral (bischoflichen Kirche) in Cremona the banks of the Adda and the river fishery against all other rights from Teuchera to its junction with the Po. " . . . ripas et piscarias cum molendinis et portubus a Teucaria usque ubi Addua in Padum defluit et caput Addue nominatur, per nostri precepti paginam predicte Cremonensi ecclesie donando concederemus." *Ibid.*, p. 615. 27 May, 996.

Another similar grant: "piscatoribus autem superius exarate abbatie firma largitione concedimus, ut per Padum et per flumina alia paludesque omnes ab Papie finibus usque mare liberam piscandi ad abbatis et monachorum usus facultatem habeant, omni contradictione remota." 25 March, 997. *Ibid.*, p. 655.7 *et seq.* And on 26 April, 998, the Emperor made another grant of rights in a river fishery. *Ibid.*, p. 707.

On November 1, 1007, Henry II granted to a nunnery exclusive fishing rights in a district on both sides of the Main. "Preterea fines piscacionum sic discrevimus, ut ex una parte Mogi ab amne qui dicitur Swarzaha usque ad riwum qui dicitur Dihenbach et ex altera parte Mogi a villa qui vocatur Chellere usque ad vallem Sulzevelt nemo preter abbatissam piscandi potestatem haberet nisi qui piscandi licenciam ab ipsa inpetraret. *Die Urkunden Heinrichs II. und Arduins*, in the *Monumenta, Diplomatum, Heinrici et Arduini Diplomata* (Hannover, 1900–03), iii, 662.

The grant of a fishery was occasionally, and probably often, but one of a number of grants which were all conferred at the same time. This fact is shown in the following, which is the record of a grant made by Charles IV, to the Archbishop of Treves; it is dated 25–26 November, 1346, and bears the caption, *Scripta pro Archiepiscopo Treverensi.* It comes under a general heading, *Privilegia Tempore Coronationis Concessa.* Charles grants the "districtus, thelonia, stratas publicas, conductas per terram et aquas, ius navigandi, piscarias, aquarum decursus, ripas et ittora in dominio. . . ." *Constitutiones et Acta publica Imperatorum et Regum*, in

was a sea fishery, which Henry restored when putting into effect the judgment of the court.[1]

A case is recorded where Conrad II, in 1038, confirmed a religious institution in the possession of some island property, including a maritime fishery.[2]

One of the more important documents is a treaty or *pactum* between Otto IV and the Duke of Venice, dated 18 August, 1209, which confirms the Venetians in the possession of their property, including their fisheries:[3]

Proprietates vero et predia, que habere videntur tam ipse dux quam suus patriarcha nec non episcopi, abbates et aecclesiae sancte Dei et reliquus populus Venetus sibi subiectus infra potestatem imperii nostri, sive in campis sive in domibus, pratis, silvis, vineis paludibus, salictis, sacionibus, piscationibus et ceteris possessionibus, quiete possideant et absque cuiusquam insultantis machinatione aut lesione sive sinistra quapiam tergiversatione, ita ut nemo contrarietatem eis inde facere presumat.

A striking example of imperial favor is the following gift, which is taken from the *Acta Regni Ludewici IV. et Friderici III.*; it bears the date, 15 February, 1328:[4]

the *Monumenta, Legum Sectio* IV, viii, *pars prior* (Hannoverae et Lipsiae, 1910), 185.

In 1026 Conrad II renewed for the monastery at Bremen a grant of fisheries and of tax-free commerce in Italy. H. Breslau, *Die Urkunden Konrads II.*, in the *Monumenta, Diplomatum, Conradi II. Diplomata*, iv, (Hannover und Leipzig, 1909), 71–72. There seems to have been nothing unusual in renewing a grant of fishery and other rights and privileges. This renewal is particularly interesting because of the number of diversified things which are included within it.

Partaking of the character of a renewal is a confirmation by Conrad II, of the possession by a nunnery of certain properties. See note 2, below.

[1] The provost representing the monastery came before the court "et querelatus est supra Atto et Pandolfo comitibus de res sancti Benedicti, qui est in comitatu Termolense, et est ipsa res infra finis: capo fine Rigo plano pede fine mare cum ipso litore maris cum portora et piscaciones suas." *Die Urkunden Heinrichs II. und Arduins, op. cit.*, p. 591. In the award of Henry it is said: "Per has fines: uno capo fine. Rivo planu et pede (fine) mare cum ipso litore maris cum portora et piscacione sua," p. 593.

It will be noted that estates with coast lines frequently possess marine fisheries.

[2] H. Breslau, *op. cit.*, p. 377. All the properties of the estate "cum . . . piscationibus maris vel fluviorum . . . monasterio . . . in insula maris nomine Tremiti sito . . . concedimus donamus . . . atque corroboramus."

[3] L. Weiland, *Constitutiones et Acta Publica Imperatorum et Regum*, in the *Monumenta, Legum Sectio* IV, ii (Hannoverae, 1896), 39.

[4] *Constitutiones et Acta Publica Imperatorum et Regum, Legum Sectio* IV, vi, *Partis prioris Fasciculus I* (Hannoverae et Lipsiae, 1914), 301.

Ludowicus Dei gracia Romanorum imperator semper augustus [rewards a faithful vassal by the bestowal on him of a dukedom] cum . . . piscariis, piscacionibus . . . montibus, planis, vallibus et omnibus et singulis locis, iuribus et pertinenciis tam maris quam terre.

This phraseology seems to indicate a grant of both salt and fresh water fisheries.

The phrase, *mare oceanum*, occurs in a document in which the Emperor Charlemagne lays down the boundaries of a certain parish (Sprengel) in a newly created bishopric (Bistum) in Bremen. It is dated 14 July, 788:[1]

. . . certo eam limite fecimus terminari eique hos Terminos: mare oceanum, Albiam fluvium, et cet.

Twice on the same day, 6 February, 806, did Charlemagne name the sea to mark a boundary.[2] Otto III specified both the sea and the seashore as boundaries.[3] Henry II used the phrase *litus maris* at least once, in this connection.[4] Conrad II made use of the term, *mare salsum:*[5]

. . . et per Argaonem usque ad mare salsum,

with a guarantee of the fisheries off shore, which were part of the domain. Frederick II, in 1223,[6] granted to one of his counts com-

[1] Mühlbacher, *op. cit.*, p. 346.

[2] A. Boretius, *Capitularia Regum Francorum*, in the *Monumenta*, *Legum Sectio* II, i (Hannoverae, 1883), 127: "Divisiones vero a Deo conservati at que conservandi imperii vel regni nostri tales facere placuit . . . vallem Segusianam usque ad clusas et inde per terminos Italicorum montium usque ad mare, hos pagos cum suis civitatibus et quicquid ab eis contra meridiem et occidentem usque ad mare vel usque ad Hispanias continetur. . . . Ludovico dilecto filio nostro consignavimus."

The second, on p. 128: " . . . quicquid autem a praedictis civitatibus vel comitatibus Roman eunti ad dextram iacet de praedicto regno, id est portionem quae remansit de regione Transpadana una cum ducatu Tuscano usque ad mare australe et usque ad Provinciam, Ludovicus ad augmentum sui regni sortiatur."

[3] *Die Urkunden Otto des III.*, *op. cit.*, p. 603: "molendinum etiam postium iuxta murum civitatis, medietatem districti de littore maris cum porticio suo per quod itur ad mare. . . ."

[4] *Die Urkunden Heinrichs II. und Arduins*, *op. cit.*, p. 226: " . . . tercio lateri limes qui dicitur Arzer percurrens a Paueriano usque in stratellam et rivus qui vocatur de Fabrica definiens ac derivens usque in mare et ipsum litus maris." 25 Apr. 1009.

[5] On 4 June, 1035, Conrad confirmed the citizens of Capodistria in the possession of their property, customs, freedom from public imposts, and freedom of commerce within the empire. H. Breslau, *op. cit.*, pp. 299, 300.

[6] Weiland, *op. cit.*, ii, 121. 20–29 Apr. 1223.

plete jurisdiction with all rights appertaining thereto over a domain extending

a Folia usque ad Renum, a mari usque ad Alpes, cum omnibus iuribus, placitis et bannis, aquis et piscacionibus.

In this and similar grants, there is no extension of territorial jurisdiction out to sea. There is not even an intimation of a claim to the sovereignty of or to dominion of the sea. A claim to sovereignty in the modern sense was of course impossible, as has been pointed out, for the concept was lacking to the mediaeval mind.

On the other hand, there is evidence which points to, if it does not prove, the existence of property rights in the bays and smaller indentations along the coasts; the gulfs and great bays may also have been reduced to private property, with perhaps appropriate restrictions to guarantee their accessibility to the public. Venice is, in truth, as nearly every writer on the subject from the thirteenth to the eighteenth centuries has pointed out, the example *par excellence* of the appropriation of the sea. Allowing for a certain amount of exaggeration, the evidence of these writers indicates clearly that the Venetians owned the bays and gulfs adjacent to the land which they occupied, and claimed jurisdiction over the upper Adriatic by right of ownership. The claim to ownership of the adjacent bays and gulfs through which their islands were sprinkled seems to have been accepted by the jurists, who advanced a theory of ownership by prescription. The claim to the ownership of the sea itself seems to have been a later development, and was not readily accepted, if, indeed, it ever met with general consent. The situation seems to be that while the Venetians had the naval power to assert their claims, foreign nations could only accept them under protest; and that these claims declined in cogency with the decline of the power of Venice. The same general situation was true in the case of Genoa, the rival of Venice.

That the smaller bays and indentations were owned by the Prince or by the great vassals (under royal patents) does not seem open to doubt. The evidence of the classical Roman jurists, and the observations of the older literary men proves that it was a common habit to enclose portions of the sea to form fish preserves. This practice received legal approval from the Emperor Leo in the East, four of whose Novels make express provision for the protection of the property rights so acquired.[1] The evidence in regard to the larger bays and gulfs is not perhaps of a character finally and definitely to prove that these bodies of water, or a large part of them, were reduced to private ownership; but on the other hand the presumption is strong that such was the case. It does not seem necessary to suppose that the practices noted in connection with inlets of the sea and enclosed fish preserves were always pursued only within small indentations of the coast. The possession by the great lords of vast domains, many of which must have had an extended frontage on the sea; the possession of private fisheries in the sea; the grant of privileges and immunities in connection with jurisdiction over the land and the cities on it which also had come into the lord's possession by virtue of a royal or imperial grant; the right to levy customs and taxes on foreigners — all of these rights and powers together would naturally produce in the mind of the ruler possessing them a sense of proprietorship of the things over which he exercised them. Such a lord would not be apt to make a distinction between a large bay and a small one; indeed, he would find it difficult to discover a reason for making such a distinction, in the great majority of cases. The lord or prince would own fisheries in both alike; he would levy harbor dues in both alike, provided that there were ports at which ships were accustomed to call; both alike would be on the coast which bounded his domain; the larger bay would possess no sanctity which the smaller one did not also possess.

There is one piece of evidence from an eye-witness that as a matter of fact the great nobles did profess to own the bays which indented the coasts of their great estates as early as the fourth century — that is, six centuries before the age of feudalism. It comes from St. Ambrose, Bishop of Milan:[2]

[1] To be found in D. Gothofredus, *Corpus Iuris Civilis*, in 2 vols., Amstelodami, 1663, under the title: *Justiniani Edicta*, item, *Novellae Constitutiones Imperatoris Leonis Augusti*, in vol. ii. Novels 56, 102, 103, 104.

[2] S. Ambrosius, *Hexameron*, ed. by R. O. Gilbert (Lipsiae, 1840), p. 116, sec. 27, bk. v.

In his *De Officiis Ministrorum* (ed. by Gilbert as *De Officiis Clericorum*, Lipsiae,

Spatia maris sibi vindicant iure mancipii, pisciumque iura sicut vernaculorum conditione sibi servitii subiecta commemorant. Iste, inquit, sinus maris meus est; ille alterius. Dividunt elementa sibi potentes.

In one of his constitutions, Frederick II uses the phrase, *nostra terra marique.*[1] The date of the document is September 22, 1245. The passage in which the words occur, follows:

Nichilominus tamen, si forte quod absit discrimen presentis discordie inter nos, ecclesiam et Lombardos durare contigerit, predicto regi ac omnibus crucesignatis cum eo, quatenus presentium negotiorum et temporum qualitas patitur et tempestas, presidia nostra terra marique, tam in navibus quam victualibus, promptis affectibus offerimus per presentes.

The use of the enclitic instead of the conjunction, *et*, is significant. -*Que*, of course, unites the word to which it is attached with the preceding word in one conception. Consequently the Emperor must be writing of "our sea" as well as of "our land."

It is perhaps permissible to quote an apposite fragment of the epitaph of the Emperor:[2]

Qui mare, qui terras, populos et regna subegit
Cesareum nomen subito mors improba fregit.
Iusticie lumen

and so forth.

In 1245, the doctrine of the extension of territorial jurisdiction over the sea adjacent to the territory from which the jurisdiction emanates, was yet to be formulated.[3] Maritime jurisdiction of

1839), p. 65, sec. 132, bk. i, he says: "Deinde formam iustitiae putaverunt, ut quis communia, id est, publica pro publicis habeat, privata pro suis. Ne hoc quidem secundum naturam; natura enim omnia omnibus in commune profudit. Sic enim Deus generari iussit omnia, ut pastus omnibus communis esset et terra foret omnium quaedam communis possessio. Natura igitur ius commune generant, usurpatio ius fecit privatum. Quo in loco aiunt placuisse Stoicis, quae in terris gigantur, omnia ad usus hominum creari; homines autem hominum causa esse generatos, ut ipsi inter se aliis alii prodesse possint."

[1] Weiland, *op. cit.*, p. 371.

[2] *Ibid.*, p. 384, n. 5.

[3] The present writer is indebted to Sir Graham Bower for drawing his attention to a passage in Polybius in which that historian quotes a treaty concluded between Carthage and Rome in 509–508 B.C. The pertinent passage follows: "The Romans and their allies not to sail with long ships beyond the Fair Promontory unless forced by storm or by enemies: it is forbidden to anyone carried beyond it by force to buy or carry away anything beyond what is required for the repair of his ship or for sacrifice, and he must depart within five days." This is the first of a series of three

this character and origin was exercised by the states of Venice and Genoa long before claims for the exercise of a similar jurisdiction became general, and long before it received wide recognition from the great jurists. At this time the glossators controlled Roman Law. The feudal law of things dealt only with those capable of becoming the objects of private property. The genius of the system of land tenure was antagonistic to community of use. The products of the sea could be owned; they were known to the *ius feudale*. Only if the sea were capable of being appropriated, and not only that, but also, only when the sea had been reduced to ownership, could feudal law take cognizance of it, and then only of those parts over which property rights had been established. In the case of the sea and with regard to feudal law, ownership must be *de facto*, a *fait accompli*, before it could be *de jure*.

The question of the bays and other indentations along the coast is quite a different one from that of the open sea, as Grotius pointed out some centuries later — only to fall foul of such men as Selden and Welwood. Nevertheless the distinction is apparent. The rights and privileges connected with the use of bays and harbors were frequently used as instruments to satisfy imperial or royal generosity. A characteristic means of discharging an obligation to a loyal vassal, or, indeed, of safe-guarding the complicated interests of the ruler of a kingdom, was the granting of the right to collect the port dues. Several instances of this practice are on record, and may be cited here.

treaties embodying these provisions, the last of which was negotiated in 279 B.C. See *The Histories*, transl. by W. R. Paton (New York, 1922), iii, 22.

Sir Graham comments, "It made the western half of the Mediterranean to the west of Cape Bon a *mare clausum*."

These treaties furnish valuable proof of an early example of a practice which, in developed form, was to furnish the subject for heated controversy in the seventeenth century. It is important to note that the portion of the Mediterranean specified was closed to Rome, not by an act of sovereignty on the part of Carthage, but by a treaty with the power excluded, i.e., Rome. A *mare clausum* was established, in fact; but it was established as an arrangement made between the parties concerned. In essence, these treaties seem to be agreements concerning the use or navigation of the sea made between the two chief Mediterranean powers, one of which was dominant at the time the treaties were made.

On the 18th of March, 1030, Conrad II turned over the government of the city of Cremona to the Cathedral Church there, together with the right to collect, and, presumably, to retain, the port dues.[1]

Rudolph made a similar grant in 1291, which is recorded in a document entitled, "Confirmatio Pacis generalis," 8 Apr. 1291:[2]

19. Alle die die zolle nement uf wazzer oder uf lande, die sulnt den wegen und den bruggen ir reht behaben mit machend und mit bezzerunge, und von dem si nement den zol, die suln si befriden und beleiten nach ir maht, als ir geriht gat, daz si nit ferliesen. . . .

This paragraph obviously included inland waterways within the scope of its provisions.

Harbors appertaining to a domain seem generally to have been included with the grant of the land as part of the appurtenances thereof. Several instances of this have been given.

A sweeping grant was made by Henry II, in 1020, in which he renewed a *pactum* with Benedict VIII, which had been made by Otto I. This grant is an illustration of those in which harbors or ports are included merely as one of the items of the grant:[3]

In nomine domini dei omnipotentis patris et filii et spiritus sancti. Ego Heinrichus dei gratia imperator augustus spondeo at promitto per hoc pactum confirmationis nostre tibi beato Petro principi apostolorum et clavigero regni celorum et per te vicario tuo domno Benedicto summo pontifici et universali pape, sicut a predecessoribus vestris usque nunc in vestra potestate atque ditione tenuistis et disposuistis: civitatem Romanam cum ducatu suo et suburbanis atque viculis omnibus et territoriis eius montanis ac maritimis, litoribus ac portubus, seu cunctis civitatibus, etc.

The treaties with the Venetians offer interesting examples of general provisions for freedom of travel and commerce. The privileges granted are usually operative both on land and sea.

In the treaty between Otto IV and the Duke of Venice, 18 August, 1209, already cited, Article 10 is as follows:[4]

Ripaticum autem et quadragesimum Venetis detur secundum antiquam consuetudinem. Ipse vero Veneti per totum imperium et per totam terram,

[1] Breslau, *op. cit.*, p. 197. See also, p. 213.

[2] L. Schwalm, *Constitutiones et Acta Publica Imperatorum et Regum*, in the *Monumenta, Legum Sectio* IV, iii (Hannoverae et Lipsiae, 1904–06), 445.

[3] *Die Urkunden Heinriche II. und Arduins*, *op. cit.*, p. 544.

[4] Weiland, *op. cit.*, pp. 40, 41.

quam vel nunc habemus vel in posterum Deo auctore habituri sumus, liberi sint ab omni exactione et datione; et licentiam habeant homines ipsius ducis ambulandi per terram seu per flumina totius imperii nostri; similiter et nostri per mare usque ad eos et non amplius.

17. Et hoc stetit de capulo, quod Rivoaltenses, Metamaucenses, Albionenses, Torcellenses, Amianenses fecerunt retro ab annis multis: habeant licentiam faciendi secundum antiquam consuetudinem, sive per flumina sive per mare.

The last clause of Article 10 conveys the impression that the subjects of the Emperor are being given a treaty right to navigate in the territorial waters of Venice, or, in other words, that the sea fronting Venice is in the possession of that state; in fine, that the Emperor is recognizing the property rights of the Venetians in the parts of the Adriatic claimed by them. If this is not so, it is difficult to understand why the subjects of the Emperor should need treaty protection in order to sail their vessels on the high seas. The Venetians were not a pirate nation; there is no intimation here that they were pledging themselves to refrain from depredations on the ships of the subjects of Otto IV.

Similar provisions, with marked similarity of language occur in a treaty between Frederick II and the Duke of Venice, 20 September, 1220.[1]

Finally, the following document should be cited. It bears the title, "Promissiones Alfonsi et Nuntii Pisanorum," and is dated, 18 March, 1256.[2]

3. . . . et quod omnia et singula, que alicui Romanorum imperatorum antecessorum vestrorum dictum comune fecit vel tenetur facere seu consuevit, faciet vobis et vestris filiis legittimis, qui vobis in hoc honore succes-

[1] Weiland, *op. cit.*, pp. 93–97. The provision, "Proprietates vero — facere inde presumat," which is Article 1 of this treaty, is repeated. In Article 10, "Ripaticum autem — et non amplius" recurs with the addition of " 'et regnum nostrum' after 'per totum imperium.' 'Per terram' becomes 'per terras' after 'ambulandi.' 'Et regni' is introduced after 'totius imperii.' 'Et hoc stetit — sive per mare,' " *i.e.*, clause 17, is retained in its entirety.

[2] Weiland, *op. cit.*, pp. 493, 495, 496. The following examples may be added to those in the text; they contribute nothing which is not touched on there, but they round out the subject.

On the 26th of April, 998, Otto III granted freedom of traffic to the vessels belonging to a certain monastery, and also certain river fisheries. The part relating to the ships follows: "Naves etiam ipsius monasterii quae a fratribus vel eorum missis causa piscationis vel emptionis sive alicuius rei commutatione ad Ferrariam vel ad

serint, tam per mare quam per terram bona fide, sine fraude, remota omni malita.

. . . et eos faciet sanos et salvos in personis et rebus terra et mari et eorum privilegia omnia confirmabit.

17. . . . Et quod in brevi consulum ordinis maris dictum comune mitti faciet et ab eis iurare, quod unaqueque navis et galea Pisana portabit una cum vexillo Pisano vexillum de armis suprascripti domini regis.

Comaclum vel Ravennam se (u) i(n) quasecumque partes Italiae missae fuerint, ita nostr(o) dono et auctoritate sint securae et nullus cuiusque dignitatis vel ordinis homo ab eis aliquod tributum vel censum vel aliquam dacionem requirat vel tollere presumat." *Die Urkunden Otto des III.*, *op. cit.*, p. 708.

Following is an imperial confirmation of the papal domains, dated 817. It will be observed that this antedates the document given in the text. There is little to choose between them. The one given in the text is perhaps a little more interesting. Henry II and Benedict VIII were on intimate terms, both desirous of church reform. Lothair sent his confirmation of the papal privileges to Paschal I, upon receiving news of his consecration, in 817, and assurances that it had taken place in due form: "Ego Hludowicus, imperator augustus, statuo et concedo per hoc pactum confirmationis . . . civitatem Romanam cum ducatu suo et suburbanis atque viculis omnibus et territoriis eius montanis ac maritimis, littoribus ac portubus. . . ." Boretius, *op. cit.*, p. 352.

Here is one of the capitularies of Lothair, dated 822–823. "Ut nullius negotium suum infra mare exercere presumat, nisi ad portura legitima, secundum more antiquo, propter iustitiam domni imperatoris et nostram; et si quis aliter fecerit, omnem negotium suum perdat." Boretius, *op. cit.*, p. 319.17.

Concerning the protection of the shore: "Capitula comitibus Papiae ab Hludowico II. Proposita. 850 exeunte. Naves autem, quae propter custodiam littoris per mare sunt antiquitus, ordinatae ad precavendas adversariorum insidias, qualiter secundum ordinem eundem reparatae fiant, opportune consulimus, quoniam hac desidia non modica ex parte populus noster inimicorum insidias sustinet." Boretius et Krause, *Kapitularia Regum Francorum*, in the *Monumenta*, *Legum Sectio* II, ii (Hannoverae, 1897), 85.6.

A treaty with Venice containing provisions for harbor privileges, negotiated between Lothair I and Duke Peter in 840: 24. "Et hoc stetit, ut de capulo (quod) Rivoaltenses, Amorianenses, etc., etc., fecerunt, ab hodie in annos XXX, ubi capulaverunt, habeant licentiam capulandi, sicut supradictos annos habuerunt consuetudinem, sive per flumina, sive per mare; et flumina, que aperta habuerunt in fine Tarvisiana, ab hodie in annos triginta reaperiantur," *ibid*, p. 134.

Frederick II concluded *a pictum cum Soldano Tuneti*, by name Yahia-Abu-Zakaria (corrupted into Abuissae), on 20 April, 1231, touching the rights and duties of Christian merchants trading in Africa and their personal security there. Weiland, *op. cit.*, p. 187.

CHAPTER V

THE FEUDAL LAW

I. The Feudal System

Occasion has arisen in the course of the investigation recorded in the preceding pages to notice something of the character and quality of feudal law in so far as that law may deal either generally or directly with the status of the sea and with maritime jurisdiction of fisheries. It is apparent that what the law may have to say on these subjects must be conditioned by the nature of the law itself, and that the nature of the law must be, at least at bottom, the result of its origins. Feudal law was developed from and by circumstances which were sufficiently powerful in themselves to dominate the whole cast of the legal fabric throughout the period of its effectiveness, and to restrict within narrow limits the ability of the system to adapt itself to an environment of a nature different from that which gave it birth.

Feudal law governed the jural relations of a social order which was marked by distinct, temporary, and in some respects unique characteristics. This social order was of course itself the product of its past. Its rise to dominance in Europe was accompanied with a corresponding elimination of conflicting social orders. The aristocratic institutions of the feudal age were dominant because they had for the time eliminated the rivalry of antagonistic democratic and monarchical institutions in government and in society.

Mr. Abdy, in his book on Feudalism,[1] thus summarizes the essence of this conflict, and its result:

> Thus, very early in the history of social order in Europe free institutions, aristocratic institutions, and monarchical institutions appeared side by side. So too appeared three forms of national administration: that derived from the assemblies of the freemen; that claimed by the proprietors in their own localities; and that claimed by royalty. There were also three lower classes in the social organization — citizens, vassals, and subjects.

[1] J. T. Abdy, *Feudalism: Its Rise, Progress, and Consequences* (London, 1890), p. 106.

These three rival institutions were never united, were constantly and incessantly at variance. The first to give way was the system of free institutions. Between the other two the strife continued. At the end of the Merovingian dynasty the monarchical system was at the point of death. Charlemagne arrested its fall for a while, but his successors were unequal to the contest. The aristocratic principle remained master of the political situation and so at the end of the tenth century there was left neither citizen nor subject. Lordship and vassalage or serfdom was what remained, and feudalism became the dominant idea.

Since feudal law governed the jural relations of feudal institutions, and since the feudal system was characterized by elements of a peculiar and pronounced sort, a clear definition of feudalism is necessary. The definition following is that of Mr. Frederic W. Maitland:[1]

What do we mean by feudalism? Some such answer as the following is the best that I can give — A state of society in which the main social bond is the relation between lord and man, a relation implying on the lord's part protection and defence; on the man's part protection, service and reverence, the service including service in arms. This personal relation is inseparably involved in a proprietary relation, the tenure of land — the man holds land of the lord, the man's service is a burden on the land, the lord has important rights in the land, and (we may say) the full ownership of the land is split up between man and lord. The lord has jurisdiction over his men, holds court for them, to which they owe suit. *Jurisdiction is regarded as property, as a private right which the lord has over his land. The national organization is a system of these relationships.*[2] At the head there stands the king as *lord*[2] of all, below him are his immediate vassals, or tenants in chief, who again are lords of tenants, who again may be lords of tenants, and so on, down to the lowest possessor of land. Lastly, as every other court consists of the lord's tenants, so the king's court consists of his tenants in chief, and so far as there is any constitutional control over the king, it is exercised by the body of these tenants.

It appears from this definition that two principles governed feudal relationships, the principle of personal loyalty and devotion or reverence, and the principle of the contractual relation of lord and vassal.[3] The system which was in theory the expression or the carrying into effect of these two principles embraced almost every aspect of mediaeval life.[4] It is important to note

[1] F. W. Maitland, *Constitutional History of England* (Cambridge, 1908), p. 143.

[2] Italics are the present writer's.

[3] On this see Carlyle, *op. cit.*, iii, 21.

[4] *Ibid.*, p. 19.

what has been observed before, that the modern conception of sovereignty was not present to the mind of the mediaeval jurist. Law was not made; it was not the mere command of a law-maker. The law was essentially custom. An act of legislation did not create a law, it recorded or promulgated a law which was already recognized as binding. Not even the king or the emperor was above the law.[1] The statement that the law was conceived of as already existing in the community, that it was stated and not made, is subject to two qualifications. In the ninth century there are traces recorded of a conception of law as being made,[2] although this idea died out again. In the thirteenth century the idea reappears. It is believed that law may be made under certain conditions and by the proper authority.[3] The old idea of customary law does not disappear. The growth of the new idea is gradual. The significant thing is that both conceptions exist together, for this time the new idea does not again disappear.

> It is difficult to say how far the development of this was due to the pressure of circumstances compelling men deliberately to make new laws, or to modify old ones, how far it may have been facilitated by the revived and extended study of the Roman jurisprudence, and by the systematic development of the Canon law. . . . Whatever may have been the circumstances which produced this great change, it is of the first importance in the history of political theory to observe the fact of the change.
>
> We have here arrived at the beginnings of the modern conception of sovereignty, that is, of the conception that there is in every independent society the power of making and unmaking laws, some final authority which knows no legal limits, and from which there is no legal appeal.[4]

The acquisition of property rights in the sea presented a problem which pure feudal jurisprudence could not overcome. The classical Roman law stated expressly that the sea was open to all men, and that it was incapable by the law of nature of becoming the object of private property. This dictum was positive and clear. The Roman lawyer must adulterate his sources before he could countenance any ownership, any *dominium*, of the sea.

[1] Carlyle, *op. cit.*, p. 41. Also, Gierke, *Political Theories of the Middle Age*, *op. cit.*, *passim*. [2] Carlyle, *op. cit.*, p. 41 and note. [3] *Ibid.*, p. 45.

[4] *Ibid.*, p. 45. Compare Wilson, *International Law*, 8th ed. (New York, 1922), p. 47: Sovereignty is that "supreme political power beyond and above which there is no political power."

Feudal law could not take any other than a negative position, although it was in agreement on this point with the Roman law. Feudal law took no cognizance of the sea for the reason that the sea was not the object of private property. Feudalism was based upon the ownership of land. On this basis was erected its system of personal and contractual relationships. The hierarchy of landowners which feudal jurisprudence contemplated would not have existed had there been no owners of land. There had been landowners both great and small in the past, and they had had relations with one another. But before the tenth century these had not been feudal relations. The peculiar relationships which are embraced under the name of feudalism could not exist apart from landownership carried on under any other system. Nor could they exist apart from the existence of private property. While therefore it is true that the fact of landownership did not create feudalism, it is also and equally true that feudalism was bottomed upon the ownership of land. These self-evident observations have this in point: that the sea was not included within the term, land. It would have been possible for a different system of law to have included the two under one generic term. It is conceivable that the Roman law could have sanctioned the acquisition of property rights in the sea instead of having forbidden it. But this is not true of feudal law. Within the complicated system of property rights which were governed by feudal law, including property rights in jurisdiction, there is no mention of property rights in the sea, that is, in the sea itself as distinct from the products thereof. The feudal law was a territorial law, because the feudal system was a territorial system.

The king or the emperor was the ultimate landowner in the state. In him was vested the title to all the lands of his subjects. If there was to be ownership of the sea, then he must be the first owner. Later on, as the modern state rose on the ruins of feudalism, the king, as the representation and embodiment of the state, must own the sea. In the first instance the king, in the second instance the kingship, would have to possess all proprietary rights. The method taken to justify and to sanction such a proprietorship would naturally be that of an expansion of the territorial idea, with an accompanying appeal to customary law, or to usage, or to both. Jurisdiction on the sea there had, of course, always been. But it had been a special kind of jurisdiction, separate and independent of territorial jurisdiction. Its object had been to police the seas, that is, to suppress piracy and to make the seas safe for navigation and commerce. If there was to be a legally recognized proprietary right in the sea, then this jurisdiction must be rooted on land, or, in effect, there must be an extension of territorial jurisdiction over the sea. The coastal waters would be the first to feel this jurisdiction. The adjacent sea would be the first over which or in which proprietary rights would be asserted. These coastal waters would become, according to the developing theory, territorial waters. Roman law in its purity offered an uncompromising opposition to the development of such a theory, because of its direct statement of the opposite one. Feudal law, though also inhospitable ground for the growth of such a theory, because of its silence offered an obstacle less difficult to overcome. It did more than this; it provided a means by which the necessary sanctions could be obtained. Feudal law attributed to the king regalia — exclusive rights, privileges, and prerogatives. He was the focus of the life and power of the state, the ultimate landowner, and the source of concessions and privileges. He was the pivot of the feudal system. Through him, then, a property right in the sea could be asserted. He provided in a system of proprietary rights the necessary lodging place for a similar right in the sea. Feudal theory was unhampered by a statement that such rights were unknown to the law. Material for appeals to custom were ready to hand. Almost always, when a Roman or feudal jurist considered the status of the sea in connection with the legal possibility of acquiring rights of ownership in it, the problem presented by the claims and practice of Venice and Genoa in the Adriatic arose either to plague or gratify him, and his explanation of the facts would be conditioned by the purpose which he had in observing them. Additional justification was to be found in appeals to the laws governing the acquisition of property rights by prescription. Feudal law made it possible to invest the king with a prescriptive title to the adjacent sea.

II. The Law

The "Consuetudines Feudorum," or the "Libri Feudorum," refers to itself as *ius*.[1] This *ius* is customary law, *solita feudi jura*,[2] *mores*, *consuetudines*, *usum feudi*.[3] It is *ius feudi*. Its origin is *antiquissimo tempore*, and it takes precedence over Roman law.[4]

The *ius feudale*, however, contains written law. It is in part composed of imperial constitutions or statutes. The *Constitutiones* contains constitutions attributed to Conrad, Henry *Imperator*, Lothair I and III, and Frederick I and II.

Part of its terminology was created by custom, *mos*.[5]

Practice is a source of law,[6] just and true practice.[7] A *consuetudo*, however, may be abrogated by a *lex* of the emperor.[7] Reference to practice is frequent, and is made in different terms. The practice, it is clear, must be both ancient [8] and reasonable.[9] But modern practice may be accepted as a source of law.[10] There is reference to a practice which was formed by wise men of anti-

[1] K. Lehmann, *Das Langobardische Lehnrecht*, Göttingen, 1896. Figures in parenthesis refer to the books of the vulgate. p. 85.25 (i. 1. 4.). p. 89.20. (i. 4.5.). p. 172.30 (ii. 48.). p. 189.20. (*Capitula extraordinaria* I. 14.). p. 194.10. (*Ibid.*, I. 31.).

[2] *Ibid.*, p. 84.2 (i. 1.1).

[3] *Ibid.*, p. 115. (ii. 1. pr.).

[4] *Ibid.*, p. 115 (2. 1. pr.). Arnoldus Corvinus, *Ius Feudale, editio tertia* (Amstelodami, 1580), p. 5: "Quod si controversiae non sint feudales, aut jure feudali, nec verbis expressis, nec commoda argumentatione vel ratione per consequentiam, in Foro Civili sequendum jus Commune seu Justinianeum; in foro Canonico Pontificium. See also, Feud. ii. 1. (Libri Feudorum, Lib. II, sec. or art. 1.) Excepta (p. 6) juramenti materia; in qua, cum ea spiritualis sit & salutem animae concernat, etiam in solo Civile jus Canonicum est attendum." It is noteworthy that the Roman law is called the common law. Corvinus is not alone in his use of this term.

The best text of the *Libri Feudorum*, or, better, the *Consuetudines Feudorum*, is that of Karl Lehmann, *Das Langobardische Lehnrecht*, Göttingen, 1896.

The *Ius Feudorum Longobardicum*, with the title, *Consuetudines Feudorum*, under the heading IX, with a different system of typing and with a different arrangement of the books, is to be found in H. C. F. von Senckenberg, *Corpus Iuris Feudalis Germanici, oder, Vollständig Sammlung der Teutschen Gemeinen Lehens-Gesetze . . . herausgegeben von D. Iohann. Friedrich Eisenhart*, Halle im Magdeburgischen, 1772.

[5] 2.10.

[6] 1.14.

[7] 1.12.

[8] 1.7.1.

[9] 1.12.

[10] 1.7, 1.12.

quity, *usum ab antiquis sapientibus constitutum.*[1] There is reference to right custom;[2] to approved usage;[3] to what is customary;[4] to law and custom;[5] to law, custom, and long continued practice, *iuris constitutione aut consuetudine, ususque longaevi.*[6]

Where the unwritten law proves inadequate, the written law may be used to remedy the defect.[7]

The Regalia consist of the perquisites and prerogatives of the king or emperor. They are given as follows:[8]

> Regalia sunt arimanniae, viae publicae, flumina navigabilia, et ex quibus fiunt navigabilia, portus, ripatica, vectigalia, quae vulgo dicuntur thelonea, monetae, mulctarum poenarumque compendia, bona vacantia, et quae indignis legibus auferuntur, nisi quae specialiter quibusdam conceduntur, et bona contrahentium incestas nuptias, condemnatorum, et proscriptorum, secundum quod in novis constitutionibus cavetur: angariarum, parangariarumque et plaustrorum, et navium praestationes, et extraordinaria collatio ad felicissimam regalis numinis expeditionem, potestas constituendorum magistratuum ad justitiam expediendam, argentariae et palatia in civitatibus consuetis, piscationum redditus et salinarum, et bona committentium crimen majestatis, et dimidium thesauri in loco Caesaris inventi vel loco religiosi: si data opera, totum ad eum pertineat.

It will be observed that such things as *portus* and *flumina navigabilia*, which were *res publicae* in the technical sense under Roman law, and were therefore owned by the *populi Romani* considered as a whole, are now vested in or appropriated by the king or emperor, or, at most, they reside in the office. It is to be presumed that the Regalia carry with them the rights and powers necessary to give them effect. This is certainly true with respect to the *redditus piscationum*, for the feudal lawyers number the *ius piscandi* among the Regalia, even where they most carefully restrict its use.

[1] 1.1.3.

[2] 1.5.7.

[3] Cap. extraord. 1.9.

[4] 2.54.

[5] 2.23.

[6] Cap. extraord. 1.44.

[7] 2.1. Gothofredus says in Gloss 5 on 2.1, "In feudalibus negotiis finiendis spectanda est primum consuetudo si extat; deinde ad similes casus consuetudine feudorum expressos sit extenso. Post, ad legem scriptam si quae extat recurritur (ut hic), quae si non extat ad legum similia, recurrendum."

The emphasis on customary law is pronounced. For the purposes of the present study, the feudal laws of the Empire, France, England, and also Italy are fundamentally the same.

[8] Feud. 2.55. Lehmann, *op. cit.*, p. 182.

III. Theory of the Lawyers

Commentators on the feudal law books are not precisely in agreement on the subject of the relation of the king to river and sea fisheries, both of which, together with the powers of the king over them, have to be considered in connection with the Regalia.

Sir Thomas Craig, who gives particular attention to this subject, after dividing things which are *iuris humani* into *res publicae, res universales, res nullius*, and *res privatae* or *singulorum*, says:[1]

> Publicae, quae vel omnium hominum vel gentium communes sunt, ut aër, mare, littus, flumen, viae, itenera publica.

Publicae, of course, is used for *communes*. The sea, the seashore, rivers, highways, and the air are lumped together as a class of things the use of which is common to all men.[2]

The shores of the sea are *publici juris*.[3] The classical definition of their extent is treated as good feudal law—*quatenus maximus hybernus fluctus excurrit*. Harbors are *publici juris* and are numbered with the Regalia. Nevertheless any one may load and unload his goods in a port, provided only that he pay the required port dues. These dues are needed to meet the expense of the upkeep of the port; the inclusion of ports in the Regalia is justified on this ground.[4] Where no one is responsible for the maintenance of harbor facilities, so the argument runs, nothing is done to keep them in repair. But the use of the word, public, does not restrict the port to the service of the subjects of the king. On the contrary, the port is open to all men —

> tamen et privatorum, saltem universitatem proprii aliquando fiunt;[5] [the port is] pro suo arbitrio, non tantum ejusdem provinciae, et districtus, sed etiam toti humano generi, cum quibus amicitia non interrupta.[6]

[1] Thomas (sic) Cragius, *Jus Feudale*, 3d ed. (Edinburgi, 1732), Dieg. 15.13, p. 140.13.

[2] Craig's theory in regard to the *dominium maris* will be considered below.

[3] Dieg. 15.15, p. 140.

[4] The historical reason, of course, is, that the *res publicae* which classical Roman law ascribed to the *populus Romanus*, or, to the state, were gradually coming to be ascribed to the monarch, either as supreme property owner, or as representative of the state.

[5] *Ibid.*

Thus, while the seashore and ports or harbors are both *publici juris*, the ports are also included in the Regalia. But that inclusion does not affect their common character, that is, their freedom of use, which freedom is inherent in their character as ports or harbors.[1]

Craig makes a distinction between salmon and other fisheries. Salmon fisheries may not be given *in feudum* except by an express grant. There must be a special stipulation embodied in a clause in the deed granting the right of fishery, to the effect that salmon are also included among the fish which may be taken.[2] The reason for this reservation is, of course, that salmon (sturgeon and whales) were deemed to be royal fish, the especial property of the monarch, generally throughout Europe.

It is evident from the preceding classification of things that not all of them may be the object of feudal relations. Only those things may be given *in feudum* which are *in commercio hominum*. Consequently *res sacrae*, *res religiosae*, and *res publicae* are outside the scope of these relations, for they are *nullius in bonis*,[3] they are *extra commercium*. There is a further distinction of things which are *extra commercium domini*, and those which are *extra commercium vassali*. A lord may be invested with the former, and therefore bound to certain rights and obligations in respect to them. The latter, however, are incapable of being given *in feudum*. The latter are intended for the use of all the subjects, and may not be withdrawn from the reach of any of them.[4] Brussius mentions a class of *res communes*. It includes things which

[1] *Ius publica* probably means nothing more than "common right." If this is so, the shores and ports could be included under the same term because all men generally had a common right in them both.

[2] Dieg. 15, p. 256. "Quas Rex expresse non disponit, sibi retinere videtur."

[3] Alexandrus Brussius, *Principia Juris Feudalis* (Edinburgi, 1713), p. 73.2.1. "Sed ita demum res soli, quaeque his aequiparantur, in feudum dari poterunt, si in hominum fuerint commercio. Res itaque sacrae, religiosae, publicae, cum nullius in bonis sunt; nec alicujus fieri queant, alienari, & per consequentiam in feudi concedi, nequeant."

[4] P. 74. "Distingui tamen solet, an res sit extra domini duntaxat commercium; & sic valebit investitura, dominusque ad aestimationem (qua aliud sciz. comparetur feudum) obstrictus est, ad vero sit extra vassali commercium tantum; & tunc plane in feudum dari nequit."

may be bought or sold or given away. To grant these *in feudum* is not prohibited.[1]

In regard to the Regalia, Brussius writes that in his country, Scotland, the *redditus piscationum* is included. Salmon fisheries are embraced within the meaning of the term. He is in agreement with Craig in adding that these may not be granted save by a special *concessio* expressly given.[2] Furthermore, salmon themselves are the property of the king, wherever they may be found, even in rivers.

The emphasis which feudal law places upon property rights is brought out with precision in the work of M. Hervé, a French lawyer and expert on feudal law.[3] Every one knows, he writes, that ports and rivers are things common to all the world, and that every one has the right of fishing in them. But it is also true that one can acquire an exclusive right of fishing in them in a certain place, so that one may forbid another to fish before one's house.[4] This private right can be acquired equally in public rivers and in the sea. M. Hervé would recognize, of course, that this provision is to be found in the classical Roman law, and represents the result of the mixture of the Roman with the feudal systems of law.

This right of fishing is a property right and not a personal one. It reposes in the property. Under the Roman law, if every one had the right to fish in public rivers, it was because every one

[1] P. 75. "Rem communem quod attinet, cum ea & vendi, & in dotem dari, ut & donari possit, in feudum ergo concedi (pro illa sciz. parte quam quis in re communi habet) non prohibetur."

[2] P. 86. "Ad haec, Regalibus, apud nos, annumerari solent piscationum redditus: quo vocabulo, non quoscunque pisces, sed salmones duntaxat intelligi, tralatitium est. Hoc enim saltem cum aliis commune habent Regalibus, quod citra specialem concessionem haud transeant, licet clausula (cum privilegio piscandi in aqua, etc.) adjecta fuerit; at in eo a caeteris divortium faciunt, quod talis clausula, praescribendi (etiam quod salmones) inducat conditionem vasallo (sic), sciz. per 40 annos continuos, salmonum piscationem quiete possidente; quod & locum obtinere Senati etiam visum est, licet emolumentorum, seu pertinentiarum duntaxat in investitura facta fuerit mentio."

See, pp. 80–86 for the Regalia. On p. 87, the application of the foregoing paragraph to salmon which have ascended rivers.

[3] Hervé, *Théorie des Matières feodales et censuelles*, 8 vols., Paris, 1785–88.

[4] *Ibid.*, vii, 358–361.

owned those rivers. Under a monarchy, where the sovereignty resides in a single person, such common rights are also concentrated in him. He alone may exercise them, in the name of all.[1] It follows that the right of fishery is not a right essentially feudal.[2] It is not as *Seigneur de fief* that the king possesses it; he would still have the right were he neither lord nor suzerain. As a matter of fact and of usage, this right is generally exercised by the lords of fiefs, and a feudal character is given it. Yet it remains a right of property. All rights inhering in public property reside in the king.[3]

Under a monarchy — the feudal system, however, was not a monarchical system; it was aristocratic. The essence of the law as stated above, namely, that property was the basis and is the basis of all rights, is true of the whole of the feudal period. Yet some qualification should perhaps be made, and the nature of this modification is indicated by the use of the word, monarchy. It was toward the end of the feudal age that the king established a dominant position over against his great barons.

German and Italian commentators on the feudal law must deal with the Emperor — a personage who does not appear in the pages of the British and French commentators. The influence of the Roman law is perhaps a little more conspicuous. This is certainly true in contrast to the British Isles. The law governing public fisheries remains in principle the same.

Public navigable rivers are open to all men, with the usual restriction that no private person may hinder or impede their use by the public. Rosenthal refers this freedom to the *ius gentium.* The right of navigation, the *ius piscandi*, and other similar common rights are permanent in character. This statement is subject, however, to two qualifications. It is possible for the Emperor to forbid fishing in the rivers; and it is possible that the *ius piscandi* may have been granted to some one. In the latter case,

1 Hervé, *op. cit.*, p. 362.

2 *Ibid.*, p. 369.

3 *Ibid.*, p. 368. L. T., *Collection de Jurisprudence sur les Matières Feodales*, 2 vols. (Avignon, 1773), 1.89, agrees with Craig in asserting for his king sovereignty of the sea.

the fact of such a grant must be established *ex certa scientia.*[1] The Emperor alone has the power to prohibit the public use of fisheries, for they are controlled by the *ius gentium*, as noted above. Mention of the sea is not made. The "Sachsenspiegel," on the other hand, comes out definitely for the freedom of sea fisheries.[2] This statement, coming from one of the most important of the feudal law books, is a notable exception to the negative position which is generally assumed. It can leave hardly any doubt as to the attitude of feudal law on this subject.

De Afflictis, in his comments on the "Libri Feudorum," is in accord with this position. His agreement is noteworthy because he died in 1510,[3] that is, within the age of the "Sachsenspiegel." The shores of the sea are *publici iuris*, and are open to all men's use. They are under the king, nevertheless, for the purposes of jurisdiction and protection and defence, and any one may be forbidden to use them on account of having hindered the public use.[4] It is perhaps worthy of note that Craig and De Afflictis have both of them used the term *ius publica* in their treatment of the seashore. The term must have been familiar to both Scotch (or English) and Italian feudal law. Both commentators use it in the same sense. That sense seems to mean not public law, but common or public rights. The phrase, public law, carries with it modern implications which are foreign to feudal jurisprudence.

De Afflictis includes the shores of the sea among the Regalia because the king has this right of protection and jurisdiction.[4]

[1] Henricus a Rosenthal, *Tractatus et Synopsis totius Juris Feudalis* (*Taurini*, 1616). *Cap.* v. *Conclusio* xxiii, p. 85.

To state a law in an uncompromising fashion, and then seriously to qualify it by noting exceptions or limitations, is a method of analysis which is the favorite of a large number of jurists. Some of them carry the thing so far that there is almost nothing left of the law they profess to uphold.

[2] Christoff Zobel, *Sachsenspiegel* (Leipzig, 1595), p. 230, Art. xxviii and p. 231, column 1.

[3] Carolus Ferdinandus Hommelius, *Litteratura Iuris*, *Editio secunda* (Lipsiae, 1779), p. 331.

[4] Matthaeus de Afflictis, *Commentarius super tres libros Feudorum*, Francof. 1598? The title-page is missing from the copy at hand. P. 752.2 and .4.

The difference between the shore and a harbor is this:

> Littora sumuntur pro genere, quantum mare se extendit per arenam. portus sumitur pro specie, quia non omnia littora sunt portus, nam portus est locus conclusus, ubi naves & reliqua vasella absque laesione fluctuationis maris secure stare possunt.[1]

The harbor is thought of in terms of the port within it. This has the effect of emphasizing the shore line rather than the water. Apparently it is the conformation of the shore — its serviceability for accommodating the transhipment of goods, which fastens attention upon the land rather than upon the water. A sloping and firm beach, protected from storms and rough weather, would make a good port. Such a port would most likely be located in a harbor, that is, in a place where ships could take refuge.

> Sed an appellatione territorij veniat mare?

The answer is a negative. The sea is not included within the term, territory,

> Item, quia hoc nomen territorium, est generale, ideo comprehendit omnia: scilicet castra, & terras quia verbum generale generaliter est intelligendum.[2]

The fact that the question was asked is of more importance than the answer to it. Fisheries are included in the Regalia.

An unusual item in the Regalia is the

> authoritas faciendi amiratum, vel amiraglium in mari. Et credo [writes Afflictis], quod officium istud admiratus sit nomen novum, quia non memini me legisse in iure.

The duty of the admiral is to punish offences committed at sea, and to suppress piracy. The sea for this purpose is a district of the kingdom. The admiral

> cognoscit de delicto facto in mari, quod est de districtu regni. nam in mari est etiam districtus.[3]
>
> Nam sicut praeses in terra debet purgare provinciam malis hominibus, ita amiratus debet purgare cum classicis mare malis hominibus & piratis. Et hoc verum est, si ille delinquens in mari contiguo regni inveniatur.

[1] See Note 4, p. 75.

[2] By the same author, *Sanctiones, et Constitutiones Novissima Praelectio*, 2 vols. (Venetiis, 1562), i. 135.9. Jacobus Cujacius, *De Feudis*, placed at the end of vol. ii. *Opera Omnia*, 11 vols. (including index) (*Neapoli*, 1758), ii., 1192 B. Fisheries in the Regalia. Rochus Curtius, *Enarrationes* (Lugduni, 1550), p. 69.13: Custom and prohibition of no effect against the *ius piscandi*.

[3] See Note 4, p. 75.

The writer is following the doctrine of Baldus, a jurisconsult of the fourteenth century who is cited with great frequency by his successors.[1] Although most of his work lay in other fields, Baldus wrote a commentary on the feudal law.[2] He defines the Regalia as the

iura praecipua Regis, vel Imperii, seu fisci Romanorum, vel cuiuscunque Regis, qui in regno suo est monarcha, licet Imperatore minor ambitu circuli.[3]

The Prince is lord of his territory and of the sea subject to him. The portion of the sea subject to him is that which is adjacent to the coasts of his territory.

Porro territorium non est aliud quam terrae spatium minutum & armatum iurisdictione. In mari autem non dicitur territorium . . . sed dicitur districtus, id est, aquae spacium, seu latitudo similiter munita iurisdictione & imperio.[3]

Baldus injects the theory of the adjacent sea into feudal law.[4] Jurisdiction is no longer to be exercised anywhere over the sea; it is to be exercised in the sea adjacent to the territory of the Prince exercising it. This portion of the sea is not called territory. There is no claim to *dominium* or *proprietas* in it, as yet. It is a district in which the Prince has a right of jurisdiction, a district attached for certain governmental purposes to the nearest territory. The source of this jurisdiction is to be found in the Prince — the King or Emperor — himself. It is a royal or imperial prerogative. It is, in a word, included in the Regalia. Presently it was to be an attribute of the office and not of the man. This theory arose in the later days of feudalism, for Baldus died in 1400.[5] One hundred years later, Afflictis recorded the existence of an officer new to the law, the admiral, who was appointed by the Prince, and who ranked as the third of the principal officers of the realm.

It will have been noted that there were important rights in-

[1] The doctrine of Baldus will be considered in a later chapter. He was a pupil and follower of Bartolus.

[2] In *Usus Feudorum Commentaria*, Lugduni, 1585.

[3] P. 85.1–2.

[4] It originated with Bartolus of Saxoferrato; q.v.

[5] Hommelius, *op. cit.*, p. 327.

cluded in the Regalia which are not recorded in the "Libri Feudorum." According to Amicangelo, another Italian feudalist, the Regalia owe their origin to the *ius gentium*,[1] because the election of the king is by the *ius gentium*. Be that as it may, they undoubtedly had their foundation in customary law.

A distinction exists between fisheries and fishing, between the *reditus piscationum* and the *ius piscandi*.[2] The power to grant either or both in the sea or in the public rivers was lodged in the Prince. He might delegate the latter, that is, the power and authority to grant the *ius piscandi*. He could grant a fishery to a lord from which the public could not be excluded provided that they paid a certain fee to the lord. He could grant a right of fishing to a private person in a fishery which he had granted to another. He could grant to a private person or to a corporation the right to the exclusive use of a public fishery once a week, say, from sun up to sun down on every Friday in the year. Against the Prince there was one check, prescription from time immemorial. Against other private individuals, there was this check, and that of a special privilege granted by the Prince, or a special concession from him. The state of the law is too vague to be capable of precise definition. But this may be said: the *piscatio* was probably a location, a place where fish were known to gather. The *ius piscandi* seems to be the feudal equivalent for the modern right of fishery. The Prince, or the Crown, has the right of fishery in all public waters. So far as regards the public rivers, this right is a property right. With regard to the sea, the right is limited to the coastal waters for an unspecified distance off shore. The source of the right is not clear. In view of the fact that the sea had always been held to be open freely to all, it is probable that the right is a right to fish in certain parts of the sea, in certain *piscationes* off shore. On the high seas the Prince or the Crown had no rights of fishery, save those which every man had.

[1] Iosus Amicangelo, *Quaestiones Feudales*, Neapoli, 1653. Contains his *Quae Sunt Regaliae*, here cited, p. 3.3.

[2] Dominicus Arumaeus, *Discussionum Academicorum, De Iure Publica*, 5 vols. (Jenae, 1621), iii, 603. Andrea de Isernia, in *Usus Feudorum Commentaria* (Lugduni, 1579), p. 305.72. Petrus Gudelinus, *Opera Omnia* (Antverpiae, 1685), p. 33.8. Iacobus Alvarrotus, *De Feudis* (Francofurti, 1570), p. 339.6–7.

Whether the Prince's property right in the public rivers was based upon ownership of the underlying soil, or upon ownership of the flowing water, or upon ownership of both, is a problem left undefined. It is probable, having regard to the nature of the feudal system, that the Prince owned the soil. His prerogative of the right of fishery in tidal waters was not based upon a claim to ownership either of the soil or of the sea. At the most, he owned the fisheries, the places where the fish were caught. From ancient times the state had owned public fisheries, just as it — or the people — had owned the public rivers. The transference and concentration of power in the hands of the monarch which created the theory attributing to him the ownership of the rivers, as well as of the territory which composed his dominions, probably operated in a like manner to ascribe to him ownership of the sea fisheries. The theory of territorial waters which began to take shape at the close of the fourteenth century was not a theory of ownership of those waters, though it was both logical and inevitable as to reason and fact that it should issue in such a theory. The theory to which Baldus gave expression was one of the exclusive jurisdiction of the king or Emperor over the seas adjacent to his dominions. This jurisdiction, furthermore, was not to be used to force from other states a recognition of sovereignty — for there was no sovereignty — nor for the purpose of providing occasions for the gratification of royal or of national pride. It was to be used to safeguard the sea for the purposes of commerce, of navigation, and of industry. And, which is important, it was to prevent any other monarch or state from sending armed forces into those waters for that purpose. Beyond these generalizations it seems hardly safe to go. While there is a broad agreement of principles, the application of the law was bound to vary with the custom of the community. It was bound to vary, also, with the shifting relations of the king or Emperor to his great tenants in chief. A strong ruler could insist upon his prerogatives; a weak ruler could not afford to do so.

The influence of Roman legal conceptions upon feudal law is easily discernible, especially in the writings of those jurists who champion the community of use of the sea. In the Assizes of

Jerusalem, which is, perhaps, nearly pure feudal law, there is no mention of sea fisheries. No jurist could ignore the Roman law if he desired to write concerning the relation of the king to the right of fishing in the sea. The rights implicit in the possession of the Regalia had to be either restricted or expanded; the mere statement of these rights made a definition of the scope of their exercise almost inevitable. Both feudal lawyers and jurisconsults alike were faced with this problem. Their solutions of it will be considered in the following chapter, and the doctrines of which they laid the foundations will be traced to their fruition in the great work of Hugo Grotius and the classic reply of his opponent, John Selden.

CHAPTER VI

THE JURISCONSULTS

I. Classification

It is now evident that the problems which the jurisconsults had to face with respect to the question of the legal status of the sea were two. Stated in their most general terms, they are: Is it possible according to law for a state or for a private person to acquire property rights in the sea? And, secondly, to what extent may a state exercise jurisdiction over maritime fisheries? [1]

In their attitude towards these questions the jurists may be divided conveniently into three classes. The first class is composed of those who plant themselves squarely on the classical Roman law. For present purposes these jurists are styled classical or historical. The second class is composed of those whose chief object is to shape the law to fit the facts. These will be styled practical jurists. The third class is made up of men who are in sympathy with certain doctrines in both the schools. They are few in number and form an unimportant group. They may be included with the practicians, because, no matter how strong is their classical bias, they have touched with modern fingers the classic law.

It would be a mistake to apply the terms, conservative, radical, and liberal, respectively, to these three groups of jurists. The classicists were conservative, it is true. Their interest was in the past, if not in antiquity. But the practicians were not radical according to the modern meaning of the word as it is generally understood. Their desire was to preserve the past by accommodating it to the present, instead of by forcing it on the present as a complete, workable and self-sufficient system. They desired to reshape the law to make it fit the circumstances, the law and the customs of their day.[2]

[1] These two questions reappeared in somewhat altered form in the problem underlying the controversy of *mare liberum* v. *mare clausum* in the first half of the seventeenth century.

[2] The middle group is identified with them at this point.

II. Spirit of the Classicists

It will be recalled that the school of the Glossators came to an end with the death of Accursius in 1260. The doctrine of the classical law was henceforth carried on by jurists who abandoned the tradition of making brief notes to the *Corpus Iuris Civilis*, although an occasional writer recalls by his treatment that method. The texts of the Roman law which deal with the present subject were noticed chiefly by two classes of teachers: those who were interested in reconstructing the classical scheme of the division of things, and so were forced to make a place for *res communes* and *res nullius*, and those whose professional interests led them into controversy with the jurists who were advocating some aspect of the opposite opinion. For the theoretical writers, the men of first class, Justinian's statement that the sea is open to the use of all and may be owned by none was little more than a parenthetical observation given in illustration of one of the less important classifications of things. It was there, and there was nothing to be said about it except to note it, so to speak, in passing. Men who did not attempt a thoroughly systematic treatment were apt to omit it altogether. If the doctrine was repeated, however, it was repeated with a meticulous care which now and then resulted in nothing more than a paraphrase of the original. More often, the sense of the texts was conveyed in fresh words. The vast majority of the jurists who treat of this subject belong in this class of theorists. They refer to the proper texts carefully, automatically, and perfunctorily. They write no more than is required to reproduce the law, and they write no less. They all have to say the same things, and they have to say them in much the same way, and in about the same number of words. And they have to use much the same style of writing. They must use *mare*, *littora*, *piscatio*, *omnes homines*, *usus*, and, perhaps, *ius piscandi;* they will use *communis*, of course. *Flumina publica*, *aër*, *ripa*, and a few more complete the list. Occasionally a jurisconsult will note the presence of an opposing opinion, but such occurrences are rare, in comparison with the number of men who do not mention the subject at all, or, if they do, who ignore the presence of contradictory teaching. Those who belong to the other class mentioned, those, that is, whose professional interests lead them to take notice of writers of other schools, may or may not be interested in systematic expositions of the Roman law. More often they devote their scholarship to particular parts of the law which are intimately related to the life of the community. Among these jurists also those are rare who attempt a specific refutation of doctrines in conflict with the classical position; and if they do so, they do it briefly, and usually by the citation of appropriate texts.

The almost complete unanimity with which the jurisconsults of the historical school ignore their opponents is impressive. Man after man devotes his profound scholarship to monumental works of erudition, and ignores the presence of contradictory teaching, engulfing his opponents in a silence the cumulative effect of which is powerful in the extreme. The explanation of this attitude may perhaps be found in an unquestioning faith in the sufficiency of the Roman law, in its power to achieve supremacy by its own inherent greatness. If this law was adequate in every respect to meet the needs of the time, as its expositors believed that it was; if it could be presented in all its superlative beauty and completeness, then it must win recognition and adoption by its perfection. The barbaric ignorance of the times stood in the way of its acceptance. Government was chaotic, if not anarchic; social institutions were crude and unstable. The Roman law had been handled by commentators who lacked the proper training, who wrote uncouth Latin, who had but a superficial acquaintance with the subject in which they professed learning. It was now necessary to sweep aside their work, to attack the whole subject afresh, and to present the Roman system of jurisprudence for the profound and perfectly articulated thing that it was. It was not necessary to embark upon controversies. There was no need to answer heretical doctrines. Faithful and learned exposition of the law would suffice to make it a vigorous and powerful instrument for the furtherance of the eternal principles of justice.

Some such spirit as this seems to have animated the classicists. For a solution of present problems, they attempted to apply the finest product of the Roman genius for law, unchanged and *in toto*, with an implicit faith in its efficacy. This will explain after a fashion their silence in the face of men like Bartolus and his school. There was no need to answer them, for the subject which they were expounding with a detail and precision which is almost incredible, carried with it its own attack and its own defence. The paucity of their treatment of the sea and the subjects related to it is obviously due to the subject. In the whole classification of things, the *res communes* occupy an insignificant position. In the division of things which embraces *res extra patrimonium*, *res communes* are of more importance, naturally; but they are outranked by the religious and sacred things, and are of far less importance than the *res publicae*. The two latter classes, and especially, the last class, could and did present varied possibilities for the interaction of conflicting interests, for the conflict of rights and duties. But such things as the sea and the air could not easily provoke litigation. At the point where litigation might arise most readily, that is, in connection with property rights on the seashore, it will be observed that the law is most precise. At the opposite extreme is the deep-sea fishery, on which the law is silent.

Yet, even while these men were writing, the new theories were making their way. The new and vigorous states began to reach out after whatever might be appropriated, and there were great jurists with doctrines ready to justify them in their aspirations. The doctrine of Baldus has been noted in the preceding discussion of the feudal law, and he was himself the pupil of one of the greatest jurisconsults of modern times. With the growth of the great powers, the discovery of the new world, and the development of commerce and industry, the conflict became more and more intense until it broke the surface of international life in the naval wars of the United Provinces with Great Britain in the first half of the seventeenth century, the claim of England to the proprietorship of the seas around the British Isles, and the claim of the Dutch to a right of fishery off the British coasts, being, as is well known, the prizes contended for. And at the same time, each side produced a champion in the realm of jurisprudence.

The classical jurists found a master of the Roman law in Grotius, and a creator of the science of international law, besides. Their opponents were represented by John Selden, who expounded their theories both as to law and fact in their final and extreme form. The situation then became an impossible one. After 1648, a solution had to be found in compromise and adaptation, even though the staunchest defenders of each side might refuse to bend.

Such, then, is the place of the classical jurisconsults in the present study. This may perhaps be observed more particularly by a reference to several of their eminent representatives, the technique of whom is characteristic of the school.

III. *Part I. The Classical School*

Eighty years after the end of the period of the glossators, John Faber died.[1] No one in his day was more proficient in the Roman law than this celebrated jurisconsult. His method resembles that of the glossators. He is one of those upon whom later jurists placed most reliance, as is shown by the frequent appeals to him in the texts. He gives but a very brief notice to the sea: [2]

> Mare est commune, nec est in alicuius dominio, nisi Dei.
>
> Aër, aqua profluens, mare, & littora, sunt communia, nec unquam iure quidem naturali in alicuius dominio fuerunt: sed fuerunt relicta in suo iure, & esse primaevo, quae omnia erant communia. — mare est incomprehensibile, sunt aër: ideo non fuit in bonis populi applicatum, sed Dei.

In the back of his mind seems to be the consciousness that all is not well. It is significant that he places his emphasis upon *dominium*, a word which does not occur at the place in Justinian's texts, J. 2. 1. 1. and D. 1. 8. 3. where the community of the sea is asserted, or maintained, for the first time.

Again eighty years later, another great jurist, Paul de Castro,[3] lays down his doctrine. The shores of the sea, he says, are to-day in the same status in which they were placed by the *ius naturale;*

[1] *Biographie Universelle*, Paris, 1811, and after. Little is known of his life, and that much does not illuminate the subject in hand.

[2] Ioannes Faber, *Institutiones Commentarii* (Lugduni, 1557), p. 29.2–5 a. *Littorum.*

[3] Died, 1420. Hommel, p. 329.

they are *nullius in bonis*, and are capable of being occupied. *Dominium* over things caught in the air, on land, or in the sea belongs, according to natural law, to him who makes the capture.[1]

Klaas Everts, or Nicolas Everardus, was one of the better jurists of his time, and the most distinguished magistrate in Europe. He is one of those whose professional interests caused them to adopt a definite position upon the problem of the status of the sea. His span of life places him equally in the fifteenth and sixteenth centuries.[2] In connection with a dispute concerning the levying of certain duties at the port of Antwerp, he argues that by natural law the seas and public rivers are common and free to all for the purposes of navigation. Just as public highways are free, so the sea should be.

With the opening of the sixteenth century comes a series of notable attempts to reduce to order the science of the law. Franciscus Connanus,[3] whose work was cut short by a premature death, undertook this work, and the commentary which he left is the beginning of this task.

Jacques Cujas, the most eminent jurist of his day,[4] undertook a return to the sources of the Roman law. He determined to reconstruct obscure passages, to clarify the law, and to rectify mistakes caused by the ignorance or carelessness of copyists. His desire was to establish again the Roman law as its system was molded by Justinian, to substitute the law of a cultivated age for the rather more than less barbaric jurisprudence of his time. To ascertain his doctrine one need only to refer to the law books of Justinian.

His interest in the two questions under discussion is slight, for they draw from him but three remarks,[5] and these do not bear

[1] Pauli Castrensis, *In Digesta*, 6 vols., (Lugduni, 1553), i, 7.20.

[2] *Consilia* (Antverpiae, 1643), p. 8.1. 1462–1532.

[3] *Commentariorum Iuris Civilis* (Basileae, 1562), p. 220.1. His dates are 1508–1551.

[4] 1520–1590. For biographical details not otherwise credited, see the *Biographie Universelle*, cited above.

[5] Jacobus Cujacius, *Opera*, 10 vols. (Neapoli, 1758), iii, column 389 B; he states the law that one who is forbidden to fish in the sea before a private house has a right of action (*actio iniuriarum*) against the owner. x, col. 1179 D; he states the law permitting under restrictions the erection of buildings in the sea or on the shore.

upon the critical aspects of the subject. His interest in the Regalia of the king or emperor is only a little more pronounced; his doctrine on this point has been noted in the chapter on the feudal law.

Hugo Donau, or Donellus, the great contemporary of Cujas, was a member of the illustrious French school of jurists which taught in Germany,[1] seeking refuge, perhaps, from the religious wars. His purpose was to synthetize and to fuse all the elements and details of private law into one great system. The cognition of the whole, and of the interdependence of each part thereof on every other part, was for him the only proper task of science.[2] He based his system on the following definition of law:

> Recht ist jede zwingende Vorschrift, welche das gerechte gebietet und das Gegentheil verbietet.[3]

Roman law complies with this definition, and therefore is law in and for itself. But one's obedience is due it as an act of free will, because of its beauty and greatness, and because it is derived from the universal principles of the *ius gentium* and is thus capable of universal application.[4] The following quotations will illustrate his position:

> Ius divinum est, quod est de rebus ad Deum pertinentibus, quod Deo, quae sunt Dei, tribuit.[5]
>
> Id non ex hominum opinionibus, aut principum constitutionibus et decretis pendet, sed totium ex verbo Dei.[6]
>
> Habentur autem res superiores communes omnium. Merito, quia natura proditae ad usum hominum, nullius adhuc in dominium pervenerunt; ut quod in commune relictum sit, id necesse sit, usu esse omnium. . . . Nam nec aer, aut mare in ullis gentis potestatem venit unquam, aut adeo venire potest.[7]

The restrictions are aimed at safe-guarding the common use of the sea and the shore. i, col. 851 C records this law also.

[1] R. Stintzing, *Geschichte der Deutschen Rechtswissenschaft*, 2 vols. München & Leipzig, 1880–1884; a third vol. by E. Landsberg, divided into 3, 3.1, 3.2. Notes and 3.2. Text, 1896–1910, i, 385. His dates are 1527–1591 (i, 377).

[2] *Ibid.*, i, 377.

[3] *Ibid.*, i, 379.

[4] See preceding Note.

[5] Hugo Donellus, *Commentarii de Iure Civili*, 6th ed., 16 vols. (Norimbergae, 1827), ii, cap. 4.1, p. 201 (vol. 1).

[6] *Ibid.*, ii, cap. 4.2.

[7] (Vol. 2) iv, cap. 2.6, p. 299.

Populus Romanus in ea litora imperium habere intelligitur, quae ipse occupavit, ut potestatis et imperii sui faceret. Hac enim occupatione veniunt in potestatem nostram, quae ante nullius fuerant. Et merito sic occupatur dicuntur fieri populi Romani.[1]

It will be observed that the above is a restatement of the law of Justinian.

Gothofredus the elder, Dionysius Gothofredus, was a French Huguenot who was forced to flee the country.[2] His son was the last of that group of French jurists which taught in Germany in the sixteenth century, to which reference has been made. For in spite of the brilliance and devotion of the leaders, love of historical and theoretical studies was dying, and works of a practical nature were taking their place.

Gothofredus's most important work was an edition of the *Corpus Iuris Civilis*. In this collection were gathered for the first time as a typographical unity all of the law books of Justinian.[3] Gothofredus's own comments are glosses written in the margins after the model of the old Bolognese school. He writes a gloss on *mari*, D. 8. 4. 13, in which he applies the word, *liberum*, to *mare*, instead of *communis* or *publicum:*

Mare natura omnibus patet, id est, liberum est ad piscandum.

The use of this constitutes an innovation in legal terminology. *Communis* and *publicus* are of course treated as synonymous; but he makes the necessary distinction between *publicus* used in this sense, and the same word used with its technical meaning. In his gloss on D. 41. 1. 14. he distinguishes between things which are *publicae* because they are *in patrimonio populi Romani*, and those which are so because they are natural products, *proditae naturae*. The shore of the sea is public in the latter sense, and in *nullius adhuc dominium pervenerunt*. *Dominium* has replaced *bonis*. Taken in connection with the use of *liberum* above, this choice of words is significant.

The faithfulness with which the sixteenth-century jurists re-

[1] Donellus, *op. cit.*, cap. 2.7, p. 300. See also *lib.* iv, cap. 6 and V. 22 *passim* for extended discussion.

[2] Stintzing, *op. cit.*, i, 386. Gothofredus lived 1549–1622.

[3] *Ibid.*, i, 208.

produced the classical position may be seen in the following series of statements concerning the sea:

Mare & litora maris iure naturali omnium communia sunt.[1]

. . . mare . . . commune est . . . nec videtur etiam esse sub dominio Imperatoris, ut multi tenent.[2]

Mare dicitur, omnis aquarum congeries. . . . Mare etsi res naturalis, per se ad doctrinam Iuris non pertinens. & Iurisconsulti illud non considerant tanquam Mare, & in se ipso, sed in possessione & dominio. Mare respectu dominij, nullius est, quia proprietas eius est nullius . . . respectu possessionis, est omnium, non unius. Mare igitur est res publica, non jure Civili, sed jure gentium.[3]

Flumina autem omnia, & portus, publica sunt: ideoque ius piscandi, omnibus commune est: in portu, fluminibusque. . . .[4]

Mare est commune, & quicquid in eo nascitur.[5]

. . . cuilibet in mari piscari licet de iure gentium, etiam ante praetorium, & aedes alienas, nec prohiberi potest per dominium earum.[6]

At nemo ignorat flumina iure gentium & littora esse publica.[7]

Erstlich und fürnemlich ist der lufft, auch das Regenwasser, und Meer, sampt den gestatten desselben, durchaus allen lebendigen Creaturen zugleich frey und gemain. . . . Darumben kan noch mag an den gestatten des Meeres, Visch zufahen, auch perle oder adelstein zusuchen, niemands erwort werden.[8]

(M)are videtur reluctari possessioni.[9]

Littus proprii maris est, in distinction from a river bank. The sea used to be closed during the greater part of the period of the winter storms, quod tamen in praesentia non observatur; Nihil enim reliquit nostrorum temporum avaritia.[10]

The property rights of the Venetians in the gulf or sea of the Adriatic, as it was variously called, were excused, if not justified,

[1] Franciscus Duarenus . . . *Commentarius*, 2 vols. (Aureliae Allobrogum, 1608), ii, 481. This is only a brief *iuris regula*.

[2] Hieronymous Buccaferreus, *Responsorum* (Bononiae, 1645), p. 410.21.

[3] Ioannes Calvinus, *Lexicon Iuridicum Iuris Caesarei* (Genevae, 1670), p. 563.

[4] Rodericus Suarez, *Opera Omnia*, 2 vols. (Antverpiae, 1618), ii, 67.4.

[5] Johannes Althusius, *Dicaeologicae, libri tres* (Francofurti, 1618), i, 141.27.

[6] Carolus Ruinus, *Consiliorum seu Responsorum*, 5 vols. (Venetiis, 1591), i, 40, Cons. XXVIII.

[7] Franciscus Amaya, *Commentarii in Codicis . . . Iustiniani* (Lugduni, 1639), p. 550.57.

[8] Andreas Perneder, *Institutiones* (Ingolstadt, 1574), ii, 30.

[9] Henr. Zoesius, *Commentarius ad Digestorum*, 2 vols. (Lovanni, 1656), ii, 48-9, especially p. 49.8.

[10] Andrea Alciatus, *In Pandectarum, seu Digestorum Iuris Civilis . . . Commentaria*, etc., 4 vols. (Basileae, 1582), ii, 1145.

on the ground of prescription from time immemorial. They were, at most, an exception to the general rule. When they first put buildings in the sea and acquired rights over them, they were not acting in contravention of the law. Time had settled them in their rights. Nevertheless, they could not and did not possess the sea itself. They owned their real property; they had exclusive rights of *imperium;* and no more.[1] This position was partly grounded on the classical law, and partly aimed at the claims of the Venetians and of those who supported them. An awareness of current controversies occasionally colored a presumably detached exposition of the law, even in the mind of a strait classicist. This natural attitude in some of the writers appears in certain of the examples cited above, and in other cases to which attention has been directed.

Variations of the method of analytic exposition adopted by the masters were those of the paraphrase,[2] and of short comments on the texts of Justinian.[3] But whatever the method, the conclusions were necessarily the same.

The statement that the sea is common to all frequently ex-

[1] See, for example, Zoesius, *Commentarius, op. cit.*, sec. 1, 8.5. (He follows the divisions of the Digest.) For a generalization covering this point, see Hadrianus Negusantius, *Sylva Responsorum et Practicarum Disputationum* (Venetiis, 1619), p. 779.82; Benedictus Bonus, *De Censibus*, in the *Tractatus Illustrium*, 18 vols. (Venetiis, 1584), VI, Pars i, 167.40.

Occasionally a reference is made to the ascription to the Emperor of the lordship of the whole world, and the question is put, whether this lordship includes the sea also. The traces of the controversy are obscure in the writings of the jurists. It seems to have its legal foundation in D.14.2.9., where the critical sentence, as translated into Latin, reads, that the Emperor Antoninus responded, "Ego quidem mundi dominus, lex vero maris." The classical position was, of course, that the Emperor here clearly repudiated any notion of lordship over the sea. On this, see Ioannes Igneus, *Commentarii in aliquet Constitutiones Principum* (Lugduni & Aureliae), 1541), p. 203.713, and 201.692.3. I. Gothofredus wrote an entire pamphlet in affirmation of the imperial lordship, in which he develops a careful exegesis of the text in question. See *De Imperio Maris*, Genevae, 1637.

[2] As in T. Cormerius, *Henrici IIII . . . Codex Iuris Civilis Romani*, Lugduni, 1602; and Sebastian Brant, *Titulorum omnium Iuris*, Lugduni, 1560; and Ioan. Borcholten, *Ad Instituta Iustiniani Commentaria*, Lugduni, 1653.

[3] Ioachimus Mynsingerus, *Apotelesma, sive Corpus Perfectum*, &c., Venetiis, 1602; Franciscus Broeus, *Expositiones in . . . Iustiniani Institutionum*, Lutetiae Parisiorum, 1622; and Matthaeus Wesenbecius, *Institutionum . . . Iustiniani*, Basileae, 1572, illustrate this method.

hausted a jurist's interest in the subject.[1] On the other hand, on lack of interest is displayed in making the statement precise; and this is true whether or not the presence of opposition is recognized. The *ius naturale* is usually identified with the *ius gentium*, as with Wesenbecius,[2] or else it is distinguished from the *ius primaevum naturale*, as with Nicasius.[3] This latter terminology is apparently employed in order to fill the void caused by the fusion of the ideas contained in each species of *ius;* the *ius primaevum naturale* becomes in reality the old *ius naturale* in a new dress. Thus, in modern form, there is a return to the two practices represented by Gaius and Ulpian — that is, there are jurists who do not distinguish between the two laws, and there are those who do. Not that this divergence of doctrine had ever disappeared. So long as the Justinian texts were followed closely, the difference must perpetuate itself. But such doctrines have little, if any, bearing upon the present subject, and are important only in so far as they illuminate a manner of thought. The sea was held to be common to all, no matter under which concept the jurist who said so was working. As Buccaferreus said, the sea is common and is not under the *dominium* of even the Emperor himself, as many are accustomed to maintain.[4]

The English thirteenth century lawyers seem to have shared the opinions of the Continental orthodox civilians. At any rate, this is true of Bracton, and of those two later treatises, Britton and Fleta, which reflect where they do not abridge the *De Legibus*.

Bracton accepted the Roman law doctrines concerning the legal status of the sea. His writing on this subject is a close parallel to the passages on the same subject in Azo's *Summa*.[5] It is

[1] Baptista Aymus, *De Alluvionum Iure Universo*, 3 vols. (Bononiae, 1580), i.c. 2, p. 5.8; Stephanus Dacyz, *Juris Civilis Summa*, &c., 2 vols. (Mediolani, 1742), i, 98; Petrus Caballus, *Resolutionum Criminalium* (Venetiis, 1644), p. 36.485.

[2] *Op. cit.*, p. 116.

[3] Nicasius *super Institutionibus* (Lipsiae, 1541), p. 56.

[4] *Loc. cit., supra.*

[5] Maitland has placed the most Romanesque portions of Bracton's treatise and the source from which they are derived side by side in his book, cited in a previous chapter, *Select Passages from Bracton and Azo*. Bracton's reproduction is so faithful that it is not necessary to quote him. Maitland says, p. xiv, "The amount of matter that Bracton directly borrowed from the Corpus Iuris is not one-third, is

Maitland's opinion[1] that the pages which Bracton tries to fill with Roman law are his worst pages. Most of his work is a record of his experience with English law. The opinion may be ventured that when Bracton transcribed the glossator's exposition he was not consciously attempting to graft alien law on English law. It may be said further that he was not incorporating in his work a doctrine which was contradicted by English law, but rather, that he was following the doctrine which was approved by his knowledge and experience of his native law. In other words, the English law of the thirteenth century held to the doctrine of the freedom of the seas; and consequently, Bracton, in writing Roman doctrine, was writing English doctrine. It may be put in the opposite way. If Bracton, in using the Roman law, was using law which had become part of the English law, then the English law held to the community of the seas. Maitland observes in another place that Bracton was "assuming that Roman law may be and ought to be used as subsidiary or supplementary law to fill the gaps in national or provincial custom";[2] and "That Bracton's book met a want and won a splendid success there can be no doubt whatever."[3] It may be noted that one of the ways in which the Roman law spread over Europe was by filling the gaps in local customary law.

Nevertheless Bracton was conscious of the claims to some sort of lordship over the sea which were occasionally put forward in the name of the English king. This appears from the following note, which is his own marginal gloss:[4]

> Et nota de prima parte quod in Anglia minus curatur de iure naturali quam in aliqua regione de mundo quia Rex Angliae vocatur dominus marium propter potestatem suam quam habet in aquis.

---

not a thirtieth part of his book. The amount of matter that Bracton borrowed from Azo is larger; it may perhaps amount in all to a fifteenth of the treatise." The text used above is, Henricus de Bracton, *De Legibus et Consuetudinibus Angliae, Libri quinque*, ed. by Sir Travers Twiss, 6 vols., London, 1878–1883.

[1] *Bracton and Azo*, *op. cit.*, p. xx.

[2] *Ibid.*, p. xxix.

[3] *Ibid.*, p xxxi: The systematic study of Roman law had not been formally proscribed in England; p. xxvii: there is, on the contrary, plenty of evidence of the existence of professional legists. Bracton died in 1268. See pp. x-xiii for his life.

[4] Maitland, *op. cit.*, p. 125.

How much less than his Continental brethren Bracton cared for the law of nature is, unfortunately, left undetermined. The lawyer and the patriot seem to have been in conflict. And this gloss is the memorial.

The lawyers' French of the anonymous treatise called *Britton* garbs in strange gear doctrine that is essentially Bracton's. Bracton had written under Henry III. From 1249–57 he was hearing pleas *coram Rege* — as a judge holding office under a royal commission. If he wrote *Britton,* he wrote it at the end of the thirteenth century, under a new master — Edward I.[1] Three quotations from *Britton* will give the point of view; he is writing of the kinds of things:

> et aucunes communes, sicum la mer, et le heyr, et le rivage de la mer, et sicum dreit de pescher en flodz et en la mer et en communes ewes et rivers.[2]
>
> Et ausi sunt acunes choses en nuli biens naturelement, dount nul homme ne put fere douns, sicum . . . bestes sauvages, et pessouns.[3]
>
> De estourgeoun pris en nostre terre voloms nous qe il soint nostres, sauve al troveour ses mises et ses custages renables. De baleynz trovez en noster poer, volom nous qe la teste soit nostre et la cowe a nostre cumpagne solom le auncien usage.[4]

Fleta yields nothing except the usual provision in regard to the royal monopoly of sturgeon, and a provision that the customary division of whales caught on shore shall be followed — the head to the King, *et Regina caudam.*[5]

[1] *Britton,* transl. and ed. by Francis Morgan Nichols, 2 vols. (Oxford, 1865), xviii.

[2] *Ibid.*, i, 213. "Some things are common, as the sea, the air, and the seashore, and as the right of fishing in tidal waters and in the sea."

[3] *Ibid.*, i, 214. "There are also some things which in their natural state are no one's property, and whereof none can make a gift, as . . . wild beasts, and fishes. . . ."

[4] *Ibid.*, i, 68. "Sturgeons taken within our dominions shall belong to us, saving to the persons who took them their reasonable costs and expenses; and of whales caught within our jurisdiction the head shall belong to us and the tail to our consort, according to ancient usage." See also, i, 16; i, 216; and i, 84.13.

[5] *Fleta, seu Commentarius Juris Anglicani,* bound with Joan. Seldenus, *Ad Fletam, Dissertatio Historica,* 2d. ed., London, 1685. P. 61, cap. 45: "De Sturgione aliter observetur, quod Rex illum integrum habebit propter privilegium regale. Cap. 46: De Balaena vero sufficit, si Rex habeat caput, et Regina caudam."

This is the last of an English theory concerning the freedom of the seas, during the period under discussion. Plowden did not, indeed, advocate any right of property in the sea; but he entertained a pronounced theory as to the scope of the King's

Quo nunc ergo iure nostri Principes, quod Natura voluit esse liberum et commune, servum propriumque faciunt? Quo iure Venetiis mare Adriaticum, Genuensibus Ligusticum servit?

Quo iure? Balduinus had put the critical question.[1] For Balduinus died in 1573.[2] As will be seen below, the teachers of the contrary doctrine gained considerable strength during the last quarter of the sixteenth century. It has already been observed that the end of the century was a time when the love of the past was giving place to a keen interest in the present. This interest was as marked in the world of theory as it was in the world of fact. The authority of use and custom gained respect proportionally as the authority of the classic Roman law diminished in the estimation of the period. To-day, said a late writer, kings and princes are wont to claim under the name of territory the ***dominium*** of the sea, the ownership of the *sea!* [3]

Part II. The Practical School

Necessarily opposed to the jurists of the classical school were those who believed that the Roman law in the form given it under Justinian was not fitted to satisfy the requirements of the present time. To these men the pure Roman law was in reality a rigid system which had become in certain aspects of its doctrine archaic and therefore incapable of promoting justice. It is not that they felt, apparently, a lack either of reverence for or belief in the law. They seem to have been as interested in preserving it as were their colleagues of the opposite conviction — those, that is, who

jurisdiction. He will be noted below. Digges, Welwod, Boroughs and the rest went far beyond him and made it quite clear to everyone that the British seas were, at least so far as they were concerned, as British as the realm of England could possibly be.

[1] Fran. Balduinus, *Commentarii in libros quatuor Institutionum*, &c. (Parisiis, 1554), p. 159. Balduinus, or Francois Baudouin, 1520–1573, was a French *Rechtshistoriker*. He was forced to flee from France to Germany on account of the religious persecutions. The question quoted above is particularly interesting because he was rather more historian than legalist. Stintzing, *op. cit.*, i, 382, 383 and 382, note 3.

[2] Hommel, *op. cit.*, p. 334, gives 1575. See Note 1, above.

[3] Antonius Perezius, *Iuris Civilis Antecessoris*, etc., new ed. (Vesaliae, 1670), 2.1, 81. He died in 1653 (Hommel, *op. cit.*, p. 341).

maintained that the ancient law was sufficient for the needs of the time. It is, rather, that they did not believe that a clarification of the old texts, or even a reintegration of the entire fabric of the law, such as Donellus undertook, could prove efficacious. The remedy which they advanced for the preservation of the life of this law was, fundamentally, a restatement of its tenets in terms of modern thought. Accordingly they undertook the adaptation or reinterpretation of the old system in the light of the customs and usages and laws (from whatever source) of the present. They shifted the emphasis in doctrine from past theory to present practice; and, where the old theory was obsolete, they built a new theory. This procedure naturally involved a looking to sources outside of the law books of Justinian and outside of the works of the Glossators — those two great fountain heads of law for the classical jurists. These extraneous sources were, as has been intimated, the received laws and customs of the time. It will be readily perceived that this method was one of profound significance for the future. *Use* was, consciously or unconsciously, made the criterion of the law. The judicious application of this criterion presented a problem of subtle difficulty. A rigid system must be made sensitive to the needs of present social life. It must aid and not hinder the promotion of justice. Yet this fine task involved the use of a method which could very well turn freedom into license.

This danger is apparent in the subject under discussion. An appeal to international practice, or to the customs of the nations, was valid; immemorial custom could provide an unimpeachable sanction on which to ground a law. Yet all customs were not lawful. It was, further, debatable whether the mere passage of time could make an unlawful practice lawful. John Selden was to demonstrate what a powerful weapon the appeal to custom and usage could be, in the hands of a clever man, to justify a claim not only contrary to the received law, but at variance with the facts. There were other difficulties. It would be necessary to find an answer to the question, What is good usage? It would be necessary to solve the problem presented by divergent customs which were themselves the embodiment of conflicting doctrines.

And these answers and solutions would inevitably be colored by the interests of the parties offering them. Under the early Stuarts, England found herself in agreement rather with the Venetian attitude towards the lawfulness of alleged property rights in the sea, than with the Dutch doctrine as presented by Grotius. France naturally could not admit the English claims to the waters which washed her own channel coasts. Yet, if those claims were reduced within workable limits, the French could hardly be expected to refrain from making similar claims. Once the principle of appropriation was accepted, the problem would become simply one of definition. It would not be impossible to find a formula. Where international practice was inchoate, it could be freely developed. Where uniform practice did not exist, it could be created. And finally, it was almost always possible to find some sanction in the past for what justice or self-interest, under whatever names they might be called, aspired to in the present. The appeal to custom or usage, then, while it was necessary in order to vitalize the old law, was significant because it was an appeal to an inchoate and unstable element in national and international life.

It was, of course, significant for other reasons. Customary law was familiar law. Appeals had been made to usage before Bartolus began to cite his own decisions as precedents. "The Praetor says" was a phrase familiar to the classicist. The significance for the present discussion lies in the fact that Bartolus and his successors in the Roman law went outside of that law, and did not hesitate to correct it when they thought it necessary by resorting to a method of reasoning which left them untrammeled by the past, and which filled with pregnant possibilities the habits and manners of life which the young nations were beginning to form as they emerged into a self-conscious and vigorous statehood. When usage is appealed to as a sanction for a certain law, it becomes extremely important what that usage is. The lawyer who will make this appeal in a case covered by domestic or civil law, will be apt to do it in a case involving conflicting claims to jurisdiction over a body of water lying between two states. He may even advance a theory as to how far off shore the jurisdiction of a state extends — and this is precisely what Bartolus did, as will appear below. A custom for him was not merely a custom; nor was it merely a custom invested by the law with certain attributes connected with the creation of rights or duties; it was a potential source of law, to be used to correct the Roman law itself when that law was incapable of a beneficial and just application to a given set of facts. It was this which he taught, and which his followers taught after him. The process of reasoning underlying such a position is simple. If the Roman law is not applicable to the needs of the time, and as the needs of the time are based upon facts, then it is necessary to adapt the law to the new conditions so that it can be applied to the facts in a manner to satisfy the needs. The new conditions become the guide by which the law is altered. To appreciate the significance of this position, with its emphasis upon present conditions, it is only necessary to recall that it was taken first by the greatest jurisconsult of the fourteenth century.

If the importance of Bartolus and the Post-Glossators for the subject of the present study may be expressed in a single sentence, it may perhaps be said that they are important because they did not hesitate to depart from the pure Roman law. The Glossators were mere commentators on the law of Justinian, a law that was out of date as they were writing. The Post-Glossators, as their name indicates, were also Roman jurists; and the *Corpus Juris Civilis* was the field in which they, too, worked. They commented, however, not in marginal notes, or even in the traditional *Summae*, but in huge expositions. The more fully they commented, the farther they got from the text. The pure Romanists regarded this as depraved. But the one thing which these commentators were doing which the Glossators did not attempt to do was to bring the Roman law into living contact with the times. They wove together the actual juristic conditions of their day with the law of Justinian. Roman law probably could never have become the living law of Europe if this work had not been done. Bartolus saved the Roman law from becoming only a subject of study for antiquarians.[1] He and his followers were practical men. Their

[1] Grueber, in his introductory essay to Ledlie's translation of Sohm's *Institutes of Roman Law*, minimizes the importance of the Post-Glossators: "The writings of the

work was a practical, a useful work. They debased the purity of the Roman law; they were poor historians; they wrote inelegant Latin, to the scandal of the Humanists. But, with the exception of England, they made the Roman law the common law of Europe.

1. Bartolus

A. His Work

Bartolus of Saxoferrato, or Sassoferrato, 1314–57,[1] was an Italian jurist and teacher of law at Pisa and Perugia, and a counsellor of Charles IV. His fame excels that of any other jurist of the middle age. He gained his reputation by his public lectures and by his comments on the various parts of the Roman law. Abandoning the system of notes which, as has been observed, had become the traditional method of exposition, he and those who followed him wrote vast works on the Roman law and on the glosses themselves. These works were for the most part without an orderly arrangement of subjects; they are a jumble of unclassified discussions. Yet the men who wrote them were possessed of a spirit vigorous and penetrating, and they exercised a

Italian jurists who followed Accursius, the so-called commentators or post-glossators, . . . contributed nothing of importance to a real understanding of Roman law. They did, however, gradually develop the simple method of the glossators into a highly complicated and artificial system.

"The obvious tendency of this method was to split up legal knowledge into innumerable fragments. And if we take into account the fact that it was usual for a writer, while discussing his own views, to refer continually to the views of other writers on the same subject, and further that each author naturally wished to distinguish himself by raising new questions and distinctions, it will readily be understood that the performance of these numerous dialectical operations came to be his chief object, and that he completely lost sight of the whole basis of his own work, the actual text of the Corpus juris." Rudolph Sohm, *Institutes of Roman Law*, translated from the 4th ed. of the German by J. C. Ledlie, with an introductory essay by E. G. Grueber (Oxford, 1892), p. xv.

Grueber seems to blame the method for the result. A complicated and artificial method, aided by the frailty of human nature, caused the text of the *Corpus* to be lost sight of. This reasoning seems to presuppose that this loss was not intentional, on the part of the Post-Glossators.

[1] These are Savigny's figures. For the life of Bartolus see Savigny, *op. cit.*, vi, cap. 53; J. N. Figgis, *Bartolus and the Development of European Political Ideas*, and C. N. S. Woolf, *Bartolus of Sassoferrato* (Cambridge, 1913), Introduction. For Figgis's paper, see the following page, note 1.

judgment which was practical and profound. Bartolus drew his material from three sources. First and foremost, he used the *Corpus Iuris* for his starting point. In the next place, he drew freely from other jurists, developing and expounding them, adapting them to the needs of a law which should be practically effective for the Italy of his time. In the third place, he drew from his own experience. He had been an assessor in Todi and Pisa, and had thus gained personal experience in the administration of the law. He did not hesitate to cite his own opinions. In Spain and Portugal his opinions were for a long time given binding force by law. Not only is he reputed to have held first place in the schools, during his lifetime, even, but it is said that in the courts his authority was so great that the judges did not dare to contradict him. Apparently, to quote Bartolus was to silence the opposing view.

This unique influence was due not merely to Bartolus's preeminent ability. He lived at the close of one period and at the beginning of another. In the thought of the middle age there is a borderland where theology, politics and law meet. In the controversies between Church and State, and in political theory generally, this relationship is conspicuous. For example, it was possible to denounce heresy as treason. The peculiar product of the fusion of these three systems had a profound influence in the doctrines of the relation of the Prince to his people, of the relation of the Prince to the Pope, and of his relation to God. It dominated political theory during the Reformation. It was influential in determining the structure of the modern state. A cursory reading of Grotius will show that it is the foundation of international law.[1] Almost any discussion of the *ius naturale* will show an interplay between these three systems of thought. The *ius gentium* is obviously dependent on them. Bartolus was the great, if not the only channel through which this type of thought

[1] In the work of Bartolus is the beginning of international law. This is evident in his two works, *De Captivis et Postliminio*, vi, 237, and *De Represaliis*, x, 117. See on this Figgis, *Bartolus and the Development of European Political Ideas*, in *Transactions of the Royal Historical Society*, xix, 156, 159. This paper appears in an appendix to his book, *The Divine Rights of Kings*, 2d. ed., Cambridge, 1914. See, pp. 356 and 360.

flowed to the modern world.[1] The work of the middle age had been fully developed by the time Bartolus lived. The Papacy had won its conflict with the Empire; Thomas Aquinas had polished off theology; scholastic philosophy had taken its authoritative shape; the *Corpus Iuris Civilis* had achieved an ossified sanctity. With the exception of England, the new states were arising under the influence of these forces. And England was not untouched by them. The new birth was at hand, in the time of Bartolus. The world was in transition.

"Hence," says Figgis,[2] "it came about that a mind capable of that peculiar combination of scholarship and actuality which can at once distill the learning of the past and assimilate the facts of the present might easily preserve for future generations everything that was living force in the period that was drawing to its close, and at the same time suggest some of the thoughts which should dominate the future. . . ."

Bartolus possessed this peculiar combination. He was a legalist who gave keen attention to practical things. To quote Figgis again — Bartolus was a "born student with a child's delight in his subject and in himself, but a man's intellect — a spirit alive with all the tendencies of the time, which had in them anything analogous to legal questions; a mind trained in the scholastic philosophy with a faith in its method and a desire for rational explanations; a memory in which facts, personal, political, legal, stuck, observant of all existing political facts and discerning tendencies only beginning — essentially an 'intellectual,' yet without conceit, but not without vanity, with a strong grasp of the practical aspect of abstract reasoning, and no desire at all merely to weave metaphysical cobwebs; a mind alert, vivid, with an imagination indeed, but one occupied not about beauty of form or color, but about law and government. Such a mind was eminently fitted to sum up in itself the long ages of legal development, and to suggest the lines of future advance."[3] If Bartolus was this kind of a man — and the weight of authority is with Figgis — his attitude upon the legal status of the sea is of the

[1] The metaphor is Figgis's.

[2] *Transactions*, p. 151.

[3] *Ibid.*, p. 155.

first importance. It is perhaps not an exaggeration to say that no pronouncement more important had been given up to this time since the days of Justinian.

B. His Doctrine

Mare sub cuius territorio comprehenditur.[1]

In a concise and forcible manner, Bartolus injects this doctrine formally into jurisprudence. It is given more fully in the *Gemma*, a collection of his sayings,[2] as follows:

Mare dicitur illius Domini, sub cuius territorio comprehenditur.

In commenting upon the practice of certain states of driving *homines males* off the sea, Bartolus justifies it by an argument from analogy. As it is fitting for the *praeses* to drive off or to punish evil doers on land, so it is likewise fitting for him to do so at sea.[3] The word, *congruo*, probably conveys more than a mere sense of appropriateness. The *praeses* is fit to undertake this work. It is suitable to and consistent with his office. It is so eminently proper that he who suppresses crime on land should do so in the waters adjacent to his territory that it may be said that he has the right to do so. But if he has a good right, then to do so is good law, for the simple reason that it is *ius*. For *ius*, of course, carries the meaning of both right and law. Some such train of thought as this was probably in the mind of Bartolus; for this seems to be one of those "borderland" questions on which the mediaeval mind was able to focus at once theology, politics, and law. His reasoning is a compound of all three.[4]

A city-state owns the islands located not far from its coasts and may destroy pirate strongholds on them:

[1] *Omnium Iuris . . . Commentaria*, 10 vols., ed. by I. Anellus de Bottis and Petrus Mangrelia, Venetiis, 1602. *Ad decimum lib. Codicis, De Classicis. Additio, Alex. Quidam habent*, viii, 33. (C. 11.13.)

[2] *Gemma legalium . . . Opera omnia*, Venetiis, 1602, under *Mare*.

[3] "Et sic patet, quod sicut quis possit punire deliquentes in territorio suo, ita punire in mare adiacente illi civitati, vel provinciae." *Ibid.* Not, it may be noted, over the high sea.

[4] Bartolus is here getting into international law, a subject or science which is grounded in this common region. *Cf.* Grotius.

Et sic quaelibet insula quae est in provincia, est pars provinciae. Et per hoc semel Pisis dixi contra quosdam piratas, qui derobabant in mari, & reducebant se in quamdam insulam prope Pisas: quod licet dicatur, quodam mare est commune, & sic ibi non possunt conveniri: tamen ego dico, quod illa insula est pars illius provinciae, qui adhaeret: ut hic.[1]

The question of a state's property rights in the islands off its coasts arises in Bartolus's mind in connection with the suppression of piracy, just as does the question of maritime jurisdiction over the waters adjacent to its coasts. His train of thought is not dissimilar. An island is regarded as part of the mainland, as it were, sticking to it. It is a fragment of the mainland. It goes with the territory nearest to it. The state which has property rights in that territory has also property rights in the island. The state extends its jurisdiction out to sea; it extends its power to hold property out to sea. The reasoning in both cases is practical, if not pragmatic.

In neither case is Bartolus arguing for a property right in the sea itself. In the first case, the state's jurisdiction over the sea adjacent to its coasts has its source in what may be called its police power. This power is already in being, by virtue of its existence, be it vested in an emperor, king, or people. The power of a state to enforce the law within its own territory is not doubted. What law it is that is enforced is another question. Bartolus arrives at his doctrine simply by not restricting this power to the land. He is unable to see any reason why a state should not have exclusive rights of jurisdiction within its territorial waters. He has not postulated a new power or a new source of power. It is to the interest of a state to protect its coasts, and to make the neighboring sea safe for navigation. It would be more difficult for him to deny such a right to the state than it is for him to advocate it. There is no right of sovereignty over these waters; there is merely a right of jurisdiction over them.

In the second case, that of the islands, there is a property right involved. But it is a property right in the islands, not in the sea. He is aware of the doctrine that because the sea is common to all,

[1] *Opera*, ed. by P. C. Brederodius, Basileae, 1589. In *Primam Digesti Veteris Partem Commentaria, ad lib. quintum Digest., De Iudiciis, lex* IX i, 492. In Venice ed. 1602, i,151.

things in the sea are common to all and therefore no property right (of the sort he is advocating) is legally possible. But he waives this doctrine aside without troubling to refute it. The origin of this property right seems to be in the nature of the island's relations to the mainland. It belongs to it. The right existed, and the ownership of the island was a fact, before Pisa was troubled by the band of pirates which established a base there. The question concerning which the Pisans were in doubt was whether or not the pirates were on alien territory. It is interesting to note that as he writes his doctrine, Bartolus cites one of his own opinions in support of it.

The query arises, How near must an island be in order to come within the territory of the neighboring state? Bartolus gives an answer to this question in his tract on rivers.[1]

> Ad quod videndum est, an qui habet iurisdictionem in territorio cohaerenti mari, habeat in ipso mari, & usque ad quod spacium: Et videtur quod non; quia mare est commune omnibus. In contrarium est veritas, imo sicut praeses provinciae debet purgare provinciam malis hominibus per terram,... congruit, ita etiam per aquam. Et hoc apparet quod etiam in mari habet iurisdictionem, & in Insulis, quae sunt in dicto mari, multo magis, Insulae enim illae; quae a provincia modico spacio distant, illius provinciae esse dicimus, ut sunt Insulae Italiae . . . modico autem spacio distare puto, quando distant percentum miliaria: vicinus enim locus dicitur, . . . quo inter duas dietas non dicitur locus remotus. Constat autem quod centum miliaria per mare minus est duabus dietis. . . .
>
> Sed si Insula esset in mari alto, & a qualibet regione distans, tunc videndum esset, an posset dici propinqua alteri Insulae, ut dicatur nobis vicina, vel propinqua. Et ideo Insula Sardiniae Italiae dicitur, licet ab Italia magno spacio distet, sed est propinqua insulae Corsicae; quae ab Italia modicum distat. Secundum alios autem si nec alicui regioni, nec Insulae alterius vicina est, tunc non possumus dicere, quod aliquis in ea habeat iurisdictionem nisi Imperator; qui omnium dominus est . . . dico igitur, quod talis insula occupanti conceditur quo ad dominium.

Bartolus puts a double question: whether he who has jurisdiction in territory adjoining the sea has jurisdiction in the sea itself; *and* (if so), to what distance seaward. The first part of the question is answered in the affirmative. Then, instead of answering the other half, Bartolus passes to his discussion of islands. The reasoning here differs from that above. Since a "prov-

[1] *Tyberiadis, Tractatus de Fluminibus* (Bononiae, 1576), p. 55.1.

ince" has jurisdiction over the sea, it has jurisdiction over the islands in the said sea. He goes on from this point to state almost in parenthesis that those islands are said to belong to a "province" which are but a moderate distance from it. The rest of his discussion is taken up with a definition of the phrase, "moderate distance," and with a consideration of those islands which lie outside the distance specified, that is, those which are more than one hundred miles away. He does not return to the unanswered half of his question.

This passage from the *De Fluminibus* is frequently cited by later jurists. Caepolla, who refers to it with more exactness and with a fuller treatment than does any other writer, leaves the question as Bartolus leaves it.[1] The general impression seems to be, however, that Bartolus is laying down a hundred mile limit to the jurisdiction of a state over the adjacent sea. It is probably correct to presume that this was his intention. Indeed, whether it was, or not, it follows from his reasoning. A state has jurisdiction over the sea adjacent to its territory. It has jurisdiction over islands in the said sea. It has jurisdiction over islands which are not distant farther than one hundred miles from its coast. Then the implication is plain, and the conclusion is unavoidable, that the state has jurisdiction over the sea to a distance of one hundred miles from its coast. The conclusion is inevitable because the state's jurisdiction over the islands in the adjacent sea is made to depend upon the jurisdiction of the state over that part of the sea, and not upon any property right which the state may possess in them. Suppose an island to be one hundred and ten miles distant from land, and twenty-five miles from another island which is eighty-five miles from land. Then the first island belongs to the state which owns the second island. But would the jurisdiction of the state extend over the twenty-five miles of water intervening between the two islands? Or only over fifteen of those miles? Such questions as these are left for a later day to answer.

[1] Bartholomaeus Caepolla, *Tractatus de Servitutibus*, 4th ed. (Coloniae Agrippinae, 1660), pp. 305, 306. In further support of the hundred mile distance he cites 1, *quicunque Cod. de episc. & cler.* (C. 1.3.14.)

In may be observed that the doctrine of Bartolus is at once progressive and restrictive. From the point of view of those who admitted no maritime jurisdiction of an exclusive nature, he is revolutionary rather than progressive, for he is teaching the subversive doctrine that a state has sole rights of jurisdiction over a thing on which and in which all men have equal rights. But from the point of view of Venice and Genoa, and particularly, the former, he is rather more reactionary than progressive. His doctrine is in effect a limitation upon the sweeping claims of the Venetians to the gulf or sea of the Adriatic — claims which, moreover, they were making good by reason of their naval supremacy in that sea, and claims which they did not cease to assert until the fall of Venice in the eighteenth century. As has been noted, the Venetians claimed not only a right of exclusive jurisdiction in the Adriatic; they claimed the ownership of the sea. A just appreciation of the doctrine of Bartolus will not overlook this two-fold character which it possesses.

2. Baldus of the Ubaldi

Only less famous than his master, is Bartolus's great pupil Baldus,[1] also of Perugia. A glance at the books of the jurists of later days will show what fame was his. He is one of the most frequently cited of the Italian lawyers. Figgis alludes to a story that Bartolus once declared his crowded lecture room to be empty because Baldus was absent; and to another which relates how "once the pupil so brow-beat the professor that he had to take a day to consider the point, being unequal to immediate reply." [2]

As might be expected, Baldus holds that there is a right of jurisdiction in the sea. At the same time, he makes it clear that he is not advocating a right of property in it. Some things, he says, are common to all animals, as are, for example, the air, the sea, rain and the seashore. But there is a difference between things which are *res communes*, and those which are *nullius in bonis*. The former may not, the latter may be appropriated. Consequently the sea may not be appropriated by any one.

[1] 1334–1400. [2] Figgis, *Transactions*, *op. cit.*, pp. 166, 167.

Hic ergo quaeritur, nunquid quis possit praescribere mare, id est, aliquem usum usque aliquem iurisdictione in mari?

Baldus answers in the affirmative, for appropriation and jurisdiction are two different things; so far as the sea is concerned, there may be jurisdiction over it without ownership of it by the ruler who exercises the jurisdiction.

Maxime sine titulo praescribi non potest. Item in mari est iurisdictio, sicut in terra . . . & videmus de iuregentium in mari esse regna distincta, sicut in arida terra: ergo et Ius Civile.

Since the *ius civile* is present, so to speak, at sea, what it permits or prescribes must be there also. And

sic Venetiani & Ianuenses sua maria habent distincta ex inveteratissima consuetudine.

The right to lay taxes for the use of the sea, and the right to confiscate goods on the sea — at sea — belongs to the Prince, that is, the Emperor, alone. But those cities which really recognize no superior, and who thus possess the Regalia themselves, have this right through custom. Nevertheless, *de iure*, this right is lodged in the Prince.[1]

[1] *Commentaria In primam Digesti Veteris partem*, Lugduni, 1585. *Ad lib. primum Digest. De divisione rerum et qualitate. Lex prima. Rerum omnium*, p. 48.3. (D. 1.8.1.)

Baldus has made a distinction here of fundamental importance. The Emperor possesses *de iure* the Regalia and the right to confiscate goods at sea and the right to levy certain taxes; on the other hand, there are certain cities, or city-states, such as Venice and Genoa, which possess *de facto* the Regalia and the rights mentioned, for they are independent of the Emperor, not recognizing him as their superior. In the opinion of Baldus, the *de facto* possession by the Venetians, say, of these rights and powers does not preclude their *de iure* possession by the Emperor. He alone may possess them *de iure*. He may or may not possess them *de facto* in a particular case. What Baldus is apparently trying to do is to reconcile the mediaeval theory of the unity of the Empire — a theory which carried with it the doctrine that the Emperor is *dominus totius mundi* — with the actual state of the world in his day.

His solution comes directly from his master Bartolus, who had to face the same difficulty. The opening words of the first law of the Code of Justinian are: "Cunctos populos quos clementiae nostrae regit temperamentum. . . ." The words *Cunctos populos*, Bartolus thinks, imply that there are peoples who are outside the Empire. Yet the Emperor is *dominus totius mundi* — the Emperor Antoninus said, "Ego quidem mundi dominus." This remark of his is recorded in D. 14.2.9., that passage on which I. Gothofredus wrote his pamphlet, *De Imperio Maris*, referred to in a previous section. Bartolus solves the difficulty here presented by

It follows from his statement concerning the *ius civile*, that a person who is within the limits of that portion of the sea which is under the jurisdiction of a neighboring state is within the reach of the courts of that state. He is within, as it were, the judicial limits of that state. The sea is in the mind of Baldus a judicial district in which the *ius civile* is operative. This doctrine receives illustration, as other doctrines do, from that standard example of a maritime power, the city of Venice.[1] It is lawful to charge, or

postulating a rule *de iure* and a rule *de facto*. "Aut verbum 'regit,'" he says, "hic positum intelligitur prout de jure est (et) tunc de jure (Imperator) regit omnes populos, et sic relativum ponitur declarative, 'quos' scilicet 'omnes.' Et hoc puto fuisse de mente Imperatoris. Aut vis intelligere prout est *de facto*, et tunc, quia quidam de facto non obediunt, et sic talis qualitas non competit omnibus de genere, tunc relativum ponitur restrictive." (C. 1.1.) In *Primam Codicis Partem*, Venetiis, 1602. *Ad primum lib. Codicis. De Summa Trinitate. Lex Prima. Cunctos Populos*, p. 3.1.

Bartolus says, again: "(E)go sum consuetus dicere in prima constitutione huius libri, quod cum Imperator sit, dominus totius mundi. Et, glossae dicunt dominum quo ad protectionem, quia cum alij sunt domini singulariter, plures non potuerunt esse domini in solidum. Ego dico, quod Imperator est dominus totius mundi vere. Nec obstat quod alij sunt particulariter, quia mundus est universalitas quaedam: unde potest habere dictam universitatem, licet singulae res non sint suae. Unde si alius teneret mundum, ipse Imperator posset vendicare (sic vindicare)." In *Primam Digesti Veteris Partem*, Venetiis, 1603 (1602?). *Ad lib. Sextum Digest. De rei vendicatione (sic vindicatione). Lex prima. Per hanc autem actionem*, p. 169.1. (D. 6.1.1.)

But, as appears from the foregoing, the Emperor has not the ownership of the whole world. The former statement to which he refers is in this same volume, *ad primum lib. Digest. Prima Constitutio. Omnem*, p. 4.3. The Emperor is lord of the whole world "ratione protectionis et iurisdictionis." The Emperor is "dominus mundi quia tenetur totum mundum defendere."

For the complete theory of Bartolus concerning the Emperor, see Woolf, *op. cit.*, pp. 21–53. He observes, p. 22, that "(t)his distinction between right and fact — the acceptance of the Imperial claims in right, with the accompanying recognition of their invalidity in fact — is at the basis of all the political theories of Bartolus." He adds, "But if *de jure* the Emperor's position as lord of the whole world is unassailable, this does not imply that all other '*dominium*' is merely *de facto*. The Emperor is '*dominus totius mundi vere*,' but others can be *domini* '*particulariter*,' the world considered universally is the Emperor's, but '*singulae res*' are not necessarily his."

[1] *Commentaria*, in VII–VIII–IX–X–XI *Codicis Libros*, Lugduni, 1585. *Ad lib. vii, Codicis. De sententia ex breviculo recitandis. Lex Prima. Arbitri*, p. 54.6. (C. 7.44.1.) "Et nota quod qui est in mari quod regitur per civitatem maximam, ut Genua, Venetiae non dicitur esse extra districtum, unde ibi ius reddi potest. Item in omnibus decretis quae tribuunt ius, requiritur quod iudex sedeat pro tribunali: secus si non tribuunt ius, vel non requirunt disputationem fori." "*Breviculo*" should be "*periculo*."

to require payment of money for travel at sea, just as it is for the same purpose on land. (Baldus is probably saying indirectly that the fact that the sea is common to all does not release those who use it for purposes of navigation from the payment of passage money, dues, or tolls.) But the right to make such charges is not lodged indiscriminately in any one. Only the lord of that sea — the Emperor or the king — may impose them; and he must have this right through custom so ancient that a memory to the contrary does not exist. Such a custom has the force of power;

nam talis consuetudo potestatem Principis habet.[1]

Presumably the courts may take cognizance of the refusal of a person to pay lawful charges of this sort. The Prince has the power to grant a right of jurisdiction over the sea, just as he has the power and right to do so in the case of a city, or a district, or some other domain. And all such grants are to be broadly construed.[2]

The notion of regarding the part of the sea over which the Prince has jurisdiction as a district subjoined, so to speak, to his territory, is latent in this doctrine of the *beneficia*. It would be a mistake to suppose that Baldus would attribute a property right in the sea to the Prince. He states specifically that it is jurisdiction which is within the power of the Prince to grant. There is nothing incongruous in such a doctrine, in the minds of Bartolus and Baldus.[3] Indeed, Baldus places his position beyond miscon-

[1] *Commentaria In quartum et quintum Codicis lib.*, Lugduni, 1585. *Ad libr. quartum Codicis. De nautico foenore. Lex* III, *Cum proponas*, p. 113.18. (C. 4.33.4 (3.).) "Pedagia ita soluntur in mari, sicut in terra, tamen non possunt imponi passagia nisi per dominum illius maris, puta per Principem, vel Regem: et per antiquam consuetudinem, cuius contraij memoria non existit, nam talis consuetudo potestatem Principis habet."

[2] *Commentaria in primam Digesti Veteris partem*, Lugduni, 1585. *Ad lib. primum Digest. De Constitutionibus Principum. Lex* III, *Beneficium*, p. 29.6. (D. 1.4.3.) "Beneficia sunt latissime interpretanda." If the Prince gives me jurisdiction over a city, or castrum, or county, or district, the grant is to be broadly construed. And this applies "tam in terra quam in mari, nam mare sicut terra distinguitur seu restringitur."

[3] Angelus Perusinus, *Interpretatio. Ad undecimum librum Codicis. De Classicis. 1. Clacem (sic Classem)*, p. 319. (C. 11.13 (12).1.) This book is bound and paged and indexed with Baldus on the Code. "Sicuti congruit bono Praesidi pur-

struction. He has said that the sea is common; in what sense is this so?

Dic quod est commune quoad usum, sed proprietas nullius, sicut aër est communis usu, proprietas tamen est nullius. . . . Sed iurisdictio est Caesaris et sic ista tria sunt diversa, scilicet, proprietas, usus, iurisdictio et protectio.[1] "Ista tria sunt diversa."

That statement is the root of his thought on the matter.

In one of his discussions of the nature of a servitude, Baldus finds occasion to lay down a doctrine which turned out to be of great significance for the future. It is the beginning of a doctrine occasionally met with to the effect that a state may occupy the bed of the sea, under certain conditions, of course. Its more immediate and important influence is in connection with the shore of the sea, and consists in regarding the shore as a part of the land rather than as a part of the sea. The effect of this new orientation would inevitably be in the course of time to destroy the classic doctrine of the shore by regarding it as within the territory of the maritime state. Baldus may not have been entirely unconscious of the possibility of such a development.

In the fashion characteristic of the new jurists, he opens that part of his discussion which is of interest here by the citation of a case. The Venetians granted to the Placentinians the right of transit over a certain bridge in their possession without the payment of tolls. The bridge passed into the hands of the Paduans, who presently attempted to levy charges upon the Placentinians for their use of the bridge. The Placentinians refused to pay them, on the ground that when the Venetians granted them the right of free transit over the bridge, they created a perpetual servitude in favor of the Placentinians. The Paduans argued that that grant was not in the nature of a servitude, but was rather a personal obligation, *quae non sequitur fundum*. From the next remark of Baldus, it appears that the bridge in question was over a river. It is interesting to note that he did not think it necessary to specify this fact in his statement of the case. He proceeds to

gare provinciam malis hominibus super terram: ita eodem modo congruit per mare." This, of course, is the doctrine of Bartolus.

[1] *Ad primum Digest. De divisione rerum et qualitate. Lex* II. *Quaedam naturali iure*, p. 51. (D. 1.8.2.)

say that the Paduans also alleged that all navigable rivers pertain *ad statum Imperii*, and are Regalia; so that there can be no servitude laid on them without the order of the Prince. But this reasoning, he comments, is not valid, because the truth is that while it is true that in *universali* all navigable rivers are *Imperii Romani*, nevertheless they may be owned in *particulari;* they are the property of that state whose territory they cross.

> Nam unum et idem est territorium, quod eminet super aquas, et quod immergitur aquis, et hoc satis probatur argumentum littora maris. Nam littora quae sunt sub Imperio alicuius pupili (sic) ut Venetorum, vel Ianuensium, sunt illius populi, et ab eo qui praeest licentia est petenda.

This comes very close to admitting a right of property in the shore.[1]

It has been noted that Baldus holds that the Emperor possesses *de iure* all the Regalia, though he does not possess them *de facto* in all parts of the world. It has been pointed out that this theory is derived from that of Bartolus to the effect that the Emperor, who is *de iure* the lord of the whole world, is *de facto* a lord of only a part of it; and further, that, upon examination, "the whole world" so far as it is inhabited by the *populus Romanus*, is coterminous with western Christendom; while, within western Christendom, there are peoples who, *de facto*, acknowledge no superior in the Roman Emperor. In accord with this distinction between

[1] *Commentaria In Sextum Cod. Lib.*, Lugduni, 1585. *De Constitutionibus Insertis*, etc., *Lex.* VI. *Si Plures*, p. 178.13. (C. 6.36.7(6).) "Item servitus est si per potestatem tuum non possim transire absque gabella mercium, quam ex usu habui a tempore cuius non extat memoria, vel ex privilegio Principis habeo. Tamen fuit magna questio: cuia Veneti, ut dicitur, concesserunt Placentinis transitum per quendam (sic) pontem, quia tunc possidebatur per Venetos absque solutione alicuius vectigalis, postea pons ille factus est de districtu Paduano, mox Paduani petunt vectigal, sed Plancentini (sic) dicunt se non teneri: quia ista servitus perpetuo fuit concessa. Paduani dicunt quod ista non est species servitutis: sed fuit quaedam obligatio personalis, quae non sequitur fundum. Item allegebant quod omnia flumena navigabilia pertinent ad statum Imperii, et sunt Regalia, quibus sine iussu Principis nulla servitus potest imponi, cum sint Caesaris. Sed haec ratio non obstat, quia verum est quod in universali omnia flumina navigabilia sint Imperii Romani, licet in particulari sint: earum civitatum, pur (sic) quarum territorium transit flumen. (N)am unum et idem est territorium, quod eminet super aquas, et quod immergitur aquis, et hoc satis probatur argumentum littora maris. Nam littora quae sunt sub Imperio alicuius pupili (sic), ut Venetorum, vel Ianuensium, sunt illius populi, et ab eo qui praeest licentia est petenda."

de iure and *de facto* lordship, or, between *de iure* and *de facto* possession of the Regalia, is the distinction which Baldus makes in the bridge tolls case referred to above. He says that all navigable rivers are under the Roman *imperium*, *in universali*, but that, considered *in particulari*, they belong to, or are under the *imperium* of, the state — *civitas* — through which they flow. He further applies this distinction to the shores of the sea. This mode of reasoning is of fundamental importance in the theory of the new jurists, the Praktiker. On the one hand is the relation *de iure* of the Emperor to the world considered *in universali* — as a *universitas;* on the other hand is his relation *de facto* to the world considered *in particulari*, a world in which Venice asserts and enforces exclusive rights in the Adriatic, and in which France and England do not acknowledge the supremacy of the Emperor. What is unlawful when considered *de iure* becomes lawful *de facto*. The place occupied by a *civitas* in the world considered *in universali* is different from that occupied by the *civitas* in the world considered *in particulari*. A *civitas* having no right of maritime jurisdiction *de iure* or *universaliter* is found upon analysis to possess maritime jurisdiction *particulariter de facto*. It may even possess it *de iure in particulari* through prescription or by privilege. And what is true of maritime jurisdiction is true of the *imperium litorum maris;* what is true of land out of the water is true of land under the water.

3. Bartholomew Caepolla. Alteserra

Bartholomaeus Caepolla, a native of Verona, and a professor first in Ferrara and then in Padua, was a jurist of the middle of the fifteenth century.[1] He seems to have been an adept in *iurisprudentia cautelaris;* his work, *Tractatus cautelarum*, is the first great collection of *cautelae*,[2] or, perhaps, of aids to notaries. The

[1] D. 1477. Savigny, *op. cit.*, vi, 321. See c. 17, Pt. II.

[2] Stintzing, *op. cit.*, i, 534. On the *iurisprudentia cautelaris*, he writes, p. 533: "Schon die altrömischen Iuristen haben sich in der Aufstellung von Cautelen (Heuremata) nicht darauf beschränkt, Regeln der Vorsicht zu bieten und zu empfehlen gegen die Gefahren, welche böser Wille und Leichtfertigkeit dem Erfolge einer juristischen Handlung bereiten können; sondern auch Mittel und Wege gezeigt, um den in der formalen Strenge des Rechts liegenden Gefahren auszuweichen. In

advice and suggestions which he embodied in this work were of such a suspicious character that the phrase, "Cautellae Caepollae" soon became used to denote legal chicanery.[1] Nevertheless it would seem that his reputation was not too odious to prevent him from being influential in this branch of law. He enjoyed fame during his lifetime, and the work was widely circulated.

In one of his important tractates, *De Servitutibus rusticorum*,[2] Caepolla has an extended discussion of the application of the laws of prescription to the sea. Because the sea is by nature open to all, he says,[3] a servitude may not be placed on it by a private person. But a prince may lay a servitude on the sea. However, private individuals may contract between themselves an obligation not to fish in certain parts of the sea. In the same way, a private person may obligate himself not to hinder another private person in doing a certain thing in public waters.[4] When, therefore, a servitude has not been laid on the sea, and where there are no private obligations to the contrary, the sea is open to all, and its use is common to all men. And if some one is forbidden to fish in the sea (when, of course, it is free from restrictions) or to cast in his nets and to draw them out, *nulla lege* (as Caepolla

beiden Richtungen hat die mittelaltliche Jurisprudenz sich fortbewegt. Die *jurisprudentia cautelaris* ist einer ihrer praktischen Zweige, welcher vorzugsweise vom Notariat seine Pflege empfängt, in Regeln und Formeln für Geschäfte und gerichtliche Handlungen zur Erscheinung kommt. Wenn es sich zunächst darum handelt, durch Anweisungen und Beispiele die vorsichtige Beobachtung der Vorschriften des positiven Rechts zu lehren, um den Act gegen Anfechtungen sicher zu stellen; so überschreitet die Cautelarjurisprudenz in ihrer weiteren Ausbildung allmählich diese Grenzen und bildet sich aus zu der Kunft, die Vorschriften des Rechts zu umgehen und, gedeckt durch ihren Wortlaut, Zwecke zu verfolgen, die auf geradem Wege nicht zu erreichen sind . . . (N)icht mit Unrecht sagt Budäus, dass die Ausbildung der Cautelen wesentlich die Schuld an der Entartung der Rechtswissenschaft trage."

[1] "Es mischen sich darin die Anweisungen zur klugen Vorsicht mit solchen zur ränkevollen Schlauheit in so bedenklicher Weise, dass man wohl begreift, wie der Name '*Cautelae Caepollae*' bald die Bedeutung perverser und chicanöser Ausflüchte und Behelfe annehmen konnte," p. 534.

[2] *De Servitutibus rusticorum praediorum*, in the *Tractatus illustrium*, VI, Pt. II. Venetiis, 1584.

[3] *Ibid.*, p. 237.1–2.

[4] *Tractatus, op. cit.*, p. 237.1.2. "Sed ubi non est a principe mari servitus imposita, nec a privato aliqua obligatio constituta: tunc mare possim omnibus patet . . . et eius usus communis est omnibus, ut aeris."

puts it) *privata vel publica contradicente*, he has a right of action at law.[1]

This doctrine presents the characteristically close adherence to the Roman law, modified by certain recognized restrictions not originally contemplated by that law, which is typical of the carefully progressive Roman lawyer of the practical school. Not all of the commentators handled the classic law with discrimination, of course. The retention of the familiar phraseology while the modern attitude is really dominant is a mark of the conservative element among them.[2]

The problem as to whether a state may acquire maritime property rights is handled with subtlety. Caepolla asks this question:

> Sed nunquid possit aliquis praescribere mare, vel aliquam usum maris, aut jurisdictionem?[3] [His answer is] non potest praescribere tempore,

because such places cannot be acquired under the *ius gentium* by prescription, which means long continued possession. For the same reason, one cannot acquire title by prescription through the passage of so much time as to reach beyond the memory of man. Then, having said this, he makes the following nice qualification:

> In contrarium videtur, quod imo tanto tempore possit acquiri: quia in mari est jurisdictio, sicut in terra. ergo praescribere potest. Item quia possessio vel quasi, cujus non existat memoria, habet vim tituli seu privilegii, aut juris constituti.[4]

The first part of this argument (denying prescription) is the statement of the position of his opponents. The second part is the answer to them. It is, then, the existence of this maritime jurisdiction which makes it possible for the laws of prescription to operate there — that is, at sea. The nature of this jurisdiction is, obviously, not that of the Rhodian Code. A theorist of the classical school had no difficulty with that body of law. The, to him, poisonous quality in the present doctrine lies in the fact that the jurisdiction spoken of in it is essentially territorial. Nor is the

[1] This is a set phrase, part of the legal parlance of the day.

[2] It is sometimes difficult to classify such men.

[3] *De Servitutibus*, etc., 4th ed., Coloniae Agrippinae, 1660; p. 304.5. The phrase, *nulla lege*, etc., occurs on p. 302.

[4] *Ibid.*, p. 304.5.

doctrine that the *Princeps* may lay a servitude on the sea in antagonism to all of the classic jurists. As has been noted in the preceding chapter, a certain section of them admitted the practice, and, on the whole, admitted the legality of it too, although, perhaps with some regret. Indeed, the progressive classicists and the conservative Bartolists are not far apart in their positions on this doctrine.

He goes on in the same passage to add that even a private person may have jurisdiction in the sea by means of a concession or privilege from the Prince. Here also Caepolla is in touch with the most advanced of the theorists. But what they seem to admit grudgingly, and with hesitation, he asserts. And while they take refuge in the Regalia, as the source of these somewhat dubious powers of the Prince, he takes a broadly legal basis.

The Venetians, he thinks, furnish an illustration in point, any alleged title of the Emperor to the contrary notwithstanding. This observation constitutes a rather ruthless break in the fraternization of the two parties. The passage in which he actually lays down the law regarding the Venetian claims is this:[1]

> Et ideo cum mare Adriaticum, quod Gulfus Venetorum appellatur, sit dominii Venetorum; quia in eo ipsi Veneti praedominati sunt per tantum tempus, quod non extat memoria contrarium, et per hoc dicuntur habere jurisdictionem in illo mari, quia illud tempus habet vim tituli: dicendum est, quod ipsi domini Veneti in ipso mari possint servitutem imponere, et non alii.

The passing of time gives the force and effect of a title. *Tempus habet vim tituli*. Time creates title, even in the imprescriptible. This means that the Venetians are not merely *de facto* lords of the Adriatic, but *de iure* lords. But the old provisions concerning the property rights of structures built in the sea adds strength to the position, for the Venetians are *fundati in mari*. By the *ius gentium civitates fundatae in mari sunt ipsorum aedificantium*.[2] The Digest held that individuals were; it omitted mention of *civitates* in this connection.

But understand, he says emphatically, that what has been said

[1] *De Servitutibus* etc., *op. cit.*, p. 26.3.

[2] *Tractatus*, etc. *op. cit.*, p. 237.3. But on p. 237.8 he says that the Venetians and Genoese have title or privilege in respect of use and jurisdiction from the Emperor.

refers to use and jurisdiction only, and not to ownership, for this last cannot be acquired by any prescription or custom, because the sea is under the *ius gentium* and is in public use — unless — *nisi concessio Caesaris aut senatus intervenerit.*[1] It appears, then, that ownership may be acquired. If one wishes to establish one-self *in titulo* or *in privilegio Caesari*, and, for proof of his claim alleges possession or a quasi-possession from time immemorial, it is sufficient [2] (providing, of course, that he proves such possession).

It may be questioned, he says,[3] how far one is said to have jurisdiction in the sea or to possess the sea. The answer is, that he who has the *imperium* in the sea is said to possess the sea. A clever appeal to popular usage, perhaps, to define the word, "possess," is made here; but it does not satisfy.

There is also the question whether the Venetians have the right to impose tolls and to confiscate goods in contravention of their statutes. There are two answers to this problem. The first is, that the *ius confiscandi* is a special right sanctioned by custom and by the permission granted by the Prince. The second is, that the Venetians have the Regalia in their *imperium* and the *iura fisci*. They acknowledge no superior, and thus they impose their own laws and statutes on the sea.[4] Whether these two reasons account for the levying of tolls also is not clear. It may be noted that the second reason is an appeal to the Regalia as the source of the powers questioned.

Caepolla adopts Bartolus's hundred-mile limit to the distance to which the Prince may exercise his jurisdiction over the sea.[5] This means that he holds the doctrine of the adjacent sea. The sea is ordinarily distinguished by the territory adjacent to it.

[1] *Tractatus, op. cit.*, p. 237.8. "Item praedicta intellige quo ad usum et iurisdictionem, non autem quo ad proprietatem: quia illa non potest praescribi aliqua praescriptione, vel consuetudine . . . quia sunt de iure gentium et publico, et in usu publico: ut mare, flumina navigabilia nullo tempore acquiruntur, nisi concessio Caesaris aut Senatus intervenerit."

[2] "Sed si vellet se fundare in titulo seu privilegio Caesaris, et ad ipsum probandum allegaret possessionem vel quasi tanti temporis cuius non extat memoria, sufficeret etiam ad acquirendum dominium." *Ibid.*

[3] *Ibid.*, p. 237.9. [4] *Ibid.*, p. 237.10.

[5] *Ibid., op. cit.*, p. 238.14.

Or, put in another way, the adjacent sea is comprehended in the territory of a state as a district of that state.[1] This, it will be recalled, is in agreement with the doctrine of Baldus. Caepolla observes that it is the most favored opinion. The basis of this jurisdiction is other than that of those cases where a state has acquired it by prescription.

Chapter XLII is concerned with fisheries. It is permitted to whomsoever it pleases to fish in the sea, which by nature is open to all.[2] The same is true in regard to fishing from the shore, the use of which is as free as air. He seems to be limiting the jurisdiction of the Prince or state at this point; but his statements are not such as to make it certain that he is doing so. The remainder of his doctrine does not differ from that of the conventional classic or historical position.

It is apparent that the argument that the Prince or the state (*res publica*, *regnum*, fully independent *civitas*) might acquire property or jurisdictional rights in the sea by immemorial prescription is a favorite one. Used by the majority of the theorists to explain the privileged position of the Venetians in the Adriatic, it is used freely by the Bartolists and by the practical school in general.[3] The argument that the Prince might vest at least some of the rights so acquired (or already held as of the Regalia) in private persons seems generally[4] to have been accepted.

Alteserra[5] is representative of a group of jurists whom it is difficult to place. He gives the full Roman doctrine of the community of the sea. But then, after having done this, he adds that word which takes on such significance in the mouth of even the mildest Bartolist, *tamen*.

[1] *Tractatus*, p. 238.26.

[2] *De Servitutibus*, etc., *op. cit.*, p. 330.

[3] For this and the opposed position, see Ansaldus de Ansaldis, *De Commercio et Mercatura Discursus Legales* (Romae, 1689), p. 49.

[4] *Institutiones Iuris Civilis* (Venetiis, 1578), 2.1.1; Ioan. Bertachinus Firmanus, *Repertorium*, 4 vols. (Basileae, 1573), p. 374; Jacobus Cancerius, *Variarum Resolutionum*, etc., in 3 parts (Barcinone, 1608), iii, 279 (or, Lugduni, 1626). Angelus Aretinus, *Institutionum Iustiniani Libros Commentarii* (Venetiis, 1558), p. 59 (cf. also, p. 59.4).

[5] A. D. Alteserra, *Expositio in Institutionum Iustiniani* (Tolosae, 1664), pp. 97, 98. Cancerius and Aretinus, cited in note 4 above, seem to hold the position taken by Alteserra.

Tamen [he says] maris dominium Principis beneficio, vel longa consuetudine acquiri potest, et si maris proprium ius, id est proprietas seu dominium, ad aliquem pertineat, datur ei interdictum uti possidetis, possessionis suae tuendae gratia, et si prohibeatur iure suo uti [etc.].

That the *Princeps* can lay a servitude on the sea is, of course, good Roman doctrine, at least as developed by the Glossators. But on the other hand, Alteserra has not hesitated to use *proprietas* in regard to the sea, a use which is a step in advance of D. Gothofredus, who used the word *dominium*, as does Alteserra, but who did not go beyond. It is extremely doubtful whether a historical jurisconsult would say that even the *Princeps* himself had the power to grant a *ius proprietatis* in the sea. Alteserra, in this same passage, guards himself against a misuse of his doctrine:

Quod dicitur si maris proprium ius ad aliquem pertineat, intelligendum est de sinu maris vel aestuario. . . . [And again], littora quae fundo vendito conjuncta sunt in modo fundi non computantur, quia nullius sunt, et de iure gentium omnibus vacant.

He might belong with either group, that is, either with the advanced classicist or *historiker*, or with the Bartolist. His use of the word, *proprietas*, and his apparent willingness to allow to a private person a right of property in the sea *Principis beneficio* seem to put him in the advanced position.

It is important to note the position which is here illustrated by Alteserra. He places greater emphasis on the law of Justinian than do Bartolus and Baldus. In his reliance on theory he resembles Caepolla, although the latter accepted the hundred mile limit. Alteserra, on the other hand, points out that he is speaking of bays and estuaries. He has much in common with Treutlerus and the advanced theorists, yet he outstrips them. What is true of most of the jurists which have been cited is true also of Alteserra and his group, namely, that it is practically impossible to draw from their writings a precise theory on the status of the sea. It is therefore unwise to attempt to draw too definite generalizations from their works. But this much may safely be said: that within the group of jurisconsults which has been called "practical" for the purpose of describing their doctrine in regard to the status of the sea, there is a group which emphasizes the classical position rather more than do Bartolus and Baldus; and that, when placed out of their chronological order, they form a sequence in thought between the most advanced of the historical jurists and the commentators, or those who appeal to use. It may be said further that this group grants the validity of custom, of international custom, as a source of law, where that custom contradicts pure theory as it is found in the classic Roman law. At the same time, their emphasis on legal theory, on the law, leads them to scrutinize any custom which challenges the received doctrine, and to place the burden of proof upon the custom which is questioned, rather than upon the theory which is putting the question. They restrict within narrow limits the field in which international practice operates to abrogate the old doctrine. Admitting the force of both legal theory and practice, they lean towards theory; whereas the Bartolist of more pronounced type, making the same admission, leans more heavily upon practice. It may be noted here that the great figure holding this position is Grotius.

4. The Adjacent Sea

> Et hoc ipsum mare etiam considerant Iurisconsulti, tum late diffusum, tum etiam littora eius. Siquidem et divisum mare pervaria imperia: atque iurisdictio in pelago, non omnibus, sed certis, competit. Sunt enim et mari certi fines natura per Deum constituti, et tamen terminus unus generalis. . . . Et quia navigandi usus frequens fuit, simul et navigii iura introduci oportuit, quae nec constitui debuerunt, vel potuerunt facilius, quam ab iis, qui in proximis mari locis imperant, [etc.][1]

The division of the sea into separate jurisdictions is explained on two grounds. The first one is, that there are certain natural boundaries to the sea; the second is, the necessity of safeguarding navigation. The exercise of these *imperia* is opposed by some, who say that the sea may not pertain to any territory or dominion, and that, by the *ius gentium*, it may not be divided, but is open to all.

> (T)amen maris partes, eius civitatis censeantur, quae proxima est.[2]

---

[1] Petrus Gregorius, *Syntagma Iuris Universi*, etc., 2 vols. (Lugduni, 1587), i., 3.5. Gregoire was a French savant and professor of law who died, according to Hommel, p. 335, in 1595.

[2] *Ibid.*, i, 3.5.

It is to be expected that a French jurist would repudiate the doctrine that to the Emperor alone belongs the *imperium maris*, if, indeed, there can be such an *imperium*. He would assert the right of his king to maritime jurisdiction over the sea adjacent to the French coasts. With this in mind, the *eius civitatis censeantur* is evidence of, at least, a wide-spread acceptance of the doctrine by the independent *civitates;* and it seems to indicate the existence of enough of them to make it worth while to cite them as evidence. He mentions, in the same passage the

in Gallia praefectum maris constitutuum, quem corrupta voce dicunt Admiralium . . . cuius iurisdictioni et imperio, post principem, omnes, qui maritimas incolunt oras circa Gallias, obtemperant. . . . Constituit et milites stationarios pro custodia poscatorum, ne invadantur ab hostibus.

This passage is important, of course, as showing, first, the existence of important fisheries, and secondly, that one of the chief duties of the official who is called *corrupta voce*, the Admiral was to protect them from marauders — marauders, no doubt, who were not always pirates. The existence of these fisheries should be added to the existence of ordinary commercial navigation as the object of the solicitude of the state and a cause of the exercise of maritime jurisdiction in time of peace. What was present *de facto* is now being justified *de iure*. Gregorius refers to the Venetians, naturally enough, *qui potissimum in maritimis praevalent*.[1] He calls to mind their custom of performing a ceremony at the election of a new duke which symbolized his betrothal to the sea, and the perpetual dominion of the Venetians over it.

The argument of Gregorius [2] is that the *civitas* has the right to defend and to protect the individuals — not merely the citizens or subjects of the state — who use the sea which is adjacent to its coasts. This and the arguments like it are not concerned with a state's right or duty to protect its citizens or subjects on the sea. They are directed not at these persons but at the sea itself. They are concerned with the separation of a particular section or

[1] Gregorius, *op. cit.*, ii, 66.1.

[2] And of D'Etienne Pasquier; see his *L'Interpretation des Institutes de Justinian* (Paris, 1847), pp. 170 ff.

portion of the sea from the main body of it. They are regarding as undivided what the classic law had regarded as indivisible. Some of the arguments are content with maintaining reasons for the division. Other arguments go further and specify the area which is to be marked off.

Bartolus, it will be recalled, felt that the state has an especial interest in the sea adjacent to its shores. It is to the interest of the state to suppress and to punish crimes committed in these waters. According to this theory the punishment of evil doers for offences committed at sea is analogous to their punishment for similar offences committed on land. The official who has the right to prevent violence and crime on the land has a corresponding right in the adjacent sea. This argument received support from later jurists,[1] the most notable of whom is, perhaps, Brunneman.[2] Gregorius supplements it in the passages from his works noted above by holding that the state has the right to defend and to protect navigators and fishermen in the waters adjacent to its shores. Now and then the mere assertion of the jurisdiction is made without argument.[3] These arguments generally contain, implicitly or explicitly, a statement that the Prince (or, whoever the ruler may be) has not a right of property, of *proprietas*, in the sea.[4]

Fortescue has a passage in his *Governance of England* which clearly alludes to the practice of England in safeguarding the seas off the British Isles. Fortescue was Lord Chief Justice under Henry VI. He was born at about the time that Baldus died. The passage in question is as follows:[5]

[1] For example, Iacobus Rebuffus, *Lectura super tribus ultimis libris Codicis* (Augustae Taurinorum, 1591), p. 103.2; Ioan. Garsia, *De Expensis et Molierationibus*, in the *Tractatus Illustrium*, *op. cit.*, xvii, 331.34.

[2] Who comes at the close of the period covered by this chapter. He will be considered below.

[3] Ansaldo de Ansaldis, *op. cit.* Franciscus De Ponte, *De Potestate Proregis* (Neapoli, 1611), p. 528.27.29. Horatius Carpanus, *Rerum Omnium et Vocem Memorabilius*, etc., 2 vols. (Mediolani, 1588), ii, 8.49.

[4] Arnoldus Vinnius, *In quatuor Libros Institutionum*, etc., ed. by Heineccius (Lugduni, 1726), p. 143, is an example.

[5] Sir John Fortescue, *The Governance of England*, ed. by Charles Plummer (Oxford, 1885), pp. 122, 123. Mr. Plummer, p. vii, states that this is the first constitutional treatise in English.

Nor the lesse be that reason pondage and tonnage mey not be rekenned as parcell off the revenues wich the kynge hath ffor the mayntenance off his estate, bi cause it aught to be applied only to the kepynge off the see. And though we haue alwey werre uppon the see, yet it shalbe nescessarie that the kynge haue alway some ffloute apon the see, ffor the repressynge off rovers, sauyinge off oure marchauntes, oure fishers, and the dwellers uppon oure costes; and that the kynge kepe alway some grete and myghty vessels, ffor the brekynge off an armye when any shall be made ayen hym apon the see.

It will be observed that there is no hint here of anything more than the giving of protection — no claim to *dominium*. It is perhaps worthy of note that the people to be protected are English merchants and fishermen.

In his *De Laudibus Legum Angliae*,[1] there is a passage upon which John Selden has an interesting note. Lord Fortescue is treating of the number of witnesses required in different cases by the laws. He mentions "Facts committed upon the High Sea, without the Body of any County, which may be afterwards brought to trial before the Admiralty-Court."[2] Selden observes[3] that in the time of Edward I "the Common Law had Conisans of Things done upon the British Sea, however it afterward kept its Limits *infra Corpus Comitatus*, leaving the Sea to the Admiralty."

He then proceeds with a discussion of the term, "high seas." "The sea is phrased, *altum mare*, not to lead into the vast consideration of it, but, *to state and resolve the Jurisdiction hereby intended*.[4] *Altum mare*, being *extra regnum*, is exempt from the Ordinary Jurisdiction of the Law. . . . *Altum mare* is the proper Region of the Admiral's Jurisdiction . . . *Altum mare* is thought to be, where one can see no land on either side; otherwise he is said to be *infra Corpus Comitatus*, in which Case" the common law is operative.

There is nothing in these remarks by Selden antagonistic to the theory which is being considered in this place. He goes on to

[1] "Written Originally in Latin . . . Transl. into English, Illustrated with the Notes of Mr. Selden, etc., 2d ed., In the Savoy, 1741."

[2] *Ibid.*, p. 67. ". . . quae supra altum mare extra Corpus cujuslibet Comitatus Regni . . . coram Admirallo Angliae. . . ." See Latin text (Londoni, 1737), p. 20.19.

[3] See note 2; p. 67, note 18, of English translation.

[4] Italics the present writer's.

say a few words about the claims of England. "That the Monarchs of Britain had command of the narrow Seas, is confirmed by Ancient Records" and so forth. He thinks that the first Admiral of England was created in 10 Rich. II, "and for ought that I can find, the first that carried that Title."[1] But all of this is a matter of jurisdiction, not of property, in the sea. There were (apparently, *de facto* in respect of title), Admirals (he continues) of the West, East and Northern Coasts and of the Floats in the mouth of the Thames, under Richard I. These officers, by whatever title they were known, would seem to be the English equivalent for the Praeses of Bartolus, and, even, of Brunnemann, who uses the same word after 1648, after the passage of time had made it, to say the least, quaint. It may be pointed out, furthermore, that if a spot of water is on the high seas, if an individual there can see no land in any direction, then Bartolus's hundred-mile limit reached out on to the high seas for a considerable distance. Selden's limit would appear to be the more conservative of the two.

> *Altum mare*, in the large Notion (Selden proceeds), *is said to be, Mare Liberum, nullius in Bonis.*[2] Hence because they are the Pretensions of all Nations, Who descend into them, they are to be accounted of by the Law of Nations; and the Offenses done upon them, punishable by those Laws.

These are the words of that Selden who wrote in answer to Grotius his book, *Mare Clausum.*

This theory, then, gives to the state the right to exercise jurisdiction over the adjacent sea for the purpose of safe-guarding the persons who travel or work there, and vests this jurisdiction in a particular official (recognizing, probably, a general custom). It denies to the state the power to acquire property rights there. Now, while this doctrine of the adjacent sea was winning acceptance, those theories of maritime servitudes which have been considered were also current. Given in their lowest terms, they at least permitted a monarch to grant exclusive rights of use over a thing in which he had no ownership. Whether this inconsistency made itself felt, or not, side by side with this theory, which adds explicitly or implicitly some such reservation as, *sed sine jure*

[1] *De Laudibus Legum Angliae, op. cit.*, p. 69. See Note, p. 121, *supra.*

[2] The italics are those of the present writer.

proprietatis aut dominium,[1] there is another theory according to which the sea comes within the meaning of the word, territory. In support of this theory is the notable jurist, Albericus Gentilis, His doctrine is to be found in the eighth chapter of the first book of his *Hispanicae Advocationis*,[2] which bears the significant title, "De marino territorio tuendo."

Gentilis, 1550–1608,[3] belongs to the modern Italian school of natural law.[4] He is famous, of course, for his work in the field of international law. Like Grotius, he wanted to check the barbaric wars into which the countries of Europe were so frequently drawn. His test for the lawfulness of any war was in the principle of natural justice, which had its basis in the nature of mankind.[5] But, unlike Grotius, he sought to derive his laws from the observance and appraisement of international practice.[6] After 1537 he was professor "*regius juris civilis*" at Oxford.[7]

He begins in Chapter VIII by referring to a controversy between Spain and the Dutch. The latter had made a strong protest because a Dutch vessel had been stopped on the high seas by a Spanish ship and had been forced to surrender certain booty which, it appears, had been taken from Spanish subjects. Gentilis takes an unfavorable view of their representations, and states that the word, territory, is applied both to land and sea.

> At ego, quod olim scripsi in libris bellicis, territorium et de terris dici, et de aquis.[8]

He cites the "doctors" in general as saying that the Venetians and the Genoese, and others having a port or harbor, are said to have jurisdiction and *imperium* in the whole sea near them to a distance of one hundred miles, or even more, if there are no other

[1] Vinnius, *op. cit.* He lived 1588–1657. He was a leading Dutch jurist whose commentaries were used in Italy. See *A General Survey*, in the Continental Legal History Series (Boston, 1912), p. 158.

[2] *Libri duo*, Amstelodami, 1661.

[3] *General Survey*, p. 180.

[4] *Ibid.*, pp. 179, 180.

[5] *Ibid.*, p. 18.

[6] *Ibid.*, p. 412. Stintzing-Landsberg, 3.1, 5.

[7] *General Survey*, *ibid.*, Stintzing-Landsberg, *ibid.*

[8] Gentilis, *op. cit.*, p. 32.

"provinces" near. And he adduces Bartolus as support for his statement.[1] Strictly speaking, of course, Bartolus did not lay down an indefinite limit under the condition mentioned by Gentilis. He said that if an island which was more than one hundred miles distant from a state was near an island which was within that distance and which belonged to the state, then it also belonged to the state.

The passage in his *De Iure Belli* to which he refers is as follows:[2]

> Athenienses suo mari permisissent transire Spartanos hostes. Iusta expostulatio: quoniam mare portio terrae: ut gymnosophista respondit, et agnoscunt nostri. Mare adiacens pars ditionis est, et territorium de terris dicitur et de aquis. Ne quid dicam de Venetis aliisve, qui integra maria sibi vindicarunt: sed et proditor dicitur feudatarius, qui permittit gentem transire inimicam.

Let the Dutch, he proceeds, and every one use the sea — but without violating foreign jurisdiction. Let them remember that there are things heretofore undefined which are defined to-day; and that the distinction in the *ius gentium* between dominions and jurisdictions must be most carefully observed.[3]

Gentilis credits Baldus with his theory of *mare adiacens pars ditionis*, and with justice, for the adjacent sea, in the thought of the latter, was a *districtum* appertaining to the land, in which the *ius civile* is operative.

In addition to this doctrine and the Bartolist hundred-mile limit, there is the phrase, *mare portio terrae*, and the application of the idea contained in the word *territorium* to the sea. After Gentilis it is literally correct to speak of territorial waters in international

[1] Gentilis, *op. cit.*, p. 33. "Et sic quidem Bartolus de centum illis miliariis, licet dicatur, quod mare est commune. Et sic alii incunctanter, si Comanum illum excipis refractarium. Et vides, quam protendatur Regis nostri imperium longe in meridiem, septentrionem, occasum." The coasts of other states are far distant from the coasts of Spain. "Et sic est immensum lata jurisdictio Regis nostri marina."

[2] *De Iure Belli, Libri tres*, ed. by T. E. Holland (Oxonii, 1877), iii, c. 17, p. 369.

[3] *Hispanicae Advocationis*, *op. cit.*, p. 37. "Fruantur Hollandi, fruantur mari omnes, sed citra injuriam alienae jurisdictionis. Sed et meminerint omnes, esse et modum marini, atque omnis itineris. Meminerint, alia olim indistincta, quae distincta sunt hodie, et cautissime servandam distinctionem juris gentium, dominiorum atque jurisdictionem."

law.[1] What Gentilis has to say is given additional significance because he is observing international practice and appraising it. Fortunately or unfortunately, his work remained for a long time relatively unconsidered because of the dominating influence of Grotius, "the father of international law," and Pufendorf, who followed him.

Caspar Klock [2] gives expression to this theory of territorial waters in the field of Roman jurisprudence, though perhaps in not quite so definite a fashion, or, at least, not so pointedly, as does Gentilis. He begins with public rivers. Since public rivers belong among the Regalia, it is allowable to prohibit the use of them for navigation. This is an extreme view, and the writer is the first jurist who has voiced it. The banks (*littora*) of rivers are said to be his who has jurisdiction over them. According to this statement, either the riparian owners have acquired "jurisdiction," or the lord himself is the owner of the river properties, and the tenants are only tenants, within the extent of his domain. The right of jurisdiction apparently carries with it the right of ownership, and not *vice versa*. It is difficult to believe that Klock is reliable. His use of the word *littora* instead of *ripae* is not an indication of scholarship, for that word is almost always used to denote the shore of the sea.

The sea to the distance of one hundred miles belongs to the nearest shore.

> Quamvis et mare ejus esse Imperii, cujus est territorium coadjacens.

The punishment of persons guilty of offences committed at sea is the duty of the *iudex territorii propinquioris loco delicti*. Klock then makes the usual reservation:

> Etsi quoque nihil impediat quo minus Respublica praescribet Maris Imperium, si non quoad Dominium et proprietatem, saltem quoad usum Jurisdictionis. . . . [3]

[1] It need hardly be pointed out that Gentilis is writing international law itself, and using the empirical inductive method to do it. Grotius is philosophical and deductive, and is vague on the consensus *gentium*. See the *General Survey* and Stintzing-Landsberg, *loc. cit.*

[2] Died, 1655. Hommel, *op. cit.*, p. 341.

[3] Caspar Klockius, *Tractatus de Aerario, Libri duo* (Norimbergae, 1671), p. 938. 1–4.

But in another place,[1] he seems to advocate the *proprietas* of the adjacent sea:

Quid? quod maris propinqui usum usurpationemque non jam amplius communem sed privatum factum esse, commonstrant exempla de mari Hispanorum, Lusitanorum, Gallorum, Anglorum, aliorumque populorum; item Venetorum, Genuensium, et Belgarum, qui ius navigandi in vicino mari ad se transtulerunt: Et Interpretationes nostri fatentur, tempore immemoriali usum propinqui maris, atque etiam jurisdictionem et proprietatem quaeri posse. Principem imponere posse Gabellas in mari, et eas exigere a vehentibus merces per mare, suae terrae adjacens, intra centesimum miliare.

Klock thus gives utterance to two opposed doctrines, if he means by his citation of the various national seas to imply a property right in them. That he means to do this is indicated by his saying that the sea *non . . . communem sed privatum factum esse*, and by his use of *proprietatem*. Which of the two is in fact his own, it is difficult to guess. He seems, however, rather to incline towards the territorial idea.[2]

The last writer who may be included in the period to 1648, who should be noticed in connection with the development of the doctrine of the adjacent sea, is the Dutch philosopher, theologian, and jurisconsult, Brunneman.[3] Although those works of his which will be cited here were published after 1648,[4] he was forty years old in that year, and therefore may be considered as familiar with, and a part of, the thought of the period of the early seventeenth century. His attitude is scientific. He uses a method seldom used in his day, and one which enhances the value of his work. It is not, strictly speaking, exegetical, but rather more paraphrastic. Philological and historical interests are in the background; the practical are in the foreground. He avoids subtleties, and enters controversies with discrimination.[5]

[1] *Ibid.*, p. 754.16.

[2] Other jurists including the sea within the meaning of *territorium* are: Tiberius Decianus, *Responsorum*, 3 vols. (Venetiis, 1579), i, 678.26. Julius Caponus, *Controversarium Forensium*, (Coloniae Allobrogum, 1732), p. 183.66. Probably Fulvius Pacianus, *Consilia*, (Augustae Vindelicorum, 1605), p. 812.12. Vinnius, *op. cit.*, notes the presence of this and opposed theories, p. 143.

[3] 1608–1672. Stintzing, *op. cit.*, ii, 101 ff.

[4] The Commentary on the Justinian Code in 1663; the Commentary on the Digest, in 1670. Stintzing, *op. cit.*, p. 108, *loc. cit.*

[5] Stintzing, *ibid.*, p. 109. His commentaries "zwar in ihre Form auf vergangene Zeiten zurückweisen, aber ihrem Inhalt und ihrer Tendenz nach ganz der herrschen-

Brunneman accepts the doctrine of the adjacent sea, but he says nothing concerning a possible limit to the distance off shore at which the sea ceases to be "adjacent"; and he rejects the territorial idea by basing the right of the Prince to exercise maritime jurisdiction upon the necessity of suppressing crime at sea.

He mentions[1] the care of the fleets

> quae instruendae sunt ad purgandum mare, et flumina a piratis, ut navigationes sint securae, item ad alias publicas necessitates contra barbarosi . . .

and then proceeds in language which recalls Bartolus on this point, as well as the Bartolist doctrine in general:

> Sicut Praesidi incumbit purgare Rempublicam a malis hominibus, . . . ita etiam mare a piratis purgandum est, per eum, qui adjacens territorium habet, et jurisdictionem etiam ad mare adjacens extendi, ita ut delictum in mari commissum hic possit punire Dominus terrae adjacentis.

This brief passage contains the essence of the Brunnemann doctrine. In his Commentary on the Digest he refers to the same subject in words which amplify the above to a certain extent. It is as follows:

> Mare hic inter communia refertur, cui hodie opponitur, quod Principes sibi in certos districtus jurisdictionem arrogent. Sed aliud est, usu esse commune, et aliud in jurisdictione esse. Certe littorum usus communis est, et tamen procul dubio jurisdictio est Imperii vel Principis. Quod autem recte sibi tribuant jurisdictionem Principes, ex eo patet, quia cum magna scelera patrentur in mari, utique jurisdictionem alicui competere necesse est, ne in mari ea sint permissa, quae in terra prohibita.[2]

Brunnemann's method is, as he notes on his title-page, theoretical-practical. He is positive that the ruler's interest in the sea is jurisdictional and not proprietary. A later day was to see the former made dependent upon the latter, as the notion grew up that sovereignty depended upon ownership of the soil over which the rights of sovereignty were exercised. The last of his final sentence is capable of being altered to read,

> Ne in mari ea sint prohibita quae in terra permissa.

---

den Richtung ihrer Zeit angehören, sich daher selbst als '*opera theoretico-practica*' bezeichnen, und den '*usus*' darstellen wollen."

[1] Johannes Brunnemannus, *Commentarius in Codicem Justinianeum*, 2 vols. (Lugduni, 1715), *De Classicis*, 11.12.1, p. 1003.3. The two volumes are paged consecutively.

[2] *Commentarius in Quinquaginta Libros Pandectarum*, ed. by Samuel Strykius (Coloniae Allobrogum, 1752), 1.8.2.1, p. 26.

The question as to the limits of the "adjacent" sea does not meet with anything like wide recognition in the writings of the jurists previous to the controversy over *mare liberum* and *mare clausum;* while even there, no attempt is made to place precise limits which shall be at once workable and applicable to all nations. Even Venetian lawyers did not begin seriously to defend the claims to the Adriatic which have been so often remarked until the ability of their government to act effectually on them had become seriously undermined by decay. It may safely be said that up to 1648 the problem of setting limits to the adjacent sea — to the waters comprised within that term as it came to be applied to particular powers — received slight attention from the jurists. The majority of those who discuss it, including the English lawyers of the opening years of the seventeenth century, do so in general terms, and with a strong bias in favor of their national interests. The nature of the question is pragmatic rather than legal; it is a problem in affairs before it is a problem in law books. The approach to the matter is therefore particularistic from start to finish. The finish does not come until the different claims have increased in pretensions, variety, and number, to the point where serious consideration of the general aspects of the situation has become a necessity at once imperative and obvious. The necessity is then the need for a *modus vivendi* which has been created by the conflict of these claims. The question, then, in the period to 1648 lies chiefly in the historical and diplomatic fields, rather than in that of legal theory.

Nevertheless, it has filtered into a few of the law books. Bartolus noted it, and gave a definition which satisfied the interests of Pisa. It may be too, as Fulton suggests, that he was attempting to curb the claims of the Venetians by setting a limit to them. It is probably not without significance that the proposition of the hundred-mile limit to the adjacent sea came from an Italian jurist, and, not only an Italian jurist, but one who was familiar with, and part of, the life of the city states which looked to the Adriatic. He had his followers. Occasionally a writer will refer to Bartolus on the hundred-mile limit.

Jean Bodin advocated a different limit, and for a different

purpose. While treating of the sovereignty of the Prince, he writes,[1]

> Sed quoniam aequor ac mare ipsum privatorum proprium esse non potest, iure quodammodo Principum omnium maris accolarum communi receptum est, ut sexaginta miliaribus a littore, Princeps legem ad littus accedentibus dicere potest. . . . At etiam ancoras alienis littoribus sine Principis concessu iniicere non licet: quae tamen olim iuris gentium fuerunt.

The passage referring to the sixty-mile limit is given in the French edition of his work as follows:[2]

> Mais les droicts de la mer n'appartiennent qu'au Prince souverain, qui peut imposer charges iusque a xxx lieuës loing de sa terre, s'il n'y a Prince souverain plus pres qui l'empesche.

While Bodin does not specify these *droicts de la mer*, it is evident that they are rights to levy some sort of tax on the use of the sea. Antonius Matthaeus, in referring to Bodin's sixty miles, remarks, *admodum dubito, an id ipsum obtineat.*[3]

Plowden, in his argument in Sir John Constable's Case,[4] has suggested a method by which to apportion the adjacent sea:[5]

> And to take all this matter, we ought to consider to what place the bounds of England extend. . . . Firstly, the bounds of England extend to the middle of the sea adjoining which surrounds the realm; but the Queen has all the jurisdiction of the sea between France and this realm by reason of her title to France, and so it is of Ireland; but in other places, as towards Spain, she has only the moiety. . . .
>
> But although the Queen has jurisdiction in the sea adjoining her realm, still she has not property in it, nor in the land under the sea, for it is common to all men, and she cannot prohibit any one from fishing there. . . .

Plowden transferred the principle of the *thalweg* to the sea. He did not, however, win recognition for his theory.

[1] Ioan. Bodinus, *De Republica, libri sex* (Francofurti, 1622),pp. 267, 268. Bodin died in 1596 (Hommel, *op. cit.*, p. 335).

[2] *Les Six Livres de la Republique de I. Bodin* (Paris, 1576), p. 215. In the edition of 1577, p. 180.

[3] *Commentarius ad Institutiones* (Trajecti ad Rhenum, 1672), p. 541.4.

[4] Stuart A. Moore, *History and Law of the Foreshore*, 3d ed., London, 1888. "The case of Atty *v.* Sir John Constable occurred in 17 Elizabeth, A.D. 1575. The defendant was charged with taking 'wreck of the sea' in Holderness (pp. 224–227)."

[5] *Ibid.*, pp. 227–229.

5. Dominium Maris

When the theory of *mare adiacens* hardened into a theory of exclusive jurisdiction, it made that of *dominium* inevitable. The tendency of the theory of the adjacent sea to develop a doctrine of state (or royal) ownership is apparent. The theory of territorial waters is latent, if not implicit, in the theory of littoral waters. It (the former theory) demands an extension of what today would be called the municipal law of the state concerned over the adjacent sea, and it rests upon an inclusion in the word, *territorium*, of *mare* as well as *terra*, or, precisely, of *mare adiacens* with *terra*. It will be perceived at once that the union of the adjacent sea with the land adjoining, although made primarily to facilitate the justification of a theory of jurisdiction over the former, is favorable to the growth of the notion that the state exercising this jurisdiction has a certain property right in the waters in question. A pirate, for example, caught *flagrante delicto* in the sea adjacent to the territory of State A by an officer of State A is tried in the courts of State A and by the law of State A. Furthermore, it is unlikely that an officer of State B would venture to capture the pirate off the coast of State A at the time in which the theory of the adjacent sea had become a commonplace. If he did so under pressure of immediate necessity, he would be more than likely to surrender his man to the officers of State A. The selfconscious despots of the Renaissance would hardly suffer their coastal waters to be invaded by the naval forces of another monarch for the purpose of using his arms there, on any pretext. The growth of the modern states forced the old theory of coöperation in the suppression of piracy to be abandoned. With this relationship, then, which was at once both legal and political, between a state and the sea adjacent to its shores, gradually becoming generally accepted, the rights of property recognized on land could, with the appropriate modifications and qualifications, be extended to the coastal sea in much the same way in which the criminal law of the state had been extended there. Finally, the early belief that sovereignty is inseparable from ownership of the soil, made it a simple matter to predicate ownership of the sea. In the sovereign (monarch or republic) only lay the right to exercise jurisdiction. The sovereign was the ultimate owner of all the land in the kingdom or republic. This, everyone knew. But the sovereign exercised jurisdiction over the sea. And when this theory began to receive careful attention from the jurists, he was exercising exclusive jurisdiction. It followed, therefore, that the sovereign must have a right of ownership in the sea, just as he had a right of ownership over his lands.

Now, the distance to which his rights in the sea extended was an entirely different question. The controversy over *mare liberum* versus *mare clausum*, which is about to receive attention, was serious primarily because the advocates of *mare clausum* placed an extravagant interpretation upon the meaning of the term, adjacent sea. Grotius himself admitted the rights of a state to the ownership of its gulfs and bays. What agitated him was the claim of Spain and Portugal to divide the ocean between them. Selden was reasoning on sound principles when he championed the theory of territorial waters. The menace in his argument was his definition of them.

Aside from the question as to the extent of the territorial waters of a state, there was the further problem in regard to the restraints, if any, to which the sovereign's right of jurisdiction was subject. Undoubtedly this question was on a parity with the other. But it was so because of the material interests at stake — in the one case (omitting Venice and the Adriatic), the trade with the "East Indies"; in the other, the exploitation of the abundant herring fisheries off the coast of the British Isles. In the former case, thousands of miles were involved; in the latter case, some fourteen miles. But the wealth within the two districts was very great. Those on the outside wanted such restraints on the jurisdiction of the sovereign as would give them free access to it. Those on the inside wanted to admit foreigners, if at all, only on their own terms, and consequently admitted only such restraints as would not hinder them in realizing this desire.

It may be granted that, actually, and in practice, the potential wealth involved not only colored the views of the lawyers on the question as to the extent to which a sovereign may exercise his right of jurisdiction over his territorial waters, but also that it influenced profoundly their definition of the area comprised within the meaning of that phrase — that is, the phrase, "territorial waters," or the other, "adjacent sea." But, it is submitted, that in the development of the theory of state ownership of the sea, the question of the extent of the territorial waters precedes in point of logic — as it certainly does in point of time — the theory of the powers which the local sovereign possesses in those waters. The theory of the exclusive jurisdiction of the local sovereign in the adjacent sea made possible the theory of ownership of that sea. The next step was, not to define his jurisdiction, but to define the amount or area of sea covered by it.

The prizes at stake, however, befogged the issue. The Dutch appeared as antagonists both to Portugal and England. Against Portugal they argued for freedom of navigation and of trade. Especially they wanted freedom of trade, because a free right of navigation only would serve them little. The desire for free navigation was produced by the method which the Portuguese took to prevent freedom of trade. Had protective tariffs been in effect in the East Indies, the Dutch argument would have been quite different. What the Dutch were after was, really, not the open sea, but the open door. Against England, the Dutch argued for freedom of fishery. This was in essence an argument to take freely the products of that sea the use of which is common to all, and the proprietorship of which belongs to none. Since the herring frequented the coastal waters of the British Isles, it was necessary to restrict those waters to gulfs, bays, and inlets of the sea, with perhaps a strip of open sea off shore. Or, if a greater area was admitted, then to restrict the jurisdiction of the king in a manner calculated to make it impossible for him to tax or to bar foreign fishermen. Grotius, while attacking the Portuguese, had not overlooked the fishing industry. His doctrines on the free sea were sweeping enough to provoke a number of refutations from the English. It is interesting to note that his work passed almost unnoticed on the Continent for years.[1] Of course the

[1] E. Nys, *Le Droit Romain*, etc. (Bruxelles, 1910), p. 84. Until Welwood replied in the *Abridgment*. Because the issue calling it forth was settled in a month after the book's appearance.

Spanish and Portuguese stood alone in their position. The English claims were a different matter. The principle could be admitted with advantage by other states, provided that there were placed reasonable bounds to the sea involved. And so it was that the rights of a king in his own waters were entangled with a controversy over the extent of those waters. And the former element has come down in history as the dominant element, and the controversy is called one over the freedom of the seas, following the favorite titles of the period — *mare liberum*, and *mare clausum*. This is true in spite of the fact that both sides admitted the freedom of the *high* seas — the vast ocean, as they called it. The question really was, for England and the United Provinces — and they are the important contestants — what was the main sea and what was not. The English claimed rights which could be granted only in strictly territorial waters; they knew it, and claimed an enormous area of sea as being within the realm of England. The Dutch, not taking any notice whatever of the argument from territorial waters, claimed the freedom of the seas for themselves, and opposed the English with the accusation that the high seas were being illegally enclosed, that illegal restraints were being placed upon the use of the sea. The two parties were arguing from different premises at this point, and sensing the common ground of difference without apparently being able to define it, used ambiguous adjectives and indulged in repetition. The argument became one over the rights of a king in waters not his own, when it reappeared in the autumn of 1914. That was the form it took when viewed through Dutch glasses in the seventeenth century.

The *right* of ownership, then, in *territorial* waters, was not the fundamental dispute in the controversy referred to, except in so far as unsound definitions of territorial waters made it so. The *extent* of ownership over the sea was the kernel of the dispute. What the owner could do with his sea became of crucial importance because of the amount of sea claimed by him, and not because he claimed some part of the sea. That he should claim any part of the sea at all (excepting gulfs, bays, and inlets) scandalized the Dutch and became an issue only because the waters immediately off shore were abundantly supplied with herring, and *not* because the claim marked a departure from accepted or familiar legal theory.

After due weight has been given to the distinctive characteristics of this controversy, it remains true that the lawyers who participated in it were the heirs of their past. The doctrine of *mare clausum* was made possible by the development of the theory of the adjacent sea, to which consideration has been given. The doctrine of *mare clausum* is based on that of the ownership of the sea, of *dominium maris*, and is the product of it. The word *dominium* is itself significant. In mediaeval legal Latin it connotes a mixture of the ideas expressed by the words *proprietas* and *imperium*. It signifies at once ownership and lordship. It has itself undergone a development from the original meaning of ownership, which has left it ready to hand for the purposes of the moderns who use it.

CHAPTER VII

ACQUISITION OF RIGHTS OF PROPERTY IN MARITIME FISHERIES

I. The Classic Position

There is a large number of jurists who deal primarily with the legal status of public fisheries, and only secondarily, if at all, with the legal status of the sea. These men take for granted the classic Roman doctrine of the status of the sea and of public rivers. They are concerned with the nature of the rights which may be acquired in fisheries located in these waters. These rights may be one of two kinds: rights of ownership, or rights of use. The questions which these jurists attempt to answer may be phrased in some such terms as the following: May such fisheries be owned? If so, by whom? By what process, and under what laws, is a right in one of them secured? May such a right be exclusive?

The straightest classicists hold that the right of fishery is free to all in the sea for the simple reason that the sea is the common property of all men, or for the equally simple reason that the sea is incapable of being owned in any sense of the word.[1] Either theory brings the same result. No bars can be set up against a general and unrestricted use of this right.

> De iure vero communi ius piscandi omnibus competit in mari et in fluminibus. . . .[2]

Corvinus placed himself in flat opposition to any limitation of the general freedom of fishery:[3]

> Quod rebus humano juri exemptis, vel publicis, servitutes ullae imponi nequeant.

---

[1] Suarez, *Opera omnia*, 2 vols. (Antverpiae, 1618), ii, 67.5. S. Medici, *De Venatione*, etc., *Tractatus illustrium*, xvii, 396.7, 402.1.

[2] H. Barbatus, *De Divisione Fructuum* (Neapoli, 1638), p. 26.3–4.

[3] A. Corvinus, *Digesta per Aphorismos*, etc. (Amsterodami, 1642), p. 164, D. 8.4. There is not a single writer of this group, who, if he treats of the *ius piscandi*, fails to connect it with *mare commune*, either implicitly or explicitly.

A servitude, in his thought, would include in its meaning the exclusive right of an individual to fish in public waters. Public things are those which are common to all men. Things may be public by the *ius naturale*, by the *ius gentium*, or by the *ius civile*. The air, the sea, the shores of the sea, and *aqua profluens* are common to all by the *ius naturale*. Therefore the use of these is common to all. The *ius piscandi*, however, is *iuris gentium*. He makes it none the less a right common to all. This is not in contradiction to his reasoning, because he has already made the statement that there are things which are common to all men *iure gentium*. He has also good precedent for such a distinction of sources, for Justinian himself put the use of the shore under the *ius gentium*. Now, neither the *ius naturale* nor the *ius gentium* is made by the king. He is under both of them, as are all men. Consequently he cannot alter them. They spring from sources which he cannot control. Some such argument as this is characteristic of the school of strict construction.[1] It follows, also, that if the king cannot alter the law, neither can his tenants or vassals, not even the tenants in chief.[2] Neither custom nor prohibition avails against the right of fishery.

II. The Regalia

The opposing theory takes cognizance of feudal law, in which, it has been observed, the *ius piscandi* is included in the Regalia. The general rule as to the freedom of the sea is held to be true; but it is permitted to the emperor or to a king to make exceptions to it in particular cases. The important thing to be observed at this point is, that, according to this theory, the monarch has the right of making such exceptions. This right is lodged in the royal prerogative. The jurists are content to hold it so, taking it as they find it.

It would seem reasonable to suppose that the laying down of a doctrine ascribing to the king or emperor the right and power to grant rights of fishery in the sea would be attended with diffi-

[1] *Cf.* Carolus Ruinus, *Consiliorum*, 5 vols. (Venetiis, 1591), i, 40.11; and Rochus Curtius, *Enarrationes* (Lugduni, 1550), p. 69.13.

[2] I. Cancerius, *Variarum Resolutionum*, etc. (Barcinone, 1608), p. 187, C. xiii.236.

culties which would demand careful discussion. The contrary, however, is the fact. The majority of the jurists in this group give a bare statement to the effect that the *Princeps* may prohibit the exercise of the *ius piscandi*, or that he may grant it to an individual for the latter's sole enjoyment;[1] they content themselves with this assertion even when they prefix to it a statement that any one may fish in public rivers and in the sea.[2] The former statement is taken to be a qualification of the latter, which is in reality but a perfunctory recognition of the usually accepted law of the sea. The general explanation of the possession by the *Princeps* of the *ius piscandi* is, that it is included in the Regalia. This explanation not only gives the source of the right, or, more strictly, the source of the Prince's prerogative, but it perhaps gives also the reason for the jurists' acceptance of it as a matter of fact which may be taken for granted. It will be recalled that there is a provision in the "Consuetudines Feudorum" which names the Regalia. The word is a word of feudal law. The reason why the jurists were able to take the Prince's prerogative so much as a matter of course in the face of the precepts of the law books of Justinian is perhaps to be found partly in the fact that the Roman law was forced to accept the feudal law, and partly in the fact that the royal exercise of the prerogative in question had continued over so long a period of time that they had become habituated to its existence.

The observations of Valentine Forster, one of the jurists of this group, seem to corroborate this explanation.[3] He remarks that the right of fishing is the same sort of right as that of navigation, for the reason that the sea is common to all. He no doubt means that the source of these rights is to be found in the legal status of the sea. He goes on to say that by a very new law, Frederick

[1] Marciant Natta, *Consiliorum sive Responsum*, 2 vols. (Venetiis, 1584), p. 58.30. Dn. Iacobus Menochius, *Consiliorum sive Responsum*, 4 vols., Francofurti ad Moenum, 1628.

[2] Dominicus Tuschus, *Practicarum Conclusionum Iuris*, etc., 8 vols. (Romae, 1606), p. 254.1. Regidius Bossius, *Tractatus varii* (Venetiis, 1570), p. 377.18. Dn. Hieronymus Schurpft, *Consiliorum seu Responsorum Iuris* (Francofurti ad Moenum, 1575), pp. 212.3–4, 213.

[3] Valentinus Forsterus, *De Historia Iuris Romani* (Helmaestadii, 1610), p. 499.

enumerated the fisheries in public rivers and in the sea among the Regalia. He concludes that because of this fact, those who possess the Regalia and who rule the territories which the sea washes may prohibit, regulate, and restrict the use of the fisheries in those waters.

Sola, who takes the position characteristic of this group, holds that a vassal cannot forbid fishing in a public river within his domains. He holds, further, that if the Prince invest a vassal with a public river, the investiture is invalid before the law. And if the Prince invest a vassal with the privilege of prohibiting fishing in a public river, the investiture is invalid.[1]

Barbatus takes this position also.[2] Barbatus feels the opposition between the classical Roman doctrine on the sea and the law which gives to the Prince possession of the *ius piscandi*.[3] He begins by saying that the *ius piscandi* and the revenues from fisheries are reckoned among the Regalia of the Prince. He then proceeds to say that by the common law, the truth is that the *ius piscandi* belongs to all men, both in the sea and in rivers. Therefore, as much as the use of public waters may be prohibited by barons or feudatories, the use of a fishery cannot be prohibited by them, if it is located in such waters. But now, after having broken a lance for the freedom of fisheries, he gives five exceptions to the law. These are, briefly: (1) when the rivers are private; (2) when the *ius piscandi* is prohibited, not by the barons, but by the Prince; (3) when a *conventio* is contracted with a neighbor, not to fish before the latter's dwelling; (4) when it is customary not to fish for private gain, but only for the public good; and (5) when there exists an immemorial custom prohibiting the fishing.

The fourth and fifth points are the only ones which limit the use of public waters. Both of these limitations are based upon custom, not upon the Regalia. Having conceded the *ius piscandi* to the king, Barbatus very nearly deprives him of the power to

[1] Antonius Sola, *Commentaria*, etc. (Augustae Taurinorum, 1607), p. 332.9.

[2] Horatius Barbatus, *De Divisione Fructuum* (Neapoli, 1638), pp. 26.3–4, 26.8, 27.9–12.

[3] Dominicus H. De Almeyda, *Analysis Exellentiarum in Jure*, etc. (Conimbricae, 1726), pp. 263–6. De Almeyda holds that the *Princeps* may forbid fishing in the interest of the public welfare.

exercise it. It is evident that there is some doubt in his mind on the whole subject, and that his sympathy is really with the classic position.

He is not alone in his hesitation. Treutlerus, while he admits the positive use of the *ius piscandi* by the king, is of the opinion that in strict law it should not be permitted. But long usage, inspired by the need of finding sources of revenue for the royal treasury, has sanctioned the right of a man to fish in a certain part of the sea to the exclusion of any others who may desire to fish there;[1] provided, that he has received this right from the king as a concession or as a privilege, or provided, that it is based upon immemorial custom.

Cujas, staunch classicist though he be, admits not only the *ius piscandi* among the Regalia, but the *reditus piscationum* also.[2]

Barbatus, Treutlerus, and others of their type,[3] may be said to represent the progressive element among the classicists. They form a middle group between those who admit no limitations to the right of fishery, and those who take the Regalia as a matter of course.

III. Quasi-Possession by Prescription

Closely connected with the group of jurists who have adopted the theory of the *ius piscandi* and the Regalia, is a second group.

This class of jurists is composed of those who hold that a private person may acquire by prescription exclusive rights, either of quasi-possession, or of use in public fisheries — that is to say, in fisheries which are located in public waters.

The most satisfactory treatment of the law on this subject is to be found in a tract by Balbus, named *De Praescriptionibus*.[4]

[1] Treutlerus and Schöpsius, *Consiliorum sive Responsorum* (Francofurti, 1625), pp. 160, 449.50 and .54.

[2] Jacobus Cujacius, *De Feudis*, in *Opera omnia*, 10 vols. (Neapoli, 1758), vol. ii, col. 1325 B.

[3] Angelus Aretinus, *Institutionum Iustiniani . . . Commentarii* (Venetiis, 1558), pp. 58, 59.4. Franciscus Bursatus, *Consiliorum*, 4 vols. (Francofurti, 1594), iii, 34.32. Fran. Amaya, *Commentarii in Codicis . . . Iustiniani* (Lugduni, 1639), p. 550.57.

[4] Ioannes Franciscus Balbus, *De Praescriptionibus*, in the *Tractatus Illustrium*, *op. cit.*, vol. xvii.

Balbus holds that prescription is possible in *loca publica*. He cites the Venetians and the Genoese to prove his point. This prescription must be from time immemorial.[1]

The question to which he gives this answer is, Can those things which are under the *ius gentium* be acquired by prescription?[2] His reasoning is as follows. If a person is in quasi-possession by reason of his fishing alone in a *diverticulum* in a public (that is, in a navigable) river, he can *praeoccupantis iure* prohibit another from fishing where he himself is accustomed to fish. If he is not in this quasi-possession, he cannot prohibit another from occupying the spot where he fishes, *quantumcunque tempore retro possederit*. A prescription of from ten to twenty years is not required in this case to give the right to prohibit another from fishing. What is required is *praeoccupatio*, and quasi-possession of the *ius piscandi de praesenti*.

> Et tali quasi-possessione amissa cessat ius prohibendi; quia res redijt in pristinam causam. Stat ergo regula, quod ea quae sunt iurisgentium non praescribuntur.

Balbus has stated his conception of the law covering the acquisition of exclusive rights to river fisheries. He has also stated that things under the *ius gentium* may not be prescribed. Instead of stopping with this last assertion, he proceeds to qualify it in a manner fundamentally to alter its significance. The exceptions to the rule thus laid down are of more importance than the rule, for they give the key to his doctrine on the subject. Any jurist could state the rule. The important question was, What limitations to it would he be willing to advocate?

The first limitation to this rule is, that it applies to prescription only, and not to the acquisition of the same rights by custom.

> Primo limita istam regulam, ut procedat ratione praescriptionis, sed non respectu consuetudinis. Nam licet ea quae competunt de iuregentium praescribi non possunt acquiri.[3]

Balbus holds that exclusive rights based on prescription and custom are not in law the same, even though their immediate effect

[1] Balbus, *op. cit.*, p. 98.5–6.
[2] *Ibid.*, p. 97.1.
[3] *Ibid.*, p. 97.2.

— an exclusive right of fishing in a certain spot — may be the same.

Some ask, he observes, what difference does it make whether one have a certain right *ex praescriptione* or *ex consuetudine, quia ex praescriptione ius unius quod ab eo aufertur, alteri applicatur.* The difference between these two methods of acquiring rights is this: If a person acquires his right by prescription, he has taken that right away from some one. If he has acquired it by custom, he has not.[1] The obvious result of this train of reasoning is, that what is imprescriptible may be acquired by custom. Thus the *ius piscandi* may be acquired by custom. The burden of proof is on the person alleging exclusive rights. He must have fished for at least ten years in that part of the river in which he claims exclusive rights; he must have prohibited others from fishing there during the period of his occupancy; and he must have prohibited them *saltem bis sciente et patiente populo seu maiori parte et non contradicente.*

A title, then, to exclusive rights of fishery in a particular place in a public river, is valid under the *ius gentium*, provided that this custom is of ten years' duration, and provided also that certain other conditions have been fulfilled. But such a title based on an alleged prescriptive right of ten years' duration is not valid under the *ius gentium*. The question now is, would such a title, if based on a prescription of more than ten years' duration, be valid under the *ius gentium*, and, if so, how many years are required to validate such a title? Balbus's answer to this question constitutes his second limitation on his *regula*.

The usual period of time required to validate a title based on prescription is that expressed by the stereotyped phrase, *cuius initii memoria non extat*, or *cuius initii memoria non extat in contrarium.* Balbus holds that a title based on a prescription covering the usual periods of ten, twenty, or thirty years, is not good; he holds also that prescription covering a period *longissimi temporis* is not sufficient; the period must be one *cuius initii memoria*

[1] "Sed cum aliquod ius applicatur alteri, ita quod alicui non auferatur, tunc illa proprie dicitur consuetudo. Sed in casu isto applicatur ex consuetudine prohibenti, licet aliquid proprium alicui non auferatur, ergo non dicitur praescriptio, nec istud ius ex praescriptione inducitur." P. 97.2.

non extat in contrarium.[1] This *limita* is the basis of the Venetian rights in the Adriatic, and is acknowledged by classical and practical jurist alike, to be good law. The condition, *populo sciente et patiente*, however, is not required, though some assert that it is.

Balbus, who has hitherto been writing of river fisheries, now digresses in order to vindicate the claims of the Venetians. This digression shows that it is not his intention to confine the laws which he is expounding to river fisheries. It seems that they operate equally well at sea, and not only in connection with maritime fisheries, but in regard to various other rights over the sea itself.

The Venetians, he says, have jurisdiction in *eorum mari, ex longa consuetudine.* They are in *quasi possessione gulfi maris.* The Venetians *Ianuensibus et aliis quibuscunque interdicere potentiam navigandi navigare volentibus per eorum gulfum.* They have acquired a *ius maris.*

There is still a third way in which one may circumvent the *ius gentium.* Balbus lays down a third limitation of his *regula.* It is true that those things which are in public use, and which are *res communes* under the *ius gentium*, may not be prescribed. Nevertheless,

> si ex hac longissima possessione velimus acquirere dominium eorum, quae nobis iuregentium communia sunt, sed per istam talem possessionem vel quasi bene acquirimus ius quoddam excipiendi, ut de possessione non expellamur.

This is a sweeping statement, and goes far to nullify the operation of the *regula* which it modifies. The effects of this possession are twofold.

> Primus est, quia si turbamur in ea, agere possumus contra turbantem. Secundus est: quia antequam expellamur, prohibere possumus, ne quis intret locum nobis invitis, unde prohibere possumus ratione possessionis navigationem et piscationem maris et fluminis. . . .[2]

---

[1] "Secundo limita praedictam regulam, ut procedat in praescriptione communi, vel longissimi temporis, sed non procedit in praescriptione tanti temporis, cuius initij etc., quia licet loca publica et iurisgentium non praescribantur. 10. 20. vel 30. annis. Praescribuntur tamen tanto tempore cuius initij memoria non extat in contrarium." P. 98.4.

[2] Balbus's limitations to the *ius gentium* will be found in his Sexto Quaero, p. 97 *et seq.*

Balbus goes on to add that it is impossible to acquire *dominium in locis publicis*, but that, nevertheless, the buildings which an individual constructs on, say, the seashore, or in the sea itself, are the property of the individual so long as they stand. There is nothing radical in this statement. But the rights which Balbus holds may be acquired over navigation in the sea and over maritime fisheries could not be more extensive if they were rights of property.

Balbus has, however, made a fair statement of the opinions of the jurists of this group. His extended discussion of the law is merely an expansion of the brief statements with which the others content themselves.[1]

The second group of jurists is distinguished by its emphasis on the doctrine that the *ius piscandi* is numbered among the Regalia. This is not to say that none of the jurists of the third group refers to this law, or that none of the second group mentions prescription. Jurists of both groups agree that exclusive rights of fishery may be acquired by privilege or by prescription. The distinction is, that the third group gives its chief attention to prescription, while the second group is concerned with the Regalia. For it is to the Regalia to which reference is made when the word 'privilege' is used, as the source of that privilege.

IV. Ownership of the Sea

Among those jurists who treat in particular of the relations of individuals, public and private, to maritime fisheries, two groups have been discerned: those who deny that any limitations whatsoever may be put upon the right of fishery, and those who admit certain limitations on this right. This latter group is composed

[1] See, as other members of this group: Ioan. Petrus Surdus, *Consiliorum sive Responsorum*, 4 vols. (Venetiis, 1615), i, 560.14. Pompeius Limpius, *Repetitionum in varias Iuris Civilis Leges*, etc., 8 vols. (Venetiis, 1608), i, 367.131. Joh. Otto Tabor, *Tractatuum Opus*, 2 vols. (Lipsiae, 1688), p. 273.1. Ioan. Schneidewin, *In quatuor Institutionum Imperialum . . . Commentarii* (Argentorati, 1586), p. 156. The same work appears under the following title also: Io. Oinotomus, *In quatuor Institutionum*, etc. (Venetiis, 1615), p. 33. Johannes Brunnemannus, *Commentarius in Quinquaginta Libros Pandectarum*, ed. by Samuel Strykius, Coloniae Allobrogum, 1752. 1.8.4.1., Ad L. Nemo igitur, p. 27. For a collection of opinions on the subject, see Ianus Guterus, *Florilegij Magni*, 2 vols. (Venetiis, 1625), p. 32.

of jurists who approach the subject from the point of view of the Regalia, and those who approach the subject from the point of view of the general laws governing prescription. Both groups have this in common, that they accept the classic doctrine of the freedom of the sea. The fundamental difference between the two groups is this, that one group refuses to admit the presence of lawful restrictions upon this freedom, while the other group accepts these restrictions. It is important to note that the group accepting these limitations regards them as nothing but limitations; the community of the sea remains inviolate; the general status of the sea is not affected. Both of these groups, then, have this in common, that they hold the classic Roman law doctrine in regard to the legal status of the sea, in so far as it is applicable to maritime fisheries.

Opposed to these jurists are those who hold that the sea, or some part of it, may be reduced to ownership. For the purposes of this distinction, those who hold some form of the theory of the adjacent sea may be classed with those who repudiate the theory, for the theory of *mare adiacens* is fundamentally concerned with rights of jurisdiction, and not with rights of property, in the sea. Those who hold that the sea, or some part of it, — that is, the high seas, or littoral seas, — may be owned as property, just as the land is owned as property, regard maritime fisheries as so much property, and rights of fishery as property rights.

According to this theory, the person who owns the waters where the fish are, has jurisdiction over the fish. It is a property right, this jurisdiction, vested in the proprietor.

The new theory is an evolution from the old. It has developed, broadly speaking, in each of two supplementary forms. One form has grown with the growth of the theory of territorial waters. Its progress has been traced. One form has grown in the manner indicated in the pages immediately preceding, of which the several groups of jurists distinguished therein are examples. By an expansion of the application of the ancient laws governing prescription, and by the development of the feudal doctrine of the Regalia, this growth has been accomplished. These two forms depend one upon the other; and yet they are distinct, if not independent. With the coming of the theory of *dominium maris*, these two forms combine into a unity; their separate characters disappear with the disappearance of the conflict between them.

That there had been a conflict up to the time of the emergence of the theory of *dominium maris* seems abundantly clear. On the one hand was a sea which was imprescriptible. It was incapable of being made, and any part of it was incapable of being made, the object of private property. On the other hand were the public fisheries, which, in the beginning, were open without hindrance to all men. Over both the Roman *Princeps* exercised a benevolent jurisdiction directed to the furtherance of the peaceful use of these great natural resources. But the beginnings of the conflict are discernible almost as the laws safeguarding this condition of things are formulated. At its critical stage it appears vividly in the writings of the jurisconsults, and in the clash between the doctrines of the two camps into which they were divided, the classical and the practical.

This conflict had the twofold character which has been noted above. It evidenced itself in the appropriation, first, of the inlets of the sea and of the waters found in the small indentations along the coast. These waters were appropriated because they contained fisheries, or because they were admirably situated for use as ports or harbors. This appropriation raised the question of jurisdiction in a new form. Rights of property were involved. The question of the existence of any rights of property was involved.

There were still other questions. For a while it seemed as if it might be lawful to own a fishery in a sea which could not be owned. This theory proved a hardy one, as the writings which have been examined in the preceding chapters show. At the same time that this theory was ripening into an accepted doctrine under the influence of feudal ideas, the ground was being prepared by those same ideas for the theory of *mare adiacens*. The king, the Great Landowner, indeed, the ultimate owner of the land, owned the fisheries in public waters. It was but a short step to the theory that he owned the water too; and that he controlled navigation over his water.

The question of control raised the question of jurisdiction. When this jurisdiction had existed simply and *de facto*, for the good of all and the suppression of pirates, the wielder of it was something of a servant of civilization. His jurisdiction existed apparently without a source. But customary law existed outside of the law books. The emperors found themselves doing many lawful things for which an appropriate text could not be cited. The *Princeps* of the Roman law, after undergoing an eclipse during the age of feudalism, underwent a resurrection during the Renaissance. He emerged as an absolute monarch who owned the soil. His jurisdiction then found lodgement. In the course of time — and this will be noted in the succeeding chapter — sovereignty was made to depend upon ownership of the soil. The extension of both to the adjacent sea was inevitable.

The resuscitation of Roman law played into his hands. The Roman law possessed, however, not only the absolute *Princeps*. It possessed also the doctrine of the freedom of the sea. Too much had happened in Europe since the tenth century for him to be satisfied with such a situation in the thirteenth. The customary law of the Barbarians had come; the customary law of feudalism had come. The time was ripe for Bartolus to come also. But the Roman Empire was going; feudalism was going. It was time for Bartolus to ease their departure and to facilitate the coming of the new régime — the Europe of absolute monarchs. He and his followers after him began eagerly to fit the old theories to the new facts.

But they found opposed to them that other great school of thought, which is always opposed to experimentalists, that school which was composed of men who attempted to make the facts fit the theories. The twofold character of the conflict persisted. On the one hand, there was the law governing the use of public fisheries; a law which embraced the relation of the king to these fisheries, of the subjects of the king to these fisheries, and of the relation of the king to his subjects in respect to both the ownership and the use of these fisheries. On the other hand was the relation of the king, as the embodiment of the state, as the possessor of all those rights which once the people — now, *his* people

— had possessed, to the sea which washed the shores of his kingdom. The issue was joined on these two lines, by these two types of thinkers.

During the sixteenth century, it seemed as if the school of the practicians were getting the worst of it. France produced a brilliant group of jurists who, filled with devotion to antiquity and to the historical method of research, furbished up the classical Roman law. The question of the legal status of the sea began to absorb the question of the legal status of the fisheries in it. It became apparent that the solution of the latter question depended upon the solution of the former. An ownerless sea would produce freedom of navigation, and freedom of fisheries. An appropriated sea would produce the opposite — or, at least, it might produce the opposite condition.

The discovery of a new hemisphere; the rapid increase in world-population; the rise of maritime powers in the west of Europe; the expansion of commerce; the jealousy of newly fledged and self-conscious states — or monarchs; the resulting conflict of "aspirations"; these forced the issue. The love of antiquity could make no headway; appalled, it died. The last great representative of the brilliant historical school wrote a scholarly and ill-tempered pamphlet on the *imperium* of the sea, which missed the point.[1]

The time was ready for a final statement of the argument on the question of the sea. The final statement was not, as it turned out, to close the controversy; it could, however, say every thing there was to be said at that time. An intellectual giant in Holland perceived the possibilities of the law of nature, coupled with a discriminating use of the classic doctrines of the Roman law, as a weapon to defend the sea from owners or prospective owners; another intellectual giant in England perceived the possibilities of historical records and the British common law. Grotius published a chapter from an unfinished work, and aimed it at the head of Philip II of Spain. Selden perceived his sovereign to be in the line of fire, and returned Grotius's tract with two volumes of his own.

[1] Iacobus Gothofredus wrote, *De Imperio Maris*.

On the Continent there were jurists who were not participating in the controversy. They devoted their attention to a formulation of the doctrine of *dominium maris*. One or two of them, together with Selden, laid out the foundations of a theory which has obtained a recognizable place in modern international law. Whatever may be the future of the freedom of the high seas, the freedom of territorial waters is dependent upon the will of the state possessing them. The settlement of this question was also the settlement of that other question, the nature, source, and extent of a state's jurisdiction over the fisheries located within its territorial waters.

That is to say, these two questions were settled in principle. The lines were laid out along which international practice was to move. The principles were enunciated to which appeal could be made in the controversies of the future. The question whether *mare adiacens* could be owned as property was settled in the affirmative. That was the question which had to be settled; that was the question without an answer to which nothing else could be settled.

In the development of the original theory of the freedom of the sea into that of territorial waters there is a series of critical points. The first point is the doctrine of Paulus that a private individual may possess *proprium ius* in a definite part of the sea. The second is that doctrine of the Glossators which states that this private right may be acquired by privilege or by long-standing custom — *per privilegium vel per longam consuetudinem*. The third point is the doctrine that the *Princeps* may impose a servitude on the sea. For both these doctrines the authority of Azo is given in the *Corpus Iuris*. By a broad interpretation of the rights of the king or emperor as enumerated in the Regalia, and by a wide application of the laws of prescription to the sea and to maritime fisheries, later jurists broke down the original doctrine forbidding private appropriation of what is common to all. They added important exceptions to this doctrine, or law — for such it became by its incorporation into the Digest — until they interpreted away the meaning which it had once possessed. The fourth point is the enunciation of the theory of *mare adiacens* — of the adjacent sea.

For this point Bartolus is responsible. Almost at once it received an accretion from Baldus, with his theory that the sea adjacent to a state is a district of that state over which the state's law is extended. These four points provide all the material necessary to create the theory of territorial waters, of *dominium maris*. Gentilis marked the fifth and last point when he intentionally applied the word *territorium* both to land and water. These are the five links in the chain which connects the classic doctrine of the freedom of the sea with the modern doctrine of territorial waters. Throughout the history of this development the open sea remains in theory free to all. At the beginning this freedom is sanctioned by law; at the end it is sanctioned by expediency, or even by necessity. But at the beginning, this freedom was thought to be inviolable; at the end it was no longer thought so.

The opening years of the seventeenth century form the final period of the development of the theory of *dominium maris*. After that time further development became merely modifications of existing theory. This period must now be considered in some detail.

CHAPTER VIII

MARE LIBERUM *VS.* MARE CLAUSUM

I. MARE LIBERUM

QUITE distinct from the defense which has been found to be imbedded in the theories of the classical Romanists is that now to be considered, although, naturally, the sources are the same. It is distinct because it is a studied defense, and not a mere fragment of a larger scheme of law. It is distinct, also, because it is a reasoned argument, and not a mere reproduction of the texts of the law books of Justinian. It is far from confining itself to a statement of the historical sources.

Before the opening of the seventeenth century, *mare liberum* had its protagonists. Of these is the Spanish Franciscan,[1] Alphonso de Castro, who died in 1558. He observes[2] that he suspects the opinions of those who maintain that the Genoese and the Venetians may hinder those who wish to navigate the Gulf of Genoa or the Adriatic. He does not care for the reason which they advance to cover their attitude — namely, that they have a prescriptive right in those waters. This claim, he holds, is not only contrary to the laws, but also to the law of nature itself, and to that primitive law of nations which is immutable.[3] He combats on the same grounds the opinions of the Portuguese, who assert that their King controls navigation to the East Indies, and

[1] Ernest Nys, *Les Origines du Droit International* (Bruxelles et Paris, 1894), p. 382.

[2] *De Potestate legis poenalis*, ii, c. 14, part. 572; quoted by Grotius, *Mare Liberum* (citation below), pp. 53–55; and in part, by Nys, *loc. cit.*, who gives a condensed summary.

[3] "Ex quibus apparet quam suspecta sit sententia eorum, . . . existimantium Genuenses, aut etiam Venetos posse non iniuria prohibere alios navigare per Gulfum aut pelagus sui maris, quasi aequora ipsa praescripserint, id quod non solum contra leges, sed etiam est contra ipsum ius naturae, aut gentium primaevum, quod mutari non posse diximus."

The contrast between *lex* and *ius* is noteworthy. Referring to the passage beginning "id quod," etc., Nys writes in quotation marks, "'Cette opinion est contraire

those of the Spaniards, who make a similar claim in regard to the West Indies. The *dominium maris* is not lawful, for the sea

ab origine Mundi, ad hodiernum usque diem [has been] semper in communi, nulla exparte immutatum.

He makes a point which was to be made again.

Contra reliquas vero nationes [he says] longe minus praescribere possunt, quia ius praescriptionum est mere civile. . . . Ergo tale ius cessat cum agitur inter principes vel populos, superiorem non recognoscentes in temporalibus. Iura enim mere civilia cuiuscumque regionis, quoad exteros populos, nationes, vel etiam homines singulos, non magis sunt in consideratione, quam si re vera esset tale ius, aut nunquam fuisset, et ad ius commune gentium primaevum vel secundarium recurrendum est, . . . quo iure talem maris praescriptionem et usurpationem admissam non fuisse satis constat.[1]

The great Spanish jurist, Vasquez, on whom Grotius leans heavily, covers much the same ground. He maintains that the Genoese and the Venetians cannot prohibit the navigation of "their" seas.[2] Such an act is not only against the Roman law, but

non seulment aux lois, mais au droit même de la nature, au droit primitif des gens, qui est immutable.'" A free translation. He is able to bring out the difference between *lex* and *ius* admirably.

De Castro proceeds as follows: "Quod sit contra illud ius constat, quia maria aut aequora eo iure communia erant sed etiam reliquae omnes res immobiles."

Omitting, then, the passage in the text: "Et quamvis ex Lusitanis magnam turbam saepe audiverim in hac esse opinione ut eorum Rex ita praescripserit navigationem indici Occidentalis (forte Orientalis) eiusdemque Vastissimi Maris, ita ut reliquis gentibus aequora illa transfretare non liceat, et ex nostrismet Hispanis vulgus in eadem opinione fere esse videtur, ut per vastissimum immensumque pontum ad Indorum regiones quas potentissimi Reges nostri subegerunt reliquis mortalium navigare praeterquam Hispanis ius minime sit, quasi ab eis id ius praescriptum fuerit, tamen istorum omnium non minus insanae sunt opiniones, quam eorum qui quoad Genuenses et Venetos in eodem fere somnio esse adsolent, quas sententias ineptire vel ex eo dilucidius apparet, quod instarum nationum singulae contra seipsas nequeunt praescribere. . . ."

[1] See note 2 on the preceding page. He continues: "Eam et hodie usus aquarum communis est, non secus quam erat ab origine Mundi. Ergo et in aequoribus et aquis nullum ius est aut esse potest humano generi, praeterquam quoad usum communem. . . ."

[2] Fernandus Vasquius, *Controversiarum Illustrium* (Venetiis, 1564), ii, 114.30.

The Spanish jurists differ flatly from their King, as a general rule, on the question of the moment. Solorzano is a hearty defender of Spanish colonial policy, and seems to give unquestioning approval to and endorsement of Spanish pretensions. He relies upon the papal bulls, note above.

is also a violation of the *ius naturae* and of the primitive *ius gentium*.

The position of Grotius in the history of jurisprudence has been indicated. But what is more important for present purposes is to note that his doctrine is old as Roman law. [1]

"Mare liberum" [2] was first published, anonymously, in 1608, though it was known at the time that the author was Hugo Grotius. It was written, as the title indicates, to vindicate the right of the Dutch to compete with the Spanish and Portuguese in the East Indian trade.[3] Grotius has blended a good advocate's sharpness of argument with a restrained eloquence of the sort to have a wide popular appeal, with the result that he has produced a really powerful piece of work. The treatise is the work of a fully trained and clever craftsman. In his preface, Grotius thus describes the points in controversy: [4]

> Between us and the Spaniards the following points are in dispute: Can the vast, the boundless sea be the appanage of one kingdom alone, and it not the greatest? Can any one nation have the right to prevent other nations which so desire, from selling to one another, from bartering with one another, actually from communicating with one another? Can any nation give away what it never owned, or discover what already belonged to some one else? Does a manifest injustice of long standing create a specific right?

He indicates also the basis of his argument: [5]

> The law by which our case must be decided is not difficult to find, seeing that it is the same among all nations; and it is easy to understand, seeing that it is innate in every individual and implanted in his mind. . . . For it it is a law derived from nature. . . .

[1] *I. e.*, his doctrine of the legal status of the sea.

[2] Hugonis Grotii, *Mare Liberum, sive de Iure quod Batavis competit ad indicana Commercia Dissertio*, 1608. His name was eventually added to the title.

[3] *The Freedom of the Seas*, or, The Right which belongs to the Dutch to take part in the East Indian Trade; a Dissertation by Hugo Grotius, translated with a revision of the Latin text of 1633 by Ralph Van Deman Magoffin, New York 1916. The Latin and English appear on opposite pages. See also p. 1, par. 1.

[4] *Mare liberum*, Magoffin's ed., p. 4. "Inter nos et Hispanos haec controversa sunt: Sitne immensum et vastum mare regni unius nec maximi accessio; populone quiquam ius sit volentes populos prohibere ne vendant, ne permutent, ne denique commeent inter se; potueritne quisquam quod suum numquam fuit elargiri, aut invenire quod iam erat alienum; an ius aliquod tribuat manifesta longi temporis iniuria."

[5] *Ibid.*, p. 5 of the preface.

He takes his stand:[1]

> on the following most specific and unimpeachable axiom of the Law of Nations . . . the spirit of which is self-evident and immutable, to wit: Every nation is free to travel to every other nation, and to trade with it.

The sea does not belong in the number of those things which are *in commercio*. It follows from this that no part of the sea can be considered as within the territory of any people.[2] Furthermore, it is evident from the title of his book that this sea may not be restricted as to use. It is very important, then, to define what is meant by the "sea." Grotius does this by eliminating from the purview of his discussion certain parts of the sea considered as a whole, which have, at least in appearance, a certain distinctive character of their own. By putting to one side these specified bodies of (salt) water, he is able to describe what is left as "the sea." It is this body of water, only, which he holds to be *liberum*. The parts of the sea which he excludes from his definition, and the way in which he does it, may be briefly indicated as follows.

He begins with inlets. He writes at a certain stage of his argument,[3]

> Demonstratum est nec populo nec privato cuipiam ius aliquod proprium in ipsum mare (nam diverticulum excipimus) competere posse. . . . [Inlets of the sea, therefore, are excluded by definition from "the sea." He proceeds.][4] Non de mari interiore hic agimus, quod terris undique infusum alicubi etiam fluminis latitudinem non excedit, de quo tamen satis constat locutos Romanos Iurisconsultos, cum nobiles illas adversus privatam avaritiam sententias ediderunt; de Oceano quaritur, quem immensum, infinitum, rerum parentem, caelo conterminum antiquitas vocat, cuius perpetuo humore non fontes tantum et flumina et maria, sed nubes, sed ipsa quodammodo sidera pasci veteres crediderunt; qui denique per reciprocas aestuum vices terram hanc humani generis sedem ambiens, neque teneri neque includi potest, et possidet verius quam possidetur.

In this passage, inner seas are ruled out. An inner sea, it appears, is one which is surrounded by land, and which does not, in some places, have more width than that of a river. The description of the ocean does not give much illumination, though it seems to have been intended to provide contrast. A first-class lawyer indulging in rhapsody is not without his interest. But Grotius pro-

[1] *Op. cit.*, p. 7.
[2] *Ibid.*, p. 34.
[3] *Ibid.*, p. 36.
[4] *Ibid.*, p. 37.

ceeds to name two more bodies of water which are not to be deemed a part of the sea:[1]

> In hoc autem Oceano non de sinu aut freto.

The rest of his sentence withdraws another section of the sea, and somewhat resembles a limit to the adjacent sea:

> nec de omni quidem eo quod e litore conspici potest. . . .

Grotius has used sweeping language in the passages quoted above. His abandon in his description of the vast ocean is particularly notable. It is possible that he was intentionally avoiding precision, in order to appeal to popular opinion. It does not seem unlikely that he was consciously going over the heads of the masters of foreign affairs in order to strike at some underlying current of popular disapproval of extravagant and unworkable claims to the sea. However that may be, he has admitted by implication at least that *mare adiacens* is not necessarily *liberum*, and to that extent he has granted the contention of his antagonists that it *may* be *clausum*.

He goes on to say that the Portuguese claim the whole sea which separates the old world from the new; and that, if the similar claim of the Spanish is added, nearly the whole ocean is subject to those two peoples. It is these claims which he pronounces illegal and invalid.

In his argument against the validity of the claim to an exclusive right of navigation based upon title by prescription, he associates himself with De Castro. Prescription is a matter of the *ius civile*. Consequently it has not standing between kings or between free peoples. And even if it had, it could not be applied here, because it is impossible to acquire by prescription that which cannot become the object of private property.[2]

It appears, therefore (he remarks), that Angelus and those who

[1] *Mare liberum*, *op. cit.*, p. 37.

[2] *Ibid.*, p. 47. "Nam praescriptio a iure est civili, unde locum habere non potest inter reges, aut populos liberos, multo autem ubi ius naturae aut gentium resistit, quod iure civili semper validius est. Quin et pisa lex civilis praescriptionem hic impedit. Usucapi enim, aut praescriptione acquiri prohibentur, quae in bonis esse non possunt, deinde quae possideri vel quapossideri nequent, et quorum alienatio prohibita est. Haec autem omnia de mari et usu maris vere dicuntur."

agree with him were mistaken when they held that the Venetians and Genoese could acquire by prescription certain rights in the bays (or gulfs) indenting their shores.[1] In the light of this observation, it would appear that the adjacent sea has that immunity which he ascribes to the *oceanum immensum*. If this is so, it is not clear why he withdraws littoral waters from the scope of his argument.

It is noteworthy that, instead of following the traditional custom of condoning the claims made by the Venetians in the Adriatic, Grotius frankly disapproves of them.[2]

Now, the principle which applies to navigation applies also to fishing. The right of fishing is common to all for the same reason that the right of navigation is; it is based upon the nature of the sea.

> Quae autem navigationis eadem piscatus habenda est ratio, ut communis maneat omnibus.[3]

One may enclose a small body of water by fencing off a shallow indentation in the coast line, and reserve it for one's private use; but beyond this one may not go — one may not, for example, prohibit fishing off shore in front of one's residence.

> Extra diverticulum . . . ne scilicet communis usus impediatur.[4]

The revenues which are derived from maritime fisheries are included among the Regalia according to general opinion; and Grotius seems to accept, if a little unwillingly, this opinion.[5]

> Similiter reditus qui in piscationes maritimas constituti Regalium numero censentur, non rem, hoc est mare, aut piscationem, sed personas obligant. Quare subditi, in quos legem ferendi potestas Reipublicae aut Principi ex consensu competit, ad onera ista compelli forte poterunt; sed exteris ius piscandi ubique immune esse debet, ne servitus imponatur mari quod servire non potest.

This passage presents certain difficulties. Grotius seems to mean that the taxes which provide the revenue of which he is

[1] *Mare liberum, op. cit.*, p. 48.

[2] *Ibid.*, p. 48. "Apparet . . . Angelum et qui cum Angelo dixerunt Venetis et Genuensibus per praescriptionem ius aliquod in sinum maris suo litori praeiacentem acquiri potuisse, aut falli, aut fallere. . . ."

[3] *Ibid.*, p. 32. [4] *Ibid.*, p. 33. [5] *Ibid.*, p. 36.

writing are not to be compared with those which the owner (granting the possibility of there being one) of a maritime fishery might impose on persons using his fishery. They are not imposed as a fee for the privilege of using the fishery, or for that of going to the location of the fishery. The difficulties which arise may be expressed by the questions: On what are the taxes imposed? For what are they imposed? By what right does the Crown impose them? And, Why may not the Crown impose them on foreigners, if it may do so on its subjects? The answer to the first question is, undoubtedly, that they are imposed on persons. These persons are comprised exclusively of the subjects of the Crown, so far as strict law is concerned. The answer to the second question is not given. When he speaks of foreigners, however, he says that it is the right of fishing which should be exempt from taxation. It seems reasonable to suppose, then, that it is the right of fishing possessed by the subjects which the Crown — their sovereign — is taxing. Grotius does not give his unqualified consent to the existence of this right in the Crown. Nevertheless, he admits it. The third question — by what right does the Crown impose them? — is not definitely answered. *Reditus piscationum*, however, are in *numero Regalium*. It would seem then that this right is vested in the Crown. The question then arises, What is the source of this right? Why, in other words, is the *reditus piscationum* included in the Regalia? There is no hint of an answer to this question. There is only a hint of doubt in the mind of Grotius when he says that *perhaps* the Crown has the right to tax its subjects for exercising their *ius piscandi*. The answer to the fourth question is not given. The situation, then, is this: A maritime fishery is free to all men. A sovereign taxes his subjects on the exercise of their right of fishing there. This act of his is not tyranny or even usurpation, because the right is vested in him as of the Regalia. The effect of this doctrine is to give the sovereign in question control of the fishery, so far as the use of it by his subjects is concerned. But the fishery is not subject to control. Yet the tax is lawful. If a subject cannot afford to pay it, he cannot use his right to fish. Grotius was forced to hold that the tax was not levied on the fishery, but on the subject's right to fish, in order to avoid granting the sovereign any sort of property right in the fishery. The fact is, however, that the *ius piscandi* was included in the Regalia because it was the logical outcome of the doctrine that the Crown has a property right in the fishery.[1] The doctrine of a property right in the fishery itself flows naturally from that of a larger right of ownership of the sea adjacent to the shores of the king possessing such a right. These waters are then truly territorial waters. The right of jurisdiction over the adjacent sea, without any property right in them, could not give a right to tax foreigners. The jurists could dispose of any such pretension by defining the scope of the jurisdiction exercised. Grotius was aware of that. But he could not grant any *proprietas* to the king. The result is that the requirements of his argument have forced him into a contradictory position on the fishery question where the fishery is located near the shores of any particular state. When he is discussing the freedom of the high seas, he is at ease, and he is carrying public opinion with him. But when he deals with coastal waters, and with the fisheries therein, he is not able to make the facts fit snugly into his theory. He divides the coastal waters from the high seas; he acknowledges their existence. But whatever the basis of his division may be — and he is not apparently concerned to have a basis — it is not grounded on any difference in kind from the sea proper.

Grotius partially admits in one place that the supply of fish is exhaustible, and that, therefore, and on this ground, it may be possible to prohibit fishing.[2] This fact is worth noting, because Welwood used it against him, just as he used his acceptance of the existence of *mare adiacens*.

The premises underlying his argument are these: The law of nature flows from divine Providence. Part of this law is the *ius gentium primaevum*, which is immutable. The other part is the *ius gentium secundarium* or *positivum*, which is mutable. Customs which are repugnant to the *ius gentium primaevum* have no recog-

[1] Ernest Nys, *Origines*, p. 383: "Le doctrine de la souveraineté et de la propriété de la Couronne dans les mers entourant le pays avait entrainé cette consequence que le droit de pêche etait un droit regalien."

[2] *Mare liberum*, *op. cit.*, p. 43. ". . . puta piscaturam qua dici quodammodo potest pisces exhauri. . . ."

nition from the law; they are *non leges et usus.*[1] The aim of his argument, of course, is to prove that his thesis is controlled by the *ius gentium primaevum.* And his thesis is, that *mare est liberum.*

Following is a brief summary of the entire argument.

The law of God, or divine law, being the highest of all law, is the first to which appeal is made. This law, as revealed through nature, is found to command that every locality should be supplied with the necessities of life. Each place cannot produce everything that is needed for itself; it happens also that some regions excel others in producing certain things. Therefore the various peoples must coöperate in supplying the needs of each other. This necessity results from the decree of divine justice. That this is true is proved from two facts: the first is, that the ocean is a highway to every land. The second is, that the winds blow first from one quarter, then from another. It is apparent that Nature has made the requisite provision for carrying out her purpose. This is also the belief of the ancients. It follows, therefore, that even if the Portuguese had been sovereign in those parts to which the Dutch sail, which they are not, they would have been doing them an injury by forbidding them access to those places.[2]

That the Portuguese are not sovereign in those parts of the East Indies with which the Dutch traffic is easily proved by applying the appropriate tests. The first of these is that of discovery. But they have not acquired jurisdiction by right of discovery, for "to discover a thing is not only to seize it with the eyes, but to take real possession thereof." [3] Not only did the Portuguese not discover India, for it has been known for centuries, but they maintain no garrisons there. Furthermore, "discovery *per se* gives no legal rights over things unless before the alleged discovery they were *res nullius.*" [4] Nor can it be maintained that the fact that the inhabitants are infidels gives to Christians any rights of possession; to deprive them of their civil power, or sovereignty, or

[1] *Mare liberum, op. cit.*, p. 53.

[2] *Ibid.*, p. 10.

[3] *Ibid.*, p. 11. "Invenire enim non iullud est oculis usurpare, sed apprehendere. . . ."

[4] *Ibid.*, p. 13.

property, is no less robbery than it would be in the case of Christians. This position is maintained by Spanish writers of the highest authority.

> No one is sovereign of a thing which he himself has never possessed, and which no one else has ever held in his name . . . title to sovereignty is not sufficient, inasmuch as possession is a prerequisite — for having a thing is quite different from having the right to acquire it. . . .[1]

No title to jurisdiction or sovereignty can be based on the Donation of Pope Alexander VI. In the first place, if the partition then made was intended only to settle an affair between the Portuguese and the Spaniards, then it cannot affect other peoples. In the second place, if the Pope intended to give those nations each a third of the world, he could not do so, whether or not he had the power. If he did have the power, still the gift could not make the Portuguese sovereign of those parts, "for it is not a donation that makes a sovereign, it is the consequent delivery of a thing and the subsequent possession thereof."[2] The fact is, however, that the Pope lacked the power. It was a donation of the property of others, and so of no effect. The Pope is neither the civil nor the temporal lord of the world. His power is restricted to the spiritual realm; and besides this, he can have no power over infidels, for they do not belong to the Church.[3]

Finally, the Portuguese have not acquired title by war. They have not been at war with most of the peoples with whom the Dutch trade. But even if this title could be justified, it would not give a title to sovereignty, "except by right of conquest, that is to say, occupation would be a prerequisite."[4] This requirement has not been satisfied.

Having proved that the Portuguese have no legal rights of any sort over the peoples or territory of the East Indies, it is necessary to examine the question whether they have any property right or exclusive right of navigation in the Indian Ocean, or, to put it in

[1] *Mare liberum*, *op. cit.*, p. 11. "Quia dominus nemo est eius rei quam nec ipse umquam nec alter ipsius nomine possedit . . . ad dominium titulus non suffici(e)t, quia et possessio requiritur, cum aliud sit rem habere, aliud ius ad rem consequendam. . . ."

[2] *Ibid.*, p. 15.

[3] *Ibid.*, Grotius is overlooking nothing.

[4] *Ibid.*, p. 18.

different terms, whether they have an exclusive right of jurisdiction over the sea and over navigation, or over trade. The answer to this question involves a discussion of the origin of private property.

De Mari autem prima sit consideratio, quod cum passim in iure aut nullius, aut commune, aut publicum iuris gentium dicatur.[1]

The meaning of these terms must be explained.

In the primordial ages of humanity, *dominium* and *communio* bore meanings different from those attached to them in the present day.

Nam dominium nunc proprium quid significat, quod scilicet ita est alicuius ut alterius non sit eodem modo. Commune autem dicimus, cuius proprietas inter plures consortio quodam aut consensu collata est exclusis aliis.[2]

But in the early days *commune* meant simply the opposite of *proprium*. *Dominium* signified the *facultas non iniusta utendi re communi.*[3] Moreover, *usum* referred to the actual fact, and not to a legal right. In the primitive *ius gentium*, which is sometimes called the *ius naturale*, there was no *proprium*. There was no private property. There was a kind of common possession, a community of goods, which related to use. The transition to the modern distinction of individual ownership began with the private appropriation of such necessities as articles of food and drink, ownership of which is inseparable from use. The process spread to clothing, then to movables, then to immovables, property in which comes by occupation or possession.

With the rise of states, things which had undergone this process of individual appropriation were divided into *res publicae*, which were true *propria populi*, and *res privatae*, which were owned by private persons. Thus public and private ownership arose. Two conclusions may be drawn:

Prius est, eas res quae occupari non possunt, aut occupatae numquam sunt, nullius proprias esse posse; quia omnis proprietas ab occupatione coeperit. Alterum vero, eas res omnes, quae ita a natura comparatae sunt, ut aliquo utente nihilominus aliis quibusvis ad usum promiscue sufficiant, eius hodieque condicionis esse, et perpetuo esse debere cuius fuerant cum primum a natura proditae sunt.[4]

[1] *Mare liberum, op. cit.*, p. 22.
[2] *Ibid.*, pp. 22–23.
[3] *Ibid.*, p. 23.
[4] *Ibid.*, p. 27.

This second class contains all those things which can be used by some without a loss to others. The air is thus classified, and the sea.

Et eisdem de causis commune est omnium Maris Elementum, infinitum scilicet ita, ut possideri non queat, et omnium usibus accommodatum; sive navigationem respicimus, sive etiam piscaturam.[1]

The shore partakes of the character of the sea, because the sea has torn it away from other uses than those connected with itself.[2] These things are to be understood as public in the usual meaning of that word, that is, they are, according to the *ius gentium*, not the property of any one people, but the common property of the body of human society. They are also *res nullius* in the widest meaning of that term only, for they differ from those other things which are *res nullius* in the sense that they become the property of those who seize and possess them; they are incapable of becoming the objects of private property, for they are susceptible of universal use. That is, Nature does not permit the sea to be common: she commands that it be so. Since the sea, then, is not an article of commerce, and cannot become private property, it follows strictly that no part of the sea can be considered as within the territory of any people.[3]

It is permissible, nevertheless, to fence off inlets in order to make private fish preserves, to construct breakwaters and the like, provided that they do not impede the common use of the sea. These enclosures are protected by the laws of private property and are not under the *ius gentium*. Other things which are alleged to prove a private ownership of the sea are found upon examination to prove nothing of the sort. When the ancient writers say that a certain sea belonged to the Roman people, they must be understood to refer only to protection and jurisdiction; they themselves distinguish between the right of protection and jurisdiction and that of ownership. Similarly, agreements to apportion certain areas of the sea between maritime states for

[1] *Mare liberum, op. cit.*, p. 28.
[2] *Ibid.*, p. 28.
[3] "Est igitur Mare in numero earum rerum quae in commercio non sunt, hoc est, quae proprii iuris fieri non possunt. Unde sequitur si proprie loquamur, nullam Maris partem in territorio populi alicuius posse censeri." *Ibid.*, p. 34.

the purpose of preventing piracy bind only those who are parties to them, and give no right of ownership. Revenues taken from maritime fisheries are numbered in the Regalia; but the obligation here is on the fisherman, and not on the sea or on the fishery. Finally, the case of the sea differs from that of a river, for the reason that the river is the property of the people; it is public, and the right of fishing in it can be granted by the people or by the prince. The question at issue should be carefully limited. It does not concern an inner sea, one which is surrounded by land. It does not concern a gulf or a strait. It does not even concern so much of the sea as is visible from the shore. It concerns the outer sea, the ocean.

Having concluded an examination into the origin and nature of private property, it is now possible to apply the proper tests to the claims of the Spanish and Portuguese to the sea. Between the two of them, they claim only a little less than the entire ocean.

These claims cannot be sustained. They have not succeeded in taking real possession. Their only boundary is an imaginary line. There is a complete lack of physical appropriation or corporal possession. It is ridiculous to insist that occupation of the sea consists in sailing over it before some one else does. There is no part of the sea over which some one has not already sailed Even if a man were to have dominion over the sea, he still could not diminish its common use, just as the Roman people, on the shores under their *imperium*,[1] could not forbid what the *ius gentium* permitted. And if they could have prohibited fishing, for example, still they could not have prohibited navigation, for the sea is not exhausted by that use. And this is the most weighty argument of all.

It is once more futile to invoke the Donation of Pope Alexander VI, for that act is empty of meaning. This fact is clear from what has been said before on this point.

Pleas of prescription or custom cannot be sustained. Prescription is *iuris civilis*, and can have no place as between kings or free peoples,[2] especially when it is in conflict with the law of nature or

[1] *Mare liberum, op. cit.*, p. 43. "In litore imperi."

[2] *Ibid.*, p. 47. "Nam praescriptio a iure est civili, unde locum habere non potest inter reges, aut inter populos liberos."

of nations. Usurpation, of no matter how long duration, cannot interrupt the use of a *res communis*. Nor is it possible to acquire by prescription that which cannot become the object of private property. Those illustrations which are usually cited as proving the contrary are in reality themselves illustrations of the violation of the law, if the facts are as represented. For example, those jurists who concede to the Venetians and Genoese the acquisition of rights in the bays of the sea adjacent to their shores are simply in error. For no one can raise prescriptions against rights which they already possess by nature. No nation can erect a prescription against itself. And if the Venetians or Genoese do prohibit the navigation of their gulfs and bays to foreign vessels, they are doing so with injustice, for no state can acquire the *ius prohibendi* in a *res publica* by prescription. Finally, the practice of the Venetians and Genoese cannot be cited as a precedent, nor the opinions of the aforesaid jurists who defend it, for there the question is one of bays, or of the Mediterranean, while here the question is of the ocean itself, and these are two entirely different things, from the point of view of occupation.

But even if the lapse of time could give a prescriptive right to public property, the conditions necessary for the creation of that right in the present case are absent. The essential conditions are: possession from time immemorial; exclusive use of the right of possession, except in so far as the possessor grants it to others, or it is used clandestinely; the prevention of all other persons from using the thing possessed, with the application of means or measures which are of common knowledge, and which are used with the suffrance of those concerned. These conditions are essential because the law is opposed to the acquisition of public things by prescription. A survey of Portuguese history shows that this nation has not fulfilled these requirements.

The claims of the Spanish and Portuguese in respect of the East Indies, and in respect of the ocean have been considered, and refuted. It remains to analyse their claims to an exclusive right of trade with the Indies.

By the *ius gentium*, commerce is free among all men. The arguments which have already been employed serve also to refute the claim of the Portuguese to an exclusive right to trade with the East Indies. From the character of the origins of private property, together with the resulting necessity for an exchange of goods, it follows that the universal basis of all contracts is derived from nature herself, although certain special kinds have been instituted, as, for example, the practice of the payment of money. Thus freedom of commerce is based on, and arises from the primitive *ius gentium*, — a law which has a natural and permanent cause, so that it can never be destroyed; or, if it can, then only by and with the consent of all nations. Consequently, one nation may not with justice hinder two nations which desire to make a contract between themselves.

Furthermore, an exclusive right of commerce cannot arise from discovery and occupation, because the *ius mercandi* is not something corporal. The state which is the first to trade with the East Indies does not on that account acquire any exclusive rights.

Nor can the papal Donation give an exclusive right. No one has granted the right except the Pope, and he did not have the power.[1] Liberty of commerce came from the eternal law of nature and of nations, against which the authority of the Pope has no force.

Appeal to prescription or custom as the basis of a right of exclusive commerce cannot be admitted. It has been shown that between kings and free peoples these have no binding power. Nor have they any force against those things introduced by primeval law.[2] Neither sound title nor good faith is present here. The Portuguese have no recourse but to prove coercion; but this is contrary to the law of nature and is harmful to all men. Thus it cannot be established. This coercion, moreover, must have existed from time immemorial, and this is not the fact in the present case. Again, it must be of that sort which is not resisted; but this has been and is resisted by the nation. Finally, not only some, but all must have been coerced; and this has not been done. Their usurpation is therefore unlawful.

[1] *Mare liberum, op. cit.*, p. 66. "Concessit nemo, nisi forte Pontifex, qui non potuit."

[2] *Ibid.*, p. 67. "Sed nec huius nec illius vim esse aliquam inter liberas nationes, aut diversarum gentium Principes, nec adversus ea quae primigenio iure introducta sunt. . . ."

In his "De Jure Belli ac Pacis," Grotius returns to the subject for a brief treatment with perhaps a more cautious emphasis on the inviolable character of the adjacent sea.[1] The sea, whether taken as a whole or considered in its fundamental parts, cannot become private property. The nature and manner of the origins of the institution of private property makes this impossible. This is true not only for private persons but for peoples; the reason for this is, that the cause which led to the surrender of community ownership ceases at this point to operate. Grotius calls this reason a moral one. Its basis is the magnitude of the sea: the sea is so vast in extent that it is sufficient for the every use of all peoples.[2] There is, however, a natural reason in addition to the moral one. It is this: Occupation can only take place in a thing which is bounded; the sea is not bounded; therefore occupation cannot take place in the sea.[3] The sea, of course, not only is not, it cannot be bounded.

Ideo, quae communia omnium fuerunt, et in prima divisione non sunt, ea non jam divisione, sed occupatione transeunt in jus proprium, nec dividuntur nisi postquam propria esse coeperunt.[4]

Grotius proposes a limit to the extent of the adjacent sea. It should be confined to just so much as can be protected by force from the land.[5]

Ratione territorii, quatenus ex terra cogi possunt qui in proxima maris parte versantur, nec minus quam si in ipsa terra reperirentur.

The implications of this famous passage have a clear bearing on the development of the theory of territorial waters.[6]

The failure of "Mare liberum" to evoke opposition on the Continent is well known. The explanation is perhaps threefold. In the first place, Philip II, King of Spain and Portugal, ordered the book to be suppressed within his dominions. One Portuguese jurist of eminence managed to secure a copy. His reply will be noted below. In the second place, the dispute which called forth

[1] *De Jure Belli ac Pacis, libri tres*, transl. by William Whewell, 3 vols., Cambridge, 1853.

[2] *Ibid.*, II. ii. III. 1, p. 234.

[3] *Ibid.*, II. ii. III. 2, p. 234.

[4] *Ibid.*, II. ii. III. 3, p. 235.

[5] *Ibid.*, II. iii. XIII. 2, p. 267.

[6] The fact that the author of *Mare liberum* makes such a suggestion goes far to indicate the unity of thought underlying both parties to the controversy.

Grotius's effort was settled soon after the appearance of the book. In the third place, the Continent as a whole shared the Dutch dislike of the Spanish and Portuguese claims.

It is true that this distaste was keenly felt in England. But James I was engaged in asserting far-reaching claims to the waters surrounding the British Isles. The English lawyers, however much they might repudiate the position taken by the Portuguese and Spanish, were at the same time quick to see that the argument put forward by Grotius was applicable to the claims being made by their sovereign. Their agitation consequently was great; and they bent their energies enthusiastically to the problem of vindicating the British claims without championing those of Philip II at the same time. The influence of this condition of things upon the whole controversy has been indicated. The point at issue for Grotius was the claim of Philip II to a monopoly of the East Indian trade — a point which involved subsidiary claims to the right to take the measures necessary to secure it. The point at issue for the English lawyers was a subsidiary one for Grotius, therefore, because it concerned only coastal waters. The doctrine of *mare liberum* was Grotius's answer to Philip II. It was also the answer (as *mare liberum* was defined) to the claims of James I. It need not have been, in order to achieve the primary purpose of its statement. But it was, because Grotius allowed himself to cover the whole field. That the British lawyers were not mistaken in sensing the danger to their sovereign's claims was shown when Grotius reverted to it in his later work on War and Peace, — even though his position was tempered by a realization that he was an ambassador of the Court of Sweden.

The States-General, having decided that Selden's book — the most formidable of the statements of the British position — should be formally refuted, and Grotius, now an escaped prisoner in the service of a foreign sovereign, being unavailable, gave the task to Dirck Graswinckel on the 28th of April, 1636. Graswinckel submitted his book on the 13th of April, 1637. At that time, however, the States-General believed the political situation to be clearing. They set aside the work; it was never published.[1]

[1] Fulton, *op. cit.*, p. 375.

Graswinckel, nevertheless, found an opportunity to expound the doctrine of the freedom of the seas in a book in which he defended from attack the "De Iure Belli ac Pacis." His method leads him to make a series of fragmentary and disconnected statements on the subject. He seems to place his reliance (in regard to the point in question) on positive assertion rather than on reasoned conclusions. The following is his most important delivery on the subject: [1]

> Non possunt duo, rem eandem, et insimul, et in solidum possidere: at vero mare omnibus suum, omnibus idem, usu in solidum eodem tempore, a duobus, a pluribus, ab universis possideri potest, effusum quippe, incircumscriptum, quibuscumque usibus patens, nulli clausum, nulli occludendum, semper se praebiturum sulcare volentibus, nihil proprii dominii admissurum quam dum tenetur et quatenus, occupatione locali intermissa, cuicumque occupanti vacuum, liberum est, non intercludendum.

And so, with the right of navigation:

> Manente indefiniter libero maris usu, quem in solidum, utque loquimur, privative sibi asserere nulli eorum qui virunt proclive est, nedum ut in manu id sit ac potestate.

In 1637, the same year in which Graswinckel submitted his refutation of Selden's work to the States-General another Hol-

[1] Theod. Graswinckel, *Stricturae ad censuram Joannis a Felden ad libros Hugonis Grotii De Iure Belli ac Pacis* (Amstelaedami, 1654), p. 105.

His other references to the subject are these: p. 103. "Ex praemissis probat Grotius mare in proprium jus non abire posse, quia causa non erat a communione recedendi. Feldenus (sic) ait, non ex causa a communione recessum fuisse, sed a natura." But Graswinckel says that Grotius was right, "cum mare omnibus sufficeret, ideo commune mansit."

Ibid. Felden (sic) likewise thinks that because fishing may be carried on in a manner to exhaust the fishery, private ownership of the fishery is possible, *i. e.*, legally justifiable. The same reasoning is applicable to navigation also. On the other hand, Grotius denies this. Graswinckel holds that "non quidem piscium ea copia ut omnibus sufficeret, sed quo minor copia eo majores expensae in piscando. Et sic generi humano minus conduceret mare proprii dominii facere, cum potius nemini interdici debeat, quod utile est non fiat. Interim satis a natura prospectum est ne omnes in eadem parte maris piscentur, cum unaquaeque maria suos accolos habeant, et distantia loci caeteros prohibeat. Quomodo autem de navigatione idem dicendum. . . . Sola causa cur proprietas maris urgeatur haec est, quod tributum ex concessione speretur." But tribute can be imposed only *iure victoriae*, by convention, or if the sea were in fact private property.

See also p. 104. And p. 48 for a distinction between *imperium* and *dominium*. "Imperium proprietatem rerum non continet."

lander undertook the same task on his own initiative. This was J. I. Pontanus, a professor of Philosophy and History in the college of Harderwyck in Guelderland, and Historiographer to the King of Denmark.[1] Denmark, as is well known, held pronounced views in regard to its rights over its territorial waters. Pontanus therefore found, as Grotius, Ambassador of the King of Sweden to the King of France, had found, that his official position required the exercise of caution in the statement of views contrary to those held by his sovereign.

This conflict of interest exercised a notable influence in shaping the Dutch doctrine of the freedom of the seas. It forced Pontanus (and Grotius, eventually) to make a sharp distinction between the high seas and *mare proximum*. It left them free to attack the Spanish and Portuguese claims; and it left them free to combat the doctrine of Selden that the whole ocean was capable of being expropriated, so far as its nature was concerned, provided only that a nation could gather enough force to debar other nations from it. On the other hand, it forced them to recognize the existence of territorial waters, and to grant a right of ownership in them.[2] It left open the question as to the extent of such waters, for neither Grotius nor Pontanus felt under an obligation to espouse the claims advanced by the respective sovereigns in whose service they were. Indeed, the suggestion of Grotius, vague as it was, involved a limitation of the claims of Sweden and the other maritime countries.

The argument of Pontanus, then, proceeds on the lines indicated by the above considerations.[3] He subjects Selden's work to a minute analysis. He counters Selden's appeals to history with appeals of his own; and he meets Selden's interpretation of the law with his own interpretation. He is quite clear that he believes that Selden is asserting an untenable theory, so far as the high seas are concerned. The latter's position is unsound, first, because it is based upon a false interpretation of history, and secondly, because it ascribes to the high seas a nature which properly char-

[1] Fulton, *op. cit.*, p. 376.

[2] In the case of Grotius, this is by implication only.

[3] *Discussiones Historicae.* Bound with Selden's *Mare Clausum* and other essays, Wratislaviae, 1751.

acterizes only coastal waters. It is a compound of bad history and of bad law. An analysis of the historical evidence fails to show either that British kings ever exercised the dominion over the seas which is ascribed to them, or that they have habitually made claims to the right to exercise such dominion. An analysis of the law makes it clear that the rights of property which a sovereign possesses in *mare adiacens* do not extend to *mare alterum*.[1] The conclusion is that the latter has always been, and remains, free to all men. *Mare adiacens* may be *mare clausum;* but *mare alterum* must be *mare liberum*.[2]

The theory of Pontanus may be illustrated by the following passage:[3]

> Mare autem, si ejus vastitatem videamus, esse numinis ac Dei omnipotentis ex psal. 115 constat. Nec mare tantum, sed et Terra, hoc pacto sumpta, numinis esse psalmistae eidem dicitur. . . . Sed occurrit Seldenus, dupliciter considerari dominium ostendens: Et primo quidem dominii genere nihil omnino nedum Mare, esse in hominum bonis; secundo omnia esse aut esse posse quae prehendi, occupari ac possideri queunt. Ubi probe dicitur, quae prehendi, occupari ac possideri queunt. At horum neutram, si dominium spectemus, vel in Terram, vel Mare, universaliter accepta, cadere posse jam ostensum; praesertim cum neque naturae, neque usus publici ratio occupationem permittat, occupationem dico, quae ab uno aliquo fiat. Nam de partibus singulis, deque maribus particularibus nemo negaverit, alicujus esse ea dominii posse.

When Selden says,

> Mare non minus ac Tellurem dominii privati capax esse, lubenter concedimus, si de mari singulari id capiatur, nequaquam si de universali.

The following passage should be added to the above:[4]

> Scimus enim qui imperium habet in terras et aquas, ejus lege edictisque posse impediri aliquos, ne feras, pisces, aves capere et capiendo acquirere ipsis liceat; ac ea teneri lege non indigenas tantum sed et exteros quoque. Ratio est, quia loci natura spatiumque admisit, ut id, quod fuerat jam ante commune, in proprium jus dominiumque cesserit, alias inquam commune omnibus ac liberum.

---

[1] This is an interesting reversal of the argument that the nature of the high seas is not different from that of littoral waters, saving only inlets, gulfs, and such small portions.

[2] An example of Pontanus's willingness to concede *dominium* in territorial waters is the following: Selden states that divine law approves the *dominium* of the seas; Pontanus replies, Yes, "eatenus id fieri, quatenus aliquid ejus esse capax potest." ii. c. 11, p. 164.

[3] *Ibid.*, p. 164.

[4] *Ibid.*, p. 174.

Like Grotius, Pontanus differentiated the *oceanum vastum* from *mare adiacens*. But unlike Grotius, he stated explicitly that he was in accord with Selden in the latter's doctrine of *dominium maris adiacentis*. Pontanus comes close to an accord with the milder English controversialists at this point. If the later suggestion of Grotius as to the limit to be imposed upon the extent of the territorial waters of a state be added to what has just been quoted from Pontanus, it will become apparent that Dutch theory, in the hands of these two men, makes the necessary concessions for arriving at an international settlement of the dispute.[1]

II. Mare Clausum

Thomas Digges, astronomer, mathematician, and engineer, died in 1595.[2] In 1568 or 1569 he wrote a treatise entitled, "Proofs of the Queen's Interest in Lands left by the Sea and the Salt Shores thereof." [3]

He opens his argument by quoting the familiar doctrine from the Institutes of Justinian:

> Littorum quoque usus publicus est quemadmodum et Riparum, et proprietas eorum potest intelligi nullius esse, sed eiusdem Juris, cuius est mare, et quae subiacent mari, Terra, vel Arena. Heereby yt plainly appeereth that no borderer or lord of the soyle adioyninge, may claime eny interest in the salt shore, as they may in the fressh, consyderinge that although in the use they are publyck and therein agree, yet as towchinge the propertye they are repugnannt, And therefore maye necessarily bee inferred that the Prince only hath proprietye in them. For yt is a sure Maxime in the Common Lawe that whatsoever lande there is within the kinges dominion whereunto no man cann iustly make propertye yt is the kinges by his prerogative. But the same may thus bee manifestly approoued.[4]

[1] The following passages may be noted: Pontanus, *op. cit.*, p. 182. "Nos, quae ejus fuere, excussimus superius Capite xiii. ac demonstravimus communionem constitui debere in iis praesertim quae venire in proprietatem nequeant, in ceteris et quae aliter se habent inque proprietatem deduci possunt aliter rem habere, nec eam a jurisconsultis etiam vetustionibus negari, ut est suo loco ibidem sed obiter memoratum."

Ibid., p. 184. "Etenim Mare id Liberum tantum intelligitur, quod in proprietatem occupantis venire nequit; sicuti clausum, quod jam occupantum claudi ac subjici dominio inque proprietatem venire potest."

[2] Moore, Stuart A., *History of the Foreshore*, 3d. ed. (London, 1888), p. 180.

[3] Lansdowne *MSS* No. 100, Art. 6, Brit. Mus. Reprinted in *History of the Foreshore*, p. 185 ff.

[4] *Loc. cit.*, p. 187.

The property rights of the Prince in his land are greater than the property rights of his subjects in their lands.[1] That his land should include the shore is in harmony with the dictates of the Common Law, as has been noted above; but further, it is unreasonable to admit the royal title to wrecks and to deny it to the shore.[2] Digges does not explain why this should be so.

Subjects of the Prince may own portions of the shore. But those who have a "just" possession must hold their title by letters patent from the Prince. If they have not a royal grant, then they "intrude." In such a case it is of no avail to urge title by prescription.[3]

Digges takes up the obvious objection that the

Seas by the Lawe Civill and also Jure naturali are common. True it is [he says][4] that Jure naturali the seaes are common so likewise is the earth and euerye other thinge whatsoever. . . . But the Civile Lawes and all suche as comment on them confesse that even as of olde time private men, eyther by first discouerie or antique possession, might purchase propertie in such particular tenements as theye possessed and by lawe of nature were common, even so maie kings absolute princes and comon weales do in the Seas adiacent to their Territories. And for example of Civilians is produced the Estate Venetian who have to them selues vendicate such absolute prerogative in the Adriaticke seas as it is not there lawfull for any to gather amber or other comoditie that those seas yelde, ne yet to make or sell salte of theire seas made but onlie set marcks to the use of the state. And in this estate regall of Englande wee see that the Kings of most auncient times haue in the right of theire crowne helde the seas abowte this Llande so proper and entire unto them [that all things cast up on the shore by the sea are theirs]. Nay it further appeareth that although the Kings of England haue benne content to suffer fishermen Jure gentium to enioy to theire owen use such fishe as by theire charges travill and adventure they can in the Englishe Seas take, Yet haue the Kings of England for remembrance of this theire favoure that the memorie of theire propertie in the Seas shoulde not be extinguished, alwaie res[er]ved to them selves the chief fishe as Sturgeon Whale, etc.[5]

Moore says that this argument is the

first conception of the *prima facie* theory.[6] [It first invents and sets up the claim of the Crown to the foreshore] in the right of prerogative.[7] [It is based on] the King's general ownership of the land of the whole kingdom.[7] [The shore is held to be] parcel of the waste of the kingdom and has never been *de facto* granted out, and that evidence of user and *longa possessio* avails not to give a title to it unless the grant be shewn.[7]

[1] Moore, *op. cit.*, p. 189. [2] *Ibid.* [3] *Ibid.*, p. 190. [4] *Ibid.*, p. 202.
[5] *Ibid.*, p. 203. [6] *Ibid.*, p. 180. [7] *Ibid.*, p. 182.

The shore thus takes its character from the land instead of from the sea. So far as Digges is concerned, this doctrine is laid down at the same time that the right of *dominium* in the sea is asserted. Neither doctrine, however, is essential to the existence of the other.

At about this time, Thomas Craig[1] wrote a non-controversial book on feudal law. He lays down the doctrine of the *dominium* of the seas. The sea is common to all for navigation;

proprietas tamen ejus ad eos pertinere hodie creditur, ad quos proximus continens. . . .[2]

Thus kings have divided all the seas, so to speak, among themselves, in the belief that the waters which wash their coasts should belong to them. If a delict is committed within the territorial waters of a king, the offender is tried in the courts of that king, as being within his jurisdiction. Certain seas may be acquired by prescription, as, for example, the Adriatic. In this case the Venetians have taken possession of the entire sea. Fisheries which are located in territorial waters are without doubt the property of the sovereign thereof.[3]

Piscationes vero quae in proximo mari fiunt, procul dubio eorum sunt qui proximum continentem possident. Itaque non sine summa injuria nostra Belgae circa nostras insulas piscantur. Nam licet piscationes in mari non prohibeantur, tamen hae praescribuntur, et traduntur permissae aut probitae secundum consuetudinem.

Craig is one of those jurists who, like Balbus, have no hesitation in applying the laws of prescription to the sea in a drastic manner. Like Balbus, too, he supplements prescription with custom. But, unlike Balbus, he holds the theory of *dominium maris*. The theory does not seem clear to him, for, instead of basing the right to prohibit foreigners from using a fishery which is located in territorial waters upon the fact of ownership, as an ordinary exercise of the

[1] He lived 1538–1608. Fulton, *op. cit.*, p. 357, note 2.

[2] *Jus Feudale*, 3d. ed. (Edinburgh, 1732), i, Dieg. 15, p. 140.13.

[3] *Loc. cit.* It will be recalled that Craig was a feudal lawyer. His argument furnishes an illustration of the statement made in a previous chapter to the effect that the doctrine of feudal law in regard to property, while it forced silence on the subject of the legal status of the sea, yet facilitated the rise of the doctrine of *dominium maris*.

right of ownership, he resorts to the use of prescription and custom, as if no such right of exclusion existed in the proprietary. He even goes so far as to admit that *piscationes in mari non prohibeantur*.

Craig is the first British lawyer to make the general statement that a sovereign is the proprietor of the fisheries found in his waters.[1] He is the first to complain of the pressure of Dutch competition in these fisheries. Whatever his views may be on *dominium maris*, he undoubtedly believes that his Government not only may, but ought to take measures to relieve the *summa injuria* of which he is conscious.

If the date of the outbreak of the controversy over *mare liberum* and *mare clausum* be taken as 1608, the year in which Grotius published his booklet, "Mare liberum," then the doctrine of *dominium maris* had been enunciated by two British lawyers before that time.

It had also received statement from the Continent before 1608, in the writings of Petrus Gregorius, who died in 1597.[2] He points out that the sea has been divided between various *imperia*. He is referring, it is to be supposed, to littoral waters, and not to the high seas. But he also says that jurisdiction over the open sea belongs to certain rulers. He holds, further, that there are certain

[1] But see Fulton, *op. cit.*, p. 357, note 2, who (justly) gives the laurels to Welwood for being the first "who clearly enunciated, and insisted on" this principle.

Craig's text is as follows:

P. 140.13. "Ita ut Reges inter se quasi maria omnia diviserint, et quasi ex mutua partitione alterius id mare censeatur, quod alteri proprinquinus et commodius est: in quo si delictum aliquod commissum fuerit, ejus sit jurisdictio qui proximum continentem possideat, isque suum illud mare vocat. Non negabo tamen quaedam maria praescribi posse, ut totum illud mare Adriaticum, licet terras distinctas aliorum ex utraque parte habeat, tamen praescriptione Veneti sibi totum illud vendicarunt." P. 141.15: "Et haec de mari, piscationibus maris, insulis in mari natis, et maris portubus: in quibus hoc servandum, quod licet maria indubie sint publica, neque quis privatus servitutem eis possit imponere, tamen piscationes et insulas ad eos qui proximum continentem possident pertinere. . . . Itaque . . . in feudum dari possunt."

He is not quite sure what rights a king has in *suo mari*. But he is sure that the king owns the fisheries therein.

[2] Pierre Gregorie, French savant and professor of law. The date given in the text is that of the *Biographie Universelle*. Hommel, p. 335, gives 1595.

natural boundaries to the sea, which are distinct from the one general boundary — presumably the shores of the sea considered as a whole. The increase of navigation has forced the introduction of laws of navigation. These laws cannot very well be drawn up by any one except him who rules *mare proximum*; nor ought they to be introduced by any one else. Some say that the sea cannot be comprehended within any territory or dominion, and that it cannot be divided under the *ius gentium*. But this doctrine to the contrary notwithstanding, those parts of the sea which are nearest to a state are judged to belong to that state. The king of course possesses the *ius piscandi*, and the right to levy *vectigalia*.[1]

The first British lawyer to reply to Grotius is William Welwood.[2] In 1590 Welwood published a treatise on the Sea Laws of Scotland, "which is believed to be the earliest regular work on maritime jurisprudence printed in Britain."[3] In 1613 he enlarged it and added a chapter (Title XXVII), "Of the Community and Property of the Seas." This chapter is Welwood's reply to "Mare liberum."

Title XXVI is entitled, "Of Fishers, fishing, and traffiquers therewith." In it the following passage occurs:[4]

[1] *Syntagma Iuris Universi*, 2 vols. (Lugduni, 1587), i, p. 3.5: "Et hoc ipsum mare etiam considerant Iurisconsulti, tum late diffusum, tum etiam littora eius. Siquidem et divisum mare per varia imperia: atque iurisdictio in pelago, non omnibus, sed certis, competit. Sunt enim et mari certi fines natura per Deum constituti, et tamen terminus unus generalis. . . . Et quia navigandi usus frequens fuit, simul et navigii iura introduci oportuit, quae nec constitui debuerunt, vel potuerunt facilius, quam ab iis, qui in proximis mari locis imperant. . . ." Some say that "licet mare non sit in alicuius territorio vel dominio, eo quod iure gentium divisum non sit, sed omnibus pateat, tamen maris partes, eius civitatis censeantur, quae proxima est. . . ."

He calls to mind the "in Gallia praefectum maris constitutum, quem corrupta voce dicunt Admiralium, . . . cuius iurisdictioni et imperio, post principem, omnes, qui maritimas incolunt oras circa Gallias, obtemperant. . . ."

III, cap. 14.7, p. 82.7. "Ideo ius piscandi omnibus iure gentium commune, quod pertinet ad iurisdictione, et regis sunt, vel illius domini, in cuius territorio sunt, et ideo vectigalia quoque eius ad eum pertinet."

His writings are not without ambiguities, and apparent contradictions. See, p. 4.1. The above is, however, his own view.

[2] 1578–1622. He was for a time a professor in St. Andrews University, occupying successively the chairs of mathematics and law.

[3] Fulton, *op. cit.*, p. 352.

[4] In *An Abridgement of all the Sea Lawes* (London, 1636), p. 188.9. Fulton, *op. cit.*,

Yea, now a-daies, in rivers, and in parts of the Seas neerest to the possessions of men having grant and infestment from the King, may fishing be forbidden, but no private man, without the grant of the Prince, upon any pretence, or allegation of long consuetude and prescription, may acquire the propriety of any such part of the sea, as to prohibite others to fish there also; for such prescriptions onely pertain to Princes.

This was Welwood's position in 1590, eighteen years before the appearance of "Mare liberum."

He felt in regard to "Mare liberum" that the unknown author was attacking the right of the British to own and to control the use of their fisheries, under the guise of defending the right of free navigation to the East Indies.[1] The deception seemed obvious to him, because he felt that freedom of navigation on the high seas had not been impugned. Freedom of navigation is "a thing farre off from all controversie, at least upon the Ocean."[2] The conclusion seemed forced, that the argument of the author must really be directed "against our undoubted right and propriety of fishing on this side of the Seas."[3] To defend this "right and propriety" Welwood replied to "Mare liberum," and thus began the great controversy.

Welwood notes the writer's sources — "some old Poets, Orators, Philosophers, and (wrested) Jurisconsults."[4] He makes short work of them all, at one blow, by opposing to them, in the manner of his time, certain appropriate texts from the Old Testament.[5]

He returns, however, to the jurists. Taking Ulpian and "Martian" as representative of the best class of the Roman lawyers, he attempts to prove that they wrote at the direction, or under the the orders of the Emperor himself, and so that they merely expressed his will. He draws the conclusion that the Emperor pos-

p. 357, note 2, writes that "he was the first author who clearly enunciated, and insisted on, the principle that the inhabitants of a country had a primary and exclusive right to the fisheries along their coasts . . . and that one of the main reasons why that portion of the sea should pertain to the neighboring state was the risk of the exhaustion of its fisheries from promiscuous use." But Craig preceded him in stating the principle.

1 *An Abridgement of all the Sea Lawes*, pp. 199–201.

2 *Ibid.*, pp. 201–202.

3 *Ibid.*, p. 202.

4 *Ibid.*, p. 203.

5 *Ibid.*, pp. 203–208.

sessed the power to dispose of the sea and to control the use of it — in a word, that the sea belonged to him. The rescript of the Emperor to the Formian fisherman is decisive proof of the correctness of his reasoning.

So that you see the Emperours to have been warrants to these Lawyers, and their written opinions, concerning the voyage of the sea.[1]

That the Emperors claimed the "propriety" of the sea is evident, because (1) they wrote to their own subjects, (2) on the usage of the seas and the coasts of the Empire, (3) directing that they should be common to their own subjects under the *ius gentium*, which is the law kept by all nations.[2]

The word, "common," is restricted to include only the subjects of the monarch in question.

For *commune*, there is nothing else but *publicum*, *quasi populicum;* signifying a thing common for the usage of any of one sort of people, and not for all of all nations.[3]

After a close inspection of the chief points which "Mare liberum" is designed to defend, he feels that he can embrace the position of the unknown author. He is glad to accept *mare liberum*. There is no antagonism between them on this point.[4] He will rejoice if the unknown writer will accept *his* position on the adjacent sea. Indeed, there is no serious antagonism between them on this question, either. As for himself, so far as the question of limiting the use of the littoral sea is concerned, he feels it proper to restrict the use of these waters in order to preserve the fish, the supply of which has been diminishing, to the grave danger of the country. And on this point, also, he observes with pleasure that the unknown is not unwilling to concede, not only the necessity, but the lawfulness, of measures designed to preserve the supply. Fundamentally, therefore, their positions are not irreconcilable. Finally, he is appreciative of the gracious tone in which the whole argument has been couched.[5]

[1] *An Abridgement of all the Sea Lawes*, p. 212.
[2] *Ibid.*, p. 213.
[3] *Ibid.*, p. 215.
[4] *Ibid.*, p. 228.
[5] It is probable that Welwood was only in part ironic.

Welwood returned to the subject two years later.[1] His new work is an amplification of the chapter in the "Abridgement." It is written in Latin, and seems to have been well known on the Continent. The sea, as well as the land, he holds, is capable of distinction and dominion according to both human and divine law. The publicists, poets, and orators affected by Grotius were ignorant of the true law of nature. They infected later generations "with a preposterous notion concerning some universal community of things."

It is as necessary that there should be jurisdiction over coastal waters as it is over the neighboring territory. This jurisdiction should be exercised by the neighboring Prince, so that both the land and the sea may be under a common jurisdiction.

The relation of the land to the adjacent sea is so intimate that the ruler of the land may not alienate any part of the sea, or any use of it, just as he may not alienate any part of his kingdom, or a use of it.

In the adjacent sea, the Prince has the right of navigation and the right of fishing. He may lay charges on the use of either by individuals.

Fishing in the sea is for the most part appropriated. So far as Britain is concerned, the reason for this is that God appointed the fishes to swarm along the British coasts at certain seasons. It is a benefit God has granted to the British people. Why should they be hindered from possessing it? Other nations may share in this advantage, "but only by the same law by which they possess their own, that is by a just price." As matters stand, the British are being robbed of their rights.[1]

Gerard Malynes, a contemporary [2] of Welwood, held the same views as the latter in regard to the "sovereignty" of the adjacent sea; he also makes the same distinction between the high seas and territorial waters.[3]

He arrives at his position through a consideration of the origin

[1] Quoted by Fulton, *op. cit.*, pp. 354–355. *De Dominio Maris*, etc., Cosmopoli, 1615.

[2] *Consuetudo: vel, Lex Mercatoria*, London, 1656. Malynes's dates are 1586–1641 He was a merchant and writer on economics.

[3] *Ibid.*, p. 130.

of private property. He repudiates the theory that in the beginning goods were held in common. That this theory is not in accord with the facts is proved by the Old Testament.[1]

Trading on the sea arose because the land had become overpopulated,

> which could not have been done if all things had been in common. [The sea thereupon became divisible]: but not in the maine great Seas, which is common to all Nations (Iure Gentium). . . .

The result of this situation is found to be that the traffic of the nations in commodities raised on land, and navigation in the seas adjoining, together with the

> properties of both Land and Seas are distinguished by the said Law of Nations. . . .

The different seas take their names from the countries adjacent, or from their location, as "Mare Britannicum, Mare Germanicum, Mare Hibernicum . . . Mare Mediterraneum."[2] Without going into a discussion of the subject, he cites Bartolus on the hundred-mile limit.[3]

He thinks that "this distinction of dominions" has continued for "so many hundred years," that it may be considered well settled.[4]

In applying the conclusions of the above reasoning to England, he looks to history for the proofs of rights of property in the seas around the British Isles, and for examples of acts which illustrate the exercise of these rights. He uses in a superficial way the method which Borough was to develop and Selden to perfect.

Both Welwood and Malynes wrote books on maritime law. Both championed the claims of their sovereign to ownership of the surrounding waters. Of the two, Welwood is perhaps the more important.

Serjeant Robert Callis delivered his well-known lecture on the Statute of Sewers in 1622 in Grey's Inn.[5] He supports Thomas

[1] *Consuetudo: vel, Lex Mercatoria*, p.132. [2] *Ibid.*, p. 133. [3] *Ibid.*

[4] *Ibid.*, pp. 133–134, p. 120; "Regall Fishes" pertain to the Admiral.

[5] This information appears upon the title page of his book. The citation is: *Robert Callis, The Reading of, upon the Statute of Sewers*, 23 Hen. VIII, c. 5, 4th ed., by W. J. Broderip, London, 1824. See pp. 45–47, for the argument produced above.

Digges, holding that the seas around the British Isles, together with the shores, belong to the King of England. The former part of his argument only is of importance to the present subject:

> First, touching our Mare Anglicum. . . . I hope to make it manifest by many proofs and precedents of great worth and esteem, that the King hath therein these powers and properties, videlicet,
>
> 1. Imperium Regale.
> 2. Potestatem legalem.
> 3. Proprietatem tam soli quam aquae.
> 4. Possessionem et profituum tam reale quam personale.
>
> And all these by the common laws of England.[1]

His proof consists for the most part in the citation of statutes which assert or seem to assert the points in question. The jurisdiction of the admiralty over the sea is held to be a proof in point.

His reasoning is faulty in two respects. It may be admitted without hesitation that "the common laws of England" give to the King of England certain powers over his subject on the sea. It may be admitted that the King exercises maritime jurisdiction to an unspecified distance from the shore, so that, if the subject ventures forth into the *proximum mare*, he finds himself, having committed an offense, punishable by English law. The fault in Callis's reasoning lies in confusing jurisdiction with sovereignty. He reasons that because the King exercises jurisdiction over the sea, he is sovereign over the sea. The second fault follows from the first. Having concluded that the King is sovereign over the sea, he further concludes that the King owns the sea, basing (implicitly) his second conclusion on his first. If this criticism is correct, it explains his contentment with the mere citation of statutes. It explains also the critical deduction that these statutes are binding upon the foreign fishermen. For Callis is in reality assuming what must be proved. It is one thing for, say, a Dutch trawler to be subject to British admiralty jurisdiction because he is within what the States-General have agreed to recognize as British territorial waters; it is quite a different thing for him to be subject to such jurisdiction because the King in Parliament has decided that he is within British territorial waters.

The two faults which thus seem to lie behind Callis's argument — that is to say, a confusion of jurisdiction with sovereignty, and

[1] See note on p. 178, *supra*.

the assumption that sovereignty is derived from, or depends upon, ownership of the thing over which sovereign powers are exercised — is characteristic of the British school of *mare clausum.*

The Continental civilians on the whole escaped them. The *mare liberum* school consistently preached *jurisdictio et protectio* without *proprietas*, even when they admitted the existence of *mare adiacens*. Both Graswinckel and Stypmann expressly differentiate between *imperium* and *dominium*. The latter, who advocates *mare clausum*, restricts it (of course) to coastal waters — that is, he admits *dominium* over territorial waters. Pontanus grants the rights of *dominium* over territorial waters and denies them over *mare alterum*. Grotius separates sovereignty from ownership. This position presents an emphatic contrast to that of Selden, who denied the existence of a difference in kind between territorial waters and the high seas. It contrasts also with the position of such a writer as Welwood, who admitted the freedom of the high seas, for he based his argument for territorial waters on British law and precedent. The Continentals do not appeal to the practice of any one nation; on the contrary, it is just that practice which gives them trouble, as, for example, the claims of the Venetians to the Adriatic. They appeal to the *ius naturale*, to the *ius gentium*, and to the Roman law.[1]

The effect of the injection of the concept expressed by *dominium* into that expressed by *imperium* on the development of the theory of the adjacent sea into one of territorial waters is to be observed with distinctness in a passage of Lord Coke's in the "First Institute," together with the note of the commentator upon it. Lord Coke writes:[2]

> *Infra quatuor maria*, means, within the kingdom of England, and the dominions of the same kingdom.
>
> Out of the realm, *extra regnum*, is as much as to say, out of the power of the King of England, as of his crown of England: for if a man be upon

[1] The civilians who do not conform to this characterization are to be found among those who advocate *mare clausum*, or, what amounts to the same thing, the *proprietas* in *mare adiacens*. Of these Loccenius (who will be considered below) furnishes a notable example. His argument is based on an interchangeable use of *imperium* and *dominium*.

[2] J. H. Thomas, *Systematic Arrangement of Lord Coke's First Institute of the Laws of England*, 3 vols. (Philadelphia, 1836), i, 35. Lord Coke lived, 1552–1634.

the sea of England, he is within the kingdom or realm of England, and within the ligeance of the king of England, as of his crown of England. And yet *altum mare* is out of the jurisdiction of the common law, and within the jurisdiction of the lord admiral, whose jurisdiction is very ancient and long before the reign of Edward III. . . .

The commentator writes that "The sea-dominion of our King," and its incidental rights, come within the law of nations; especially the right of salutation by striking the flag and lowering the topsail to British warships:

a ceremony, which, however it may be construed by foreigners as a mere compliment, is considered by ourselves as a recognition of sovereignty.

This comment marks the complete development of the theory of the adjacent sea into that of territorial waters.

Lord Coke expands his thought in the "Fourth Institute." His observations are given in full:[1]

It is called the sea, which is not within any County from whence a jury may come.

It is no part of the Sea, where one may see what is done of the one part of the water, and of the other, as to see from one land to the other. . . .

The land between the flowing and reflowing of the sea (belongs) to the Lord of the Mannor adjoyning. . . .

Every water, which flows and reflows, is an arme of the sea, yet it followeth not that the Admiral shall have jurisdiction there, unless it be out of every County, or else such a place whereof the County cannot take knowledge. . . .

Now for the great prerogative and interest that the King of England hath in the seas of England, and for the antiquity of the Court of the Admiralty of England, and of the name of the Admiral,

he produces documents, records, and the like, leaving the reader to draw his own conclusions — of which, of course, in view of the evidence, there can be no doubt.

One such document, which is typical of the kind on which much reliance is placed by the lawyers following Callis and Coke, asserts possession of the sea by the kings of England "long before the reign of E. 3. in whose dayes some have dreamed it began." Lord Coke found it in the Tower. It contains an account of a "cause" which "was handled in or about the 22 year of E. 1. as

[1] Edw. Coke, *The Fourth Part of the Institutes of the Lawes of England*, 4th ed. (London, 1669), pp. 140–142.

by divers parts of the Record it appeareth." The important words are,

que come les roys d'Engliterre per raison du dit Royalme du temps dont il ny ad memoire du contrarie eussent este en paiceable possession de la soveraigne Seignurie de la mer d'Engliterre et des Isles isteants. . . .[1]

In 1633 Sir John Boroughs[2] wrote his booklet, "The Sovereignty of the British Seas."[3]

It was meant for the use of Charles I, and his Ministers; but the fact that it was printed in Latin suggests that it was intended also to serve in foreign countries as a vindication of England's claim.[4]

Sir John's book presents a historical, rather than a legal argument. It is based upon the records to which he had access by virtue of his office. His position may be gauged accurately from his opening:[5]

That Princes may have an exclusive property in the Soveraigntie of the severall parts of the Sea, and in the passage fishing and shores thereof, is so evidently true by way of fact, as no man that is not desperately impudent can deny it.

Aside from the facts of the case, laws for the sea are necessary. This necessity is taught by

the notorious practise of all Maritime Countries, the necessity of Order in mutuall commerce, and the safety of men's persons, goods and lives.[5]

Princes are not going to relinquish their immemorial rights merely because of arguments opposing them. They will continue to cling to them until final judgment is brought against them. He intimates his opinion that there is no immediate likelihood of such a judgment being given.

And for his sacred Majesty our dread Soveraigne Lord the King, such is his cleare and indubitable right to the Superiority of the Seas of England,

[1] See note 1 on the preceding page.

[2] *The Dictionary of National Biography* (ii, New York, 1908) states that 'Boroughs' is incorrect. He was Keeper of the Records in the Tower of London at this time. He died in 1643.

[3] Boroughs, Sir John, *The Sovereignty of the British Seas, Written in the year 1633*, ed. by Thomas Callander Wade, Edinburgh, 1920.

[4] *Op. cit.*, p. v. The editor shows that Selden refers to all the references (with a few unimportant exceptions) given in it.

[5] *Ibid.*, p. 43.

derived and confirmed upon him by immemorable prescription, and continued in possession even until this very yeare 1633, that the hearts and consciences of all just men must necessarily subscribe to the evident truth thereof.[1]

After this beginning, he starts with Julius Caesar and works up his precedents down to his own time. This book is perhaps the first attempt to present systematically the historical argument for the British claims.[2]

Borough points out that the royal title does not depend for its validity upon title to the opposite shore of the channel. That this is true is shown by the fact that in the time of Edward I, sovereignty of the sea belonged to the English kings, although Normandy was not then annexed to the kingdom. Title rests upon the fact of "our Kings being superiour Lords of the said Sea . . . by reason of the sayd Kingdomes."[3] In other words, the sea is annexed to England; it goes with the country; it is "appendant" to it.

An essay on "The inestimable Riches and Commodities of the British Seas" follows this treatise. His exposition of these resources is followed by the conclusion,

seeing by that which hath formerly bin declared it evidently appeareth that the Kings of England, by immemorable prescription, continuall usage and possession, the acknowledgement of all our neighbor states, and the municipall lawes of the Kingedome, have ever held the Soveraigne Lordship of the Seas of England,

and that the king has jurisdiction in the seas over the fishing, and, finally, observing the strategic value of the seas from the point of view of commerce and navigation (in particular, the British Channel), the King might easily be made "the greatest Monarch for Command and Wealth," and his people, the most prosperous, in Christendom. Thus "the Soveraignty of our Seas" is "the most precious Jewell of his Majesties Crowne."[4]

Digges, Callis, and Coke presented arguments based primarily upon the common law and upon the statutes of the realm. Welwood and Malynes treated of maritime law. Sir John Borough built his argument on massed historical facts. It remained only

[1] Borough, *op. cit.*, p. 45.
[2] Fulton, *op. cit.*, p. 365.
[3] Borough, *op. cit.*, p. 61.
[4] *Ibid.*, p. 114.

for John Selden to gather these elements into a whole, and to fuse them by his brilliant work into a final statement of the British argument. After Borough, all the elements of the British argument are present. There is still wanting a brain capable of developing fully the resources which have thus gradually been accumulated. The original thinkers have done their work. The need for them has passed. What is needed now is one who can and will master with pains-taking care the enormous mass of material which is waiting, and who can, also, arrange and interpret these details so as to make them tell *his* story. This is the want which John Selden satisfied, and the work which he did.

Selden was quick to see the bearing of the argument of Grotius on the English claims. Marchamont Nedham tells the story of the inception of "Mare clausum" in the preface of his translation of Selden's work.[1] It was begun at the command of James I, and then, for some reason, laid aside. More than sixteen years afterwards "at the command of the late Tyrant" (Charles was not loved by Nedham) Selden returned to his manuscripts and completed his task,[2] dedicating the new work of his sovereign. This dedication is omitted by Nedham, who merely notes that it was dedicated to him.[2] Selden says in his own foreword that he has so thoroughly revised and enlarged the original treatise that it has become an entirely new production.[3]

The two propositions which he intends to prove are thus announced in his *Praefatio:*[4]

altera, Mare ex Iure Naturae seu Gentium omnium hominum non esse commune, sed Dominii Privati seu Proprietatis capax aeque ac Tellurem; altera, Serenissimum Magnae Britanniae Regem Maris circumflui, ut individuae ac perpetuae Imperii Britannici appendicis, Dominium esse.

He will, he says, treat his subject first as a matter of law, and secondly, as a matter of fact, giving one book to each division.[5]

At the end of the first book he finds that he has proved his

[1] *Of the Dominion . . . of the Sea,* Two Books, . . . by John Selden, transl. by Marchamont Nedham, London, 1652.

[2] *The Epistle Dedicatorie,* (a).

[3] *Mare Clausum, seu Dominio Maris, Libri Duo* (Londini, 1635), the epistle dedicatory, pp. 2–3.

[4] *Ibid.*, p. 3. The pages are not numbered.

[5] *Ibid.*, p. 1 and 2.

thesis. In the second book he finds that the facts of British history prove the soundness of his claims, for they prove that England has always held the sovereignty of the seas around the British Isles.

Selden begins his first book with a survey of the ancient writings and gives a fair statement of the usual grounds for asserting the doctrine of the freedom of the seas. Among modern jurists, in contrast to the ancients, there are, he finds, only two of prominence who champion this position.[1] The implication is, of course, that modern thought is in accord with his position.

In order to show that the law countenances the private appropriation of the sea, and before proceeding to the direct argument, Selden presents what he is pleased to call a "plain scheme of the law."[2] His intention is to fit that part of the law which permits *dominium* or ownership of the sea into this outline. His scheme turns out to be a composite structure of several kinds of law, both foreign and domestic, instead of an outline or diagram of an articulated legal system.

There are two general divisions of the law: (1) Obligatory, and (2) Permissive. The Obligatory Law is "known by such things as are commanded or forbidden."[3] It is called Preceptive. The Permissive Law is concerned with "things whose use is neither commanded nor forbidden."[3] It is called Concessive. "Both of these kinds of law concern either Mankinde in general, or not at all."[3] By the phrase, "Mankinde in general," Selden means all nations.

I. 1. Obligatory Law. Additions or enlargements permitted.

A. Natural Law.

Manifested by the light of nature or the use of right reason.[3]

B. Divine Law.

To be found in "Divine Oracles which have been committed to writing."[4]

[1] Ioannis Seldeni, *Mare Clausum, seu Dominio Maris, Libri Duo* (Londini, 1635), pp. 8–9.

[2] *Ibid.*, p. 16.

[3] *Ibid.*, p. 8. Nedham's transl., p. 12.

[4] *Ibid.*, p. 8. Nedham's transl., p. 13. This outline is constructed from his discussion of the system, which may be found in Chapter III of his work.

2. *Permissive Law.* "Various"; changeable; admits alterations.

No subdivisions or classes. It would appear to be capable of division into human and divine law.

II. Positive Law. Called also Civil Law.

It arises out of the additions made to the Obligatory Law and the alterations made in the Permissive Law. It "relates, not to all Nations or the Universality of mankinde, but only to some particulars thereof." [1]

A. Law which "is singular and peculiar to any one particular Nation." [1] This is pure Civil Law.

B. Law which "is received by divers Nations." [2]

1. The "common law of divers Nations." [2]

This law binds the nations "jointly, equally, and indifferently."

a. Law which "is *Imperative* [3] over divers Nations"; received, but not made, by them.

This law is that which "is observed or receiv's Autoritie among several Nations . . . who are subject to supreme Powers that otherwise are distinct, and this by reason of an Obligation equally common to them all, but derived from som (*sic*) other, and enjoined by som special Command, either from God or man." [4]

b. The "*Intervenient* [3] Law of Nations." [5]

This law originates "through the intervention either of som Compact, or Custom." It is "commonly styled the Secondarie Law of Nations." [5] Herein are the laws of war, of diplomacy, and the like rules.

2. The law which binds nations "singly and by accident." [6]

This law is the opposite of the common law of the nations. It binds them unequally, not jointly, not indifferently. It may be called the "Law of som or divers Nations, Civil or Domestick." [6]

There is also a *ius Caesareum*, which usually has a place in controversies over the chief points of Intervenient Law. Selden seems to have some doubts as to how to classify it; he solves the difficulty by putting it in two classes at once: in the class of "Intervenient Law for som Nations," and in the "Civil or Domes-

[1] *Mare clausum*, Nedham's transl., p. 13.
[2] *Ibid.*, p. 14.
[3] Italics the writer's.
[4] *Ibid.*, pp. 14–15.
[5] *Ibid.*, p. 15.
[6] *Ibid.*, p. 14.

tick" law "of divers Nations." The latter class seems to be identical with II.2. above, but it is not surely so. The former class may or may not be that of II.1.b. above.[1]

All laws which originate from additions to the universal obligatory law of the *ius gentium* and from the alterations (*mutationibus*) of the universal permissive law are either Imperative or Intervenient. All other laws retain the name of universal and primeval *ius gentium*.[2]

The origin of private property is to be found in some form of social compact. There was a time when no one possessed exclusive ownership of anything. Gradually, however, a certain amount of private property accrued to individuals while yet there was community of ownership. This anomalous state of affairs seems to have prepared the way for a great and universal act of distribution. This act was accomplished by the taking possession of what was unoccupied.[3] It was carried out in two different ways. According to one method, by expressed or tacit consent men agreed to own what they had at the moment of forming the compact. The arrangements then made became binding on future generations. According to the other method, the land, and things which were left vacant or unoccupied, became the property of him who seized them by occupation.[4] The act of distribution was also accomplished in another way, that is, by assignment. Those who had vast property rights — they seem cannily to have acquired them by a sort of process of infiltration before the universal act of distribution — these aided in establishing the new régime by acts of assignments or by specific grants in sporadic cases.[5] Thus by distribution and assignment was private property instituted with the appropriate rights thereof.

The question comes, What was done with the sea? At first, the sea seems to have figured only as a border or boundary line to the land.[6] It therefore could not have been distributed. The

[1] *Mare clausum*, Nedham's transl., p. 16. In the Latin text, p. 10. Both the texts are ambiguous, or else Selden was muddled.

[2] *Ibid.*, Latin text, p. 10. Nedham's transl., p. 15.

[3] *Ibid.*, English text, p. 19.

[4] *Ibid.*, p. 21.

[5] *Ibid.*, p. 20.

[6] *Ibid.*, p. 25.

question then is, Could a title to the sea be acquired by occupation? Or, in different phraseology, Is the sea susceptible of private ownership just as and in the same way that the land is? It is to the answers to these questions that Selden now addresses himself.

Selden begins with divine law. An analysis of the Old Testament leads him to the conclusion that [1]

> neither the Divine Law which is universal; nor the Positive, as it appears, in Scripture, to bee Imperative or to have a command over som certain Nations . . . doth oppose a private Dominion of the Sea; but that both of them do sufficiently allow it, and afford also very clear examples of such a Dominion, (if wee may believ the Jews themselves.)

The law natural is a part of the primitive or primeval law of nations; it is usually derived from a right use of reason. The results which have come from a right use of reason, in the effort to apprehend the law natural, can be discovered in the records of the acts and customs of the most enlightened nations — that is as much as to say, in a study of international practice. Such a study will reveal the fact that this law [2]

> doth in no wise gainsay a private Dominion of the Sea, but plainly permit it . . . becaus by the positive law of Nations of every kind, which is humane, . . . to wit, as well by the Law Civil or Domestick of divers Nations, whether it be Intervenient or Imperative; that is to say, by the customs of almost all and the more noble Nations that are known to us, such a Dominion of the Sea is everywhere admitted.

The demonstration of the truth of this assertion then follows. Time may be divided into two ages, the fabulous and the historical. While arguments cannot be grounded upon fables, nevertheless fables may clothe historic truth, and on that account must have due consideration. The fable, for example, which narrates the division of Heaven, Hell, and the Sea among Jupiter, Pluto and Neptune is such a one. The ancients assert that these characters were not gods, but men. Here, then, is most likely pre-

[1] From this point the citations in English are from *Mare Clausum; The right and Dominion of the Sea*, in two Books, Written at first in Latin by . . . John Selden, Esquire. Formerly translated into English, and now perfected and restored, by J. H., Gent. (London), 1663, p. 41.

[2] *Op. cit.*, p. 42.

served an authentic narrative of how Neptune, that is, a man, was made lord of the sea. From this fable it appears that private dominion of the sea, no less than that of the land, arose from a human act of distribution.[1]

In more recent times, there is the commission of Pompey to clear the sea of pirates. While it is true that he held his commission from the Roman people, nevertheless the Roman people were lords of the sea, just as they were of their territory.[2]

The practice of Roman sovereignty over the sea receives further study in the analysis of the historical age which is to follow. At this stage of the argument, Pompey is uncompromisingly put in the fabulous age, although toward the close of it. Pompey and Neptune, the one at the end, the other at the beginning, of this age, give the leading precedents for modern practice.

King Minos of Crete was the first ruler of the historical age to exercise and to possess dominion over the sea.[3] After him, no less than seventeen oriental nations, one after another, were lords of the sea, the combined years of their supremacy amounting to more than five hundred and sixty. It should be clear that this practice — and it was unbroken — constitutes an assumption of private dominion over the sea for a length of time amply sufficient to ground it firmly in the intervenient law of nations.

The western nations have followed the same custom. The Carthaginians, who dominated the sea for the forty years preceding the first Punic War,[4] are an illustrious example of the western nation which possessed dominion in the sea.

> In the second League or Treatie of Peace . . . it was farther provided; that no Romane should touch either upon Africa or Sardinia, unless it were to take on Provision or repair their Ships . . . so that the use of the Sea was taken away, or restrained.[5]

There is also the evidence of Caesar on the Veneti:[4]

> et in magno impetu maris atque aperto, paucis portibus interiectis, quos tenent ipsi, omnes fere, qui eo mari uti consuerunt, habent vectigales.

---

[1] *Mare clausum*, J. H.'s transl., p. 48. [2] *Ibid.*, p. 51.
[3] *Ibid.*, p. 53, *et seq.* The remaining seventeen states are each cited in turn.
[4] *Ibid.*, p. 75. [5] *Ibid.*, p. 76.

Of this, Selden observes,[1]

ob usum vicini Maris, vectigalia pendebantur illis, ut dominis.

It is not a refutation of this kind of evidence to assert, as Grotius does,[2] that nations may, by agreement, surrender a right in favor of some other nation, and that, therefore, the use of this right by that other nation does not prove possession of it except in so far as it appears in the terms of the surrender. The same thing might be said of dominion or vassalage of every kind. It cannot be admitted of examples of the kind just given that they do not prove a possession of the sea or of a right of navigation. The distinction which Grotius would make is not sound. The crux of the argument is this: [3]

If to occupie and enjoy in a private manner, by Right to hinder, and forbid others, bee not Dominion, it is nothing.

Dominion in the sea, and even private ownership of the sea, is sanctioned by Roman Law, in spite of those texts on the community of the sea which have been so often brought forward by the opponents of the view here maintained. The sea is described as a *res publica*, because it has been owned by the *populus Romanus*. There are abundant instances of the ownership of enclosed parts of the sea by private persons. Wealthy citizens enclosed portions of the sea to form fish preserves; or they caused the sea to flow into their estates and to form ponds there. Over these portions of the sea they exercised the rights of private property.[4] Besides these evidences of custom, there is the saying of Paulus which begins,

Sane si maris proprium ius ad aliquem pertineat.[5] Nothing could have been more plainly spoken, to show, that, beyond all controversie, he admits a private Dominion in the Sea, even of single persons.[6]

Ulpian himself makes what is practically the same admission in the fragment beginning,

si quem tamen ante aedes meas vel ante praetorium meum piscari prohibeam. . . .[7]

---

[1] *Mare clausum*, J. H.'s transl., p. 54, Latin text; Caesar, *lib.*, 3 *cap.* 8.

[2] In *De Iure Belli ac Pacis*, *lib.*, 2 *cap.*, 3 sec. 15.

[3] J. H.'s transl., p. 79.

[4] *Ibid.*, p. 87.

[5] D. 47.10.14.

[6] J. H.'s transl., pp. 94, 96.

[7] D. 47.10.13.7. Ulpian's doctrine of the freedom of the sea, Selden calls "a stale

Passing from this study of the historical age to an examination of the present day, one finds the Venetians exercising a thoroughgoing dominion of the sea, for it is unlawful for any other nation to use it without their permission. Almost all the important maritime states claim some form of ownership or dominion in the sea. Though it must be said that the claims of France are a vain affirmation, yet they have the merit of showing that the French believe the sea to be susceptible of appropriation.[1]

In conclusion, certain of the more weighty objections are answered. These objections are of three sorts: those based on an alleged common right to freedom of travel, commerce, and navigation; those based on the nature of the sea; and those derived from the writings of jurists.

Arguments in the first class described are based on the thesis that hospitality to strangers is required, and that, therefore, the right of peaceful passage should not be denied them. But this objection, this argument, does not concern the dominion of the thing through or over which they pass. Certainly it does not derogate from it. Arguments against denying the common use of the sea "give over the disquisition of Law and Right, to insist upon that of Charitie." [2] All aliens may be barred from entrance to or passage through his property, by the lord thereof, unless some specially granted right, or some custom intervenes, which would be violated by such an act.

The arguments based on the nature of the sea emphasize, first, that it is always in motion, and therefore is not adapted to private ownership; secondly, that those boundaries cannot be marked on it without which there can hardly be private ownership; and thirdly, because by reason of its vast extent, it is sufficient for the needs of all men.

The argument based on the mobility of the sea is disposed of by the fact that rivers and fountains, which are much more in

opinion," and adds that it was "utterly cashiered" — Emperor Leo in his Novel 56 having administered the *coup de grâce*. Grotius says, in referring to Leo, "whose laws we do not use" (*Mare liberum*, p. 33) that his enactments (he cites Novels 102, 103, 104) were "contrary to the intent of the law." (*ib.*) For the Novels, see D. Gothofredus, *Corpus Iuris Civilis*, in 2 vols. (Amstelodami, 1663), vol. ii.

[1] J. H.'s transl., p. 114.

[2] *Ibid.*, p. 124.

motion than is the sea, are owned, both by princes and by private persons. Why, then, should not the sea also become the object of private property? Fluidity can no more hinder dominion in the one than it can in the other.

As to boundaries, nothing can be more desirable in this connection than to have them.

> And why Shores should not be called and reputed lawful Bounds, whereon to ground a distinction of Dominion in the Sea, . . . I cannot fully understand.[1]

In addition to the shores there are landmarks of many sorts scattered in the sea, from which lines can be drawn. Certainly Pope Alexander VI had no scruples regarding boundaries at sea. And the King of Spain enjoyed a similar freedom from doubt when he obtained a grant of the western world.

The argument from the inexhaustible abundance of the sea rests on allegations which have no basis in fact. If the sea were really inexhaustible; then he who appropriated it could receive no injury from others' use of it. But the truth is, that

> wee often see, that the Sea it self, by reason of other men's Fishing, Navigation, and Commerce, becom's the worse for him that own's it. . . .[2]

This is particularly true in seas where there are coral or pearl fisheries. It is also true of every kind of fishing.

Nor, finally, can the writings of the jurists furnish any more secure argument for those who maintain the unlawfulness of ownership of the sea. Some of them, indeed, were and are of the opinion that the law natural and of nations makes the sea perpetually and necessarily common to all men; nevertheless, an examination of the laws and customs of most ages and nations, civil or intervenient, shows the reality to have been just the reverse. A notable example of the way in which later practice has diverged from earlier opinion is to be found in the fisheries from which states have drawn revenue, and in the laws of fishing, hunting, and fowling. So far from conforming to the earlier opinions, current practice has abrogated them, or at least, nullified them. This fact is peculiarly evident in the feudal law, by which the

[1] J. H.'s transl., p. 135. [2] *Ibid.*, p. 141.

revenues from fisheries are included in the Regalia. Further examples may be found. Whales and other fish of extraordinary size do not belong to their captors, but, by the laws of England, Portugal, and other nations, to the Exchequer, or to whomsoever the Prince shall grant a royalty of that nature. It is quite clear that the law natural and of nations is not wholly to be drawn from the law books of Justinian.

A study of a great number of modern lawyers shows that most of those who advocate a natural community of the sea treat the subject in the same manner as do those who

> have pinned their Faith, more than was meet, upon the sleev of Ulpian, or som other such antient Autor.[1]

Here again, modern usage and custom does not conform to their opinions, for

> som Seas have passed into the Dominion and Patrimonie, both of Princes and private persons. . . .[1]
>
> [Grotius] hath so warily couched this subject with other things, that whether in this hee did hit or miss, the rest however might serve to assert the point which hee was to handle.[2]

Selden believes the Grotian argument to be, none the less, not without its vulnerable points. These he exposes to the reader, as the conclusion to the argument of the first book of his treatise.

Grotius treats of title by discovery, of primary occupation, and of the Donation of Pope Alexander VI, in such a fashion that he seems to abandon the idea of a natural and perpetual community of the sea, or else, to confess that it can hardly be defended.

He admits that if any small part of the sea be enclosed and possessed, it becomes the property of him who first occupied it; yet he refuses to extend this principle to the whole sea. But mere difference in size cannot be a factor in determining capacity for private dominion, if it is physically possible to acquire such dominion.

He persistently points out that he is speaking of the open sea, of the main body of the ocean. Such a vast body of water is, admittedly, a very difficult thing to possess. But if it could be held

[1] J. H.'s transl., p. 169. [2] *Ibid.*, p. 172.

by occupation, as a narrow sea or creek may be, it might just as well pass into the hands of him who first occupied it.

When he turns in the "De Iure Belli ac Pacis" to the received customs of nations, he speaks more than once of the private dominion of the sea as a thing sometimes yielded without controversy; he observes that it was custom and not natural right or reason which prohibited the appropriation of the sea; he says, further, that if the custom changed, the reasons for a common use must be changed also. Now that this has in fact happened, abundant proof has been given.

> There remains not either in the nature of the Sea it self, or in the Law either Divine, Natural, or of Nations, any thing which may so oppose the private Dominion thereof, that it cannot be admitted by every kind of Law, even the most approved; and so that any kinde of Sea whatsoever may by any sort of Law whatsoever bee capable of private Dominion. . . .[1]

The second book, though considerably less interesting for legal theory than the first book, is the one which is responsible for the sensation which the appearance of "Mare clausum" created.

> [He intends to] discours touching the Dominion of great Britain in the Sea encompassing it about, and of those large Testimonies whereby it is asserted and maintained.[2] [He will show] from all Antiquitie, down to our times without interruption, that those, who by reason of so frequent alterations of the state of Affairs, have reigned here, whether Britains, Romans, Saxons, Danes, and Normans, and so the following Kings . . . have enjoied the Dominion of that Sea by perpetual occupation, that is to say, by using and enjoying it as their own after a peculiar manner, as an undoubted portion either of the whole bodie of the estate of the British Empire, or of some part thereof, according to the state and condition of such as have ruled it; or as an inseparable appendant of this Land. Lastly, that the Kings of Great Britain have had a peculiar Dominion or proprietie over the Sea flowing about it, as a Bound not bounding their Empire, but . . . as bounded by it; in the same manner as over the Island it self, and the other neighboring Isles which they possess about it.[3]

The boundaries of this British Sea are indefinite. It extends for some distance off the west coast of Ireland and of Scotland, and north of the Shetland Islands. It is bounded definitely on the east by the coast of France. Selden seems to make the whole shore of the Continent the eastern boundary. On the south it appears that the boundary is the northern coast of Spain.[4]

[1] Nedham's translation is used for the rest of the work. P. 179.
[2] P. 181. [3] P. 182. [4] Pp. 182–187.

He agrees at once with Grotius that the mere act of occupation is not sufficient to establish ownership. There must be in addition some external act "'from whence this Occupation may be understood.'" His arguments are therefore going to be derived

from such a private or peculiar use or enjoiment of the Sea, as consist's in a setting forth Ships to Sea, either to defend or make good the Dominion; in prescribing Rules of Navigation to such as pass through it; in receiving such Profits and Commodities as are peculiar to every kinde of Sea-Dominion whatsoever; and, which is the principal, either in admitting or excluding others at pleasure.[1]

Again, in Chapter XIII, he gives those acts which witness to Britain's ownership:[2]

I. The Custodie, Government, or Admiraltie of the English Sea, as a Territorie or Province belonging to the King.

II. The Dominion of those Islands that lie before the French shore.

III. The Leav of passage through this Sea granted to Foreiners upon request.

IV. The Libertie of Fishing therein allowed upon courtesie to Foreiners and Neighbors, and the Protection given to Fishermen.

V. Prescribing of Laws and Limits to Foreiners, who beeing in Hostilitie one with another, but both in amitie with the English, made Prize of each other in this Sea.

[He adds to the above,three classes of evidence].

VI. The Records whereby this Dominion is expressly asserted by the By, as a most undoubted Right; and that not onely by the King, but by the Parlaments of England, when they debated of other matters.

VII. The Commentaries of the Law of the Land, and common customs of the Nation, which do either assert or at least allow such a Dominion.

VIII. Some antient Testimonies of inferior note.

He adds, with truth, that clearer proof can hardly be imagined. The following chapters, up to the twenty-sixth, are devoted to the demonstration of these eight points. This demonstration necessarily takes the form of showing from the records that the English kings have habitually, and from the beginning, put in practice the first five points; and in producing the evidence indicated by the last three points. The last six chapters are taken up with showing that foreigners acknowledge the British claims, and in giving special treatment to certain aspects of the question; that is, they discuss a certain Bill of Complaint, the British claims

[1] Nedham's transl., p. 188, ch. 2. [2] *Ibid.*, p. 285.

to the Irish and Western Seas, and the claims to the Eastern and Northern Seas.

At the close of this book, he makes the final (and inclusive) statement of the bounds of the British Seas:

And without question it is true, according to the Collection of Testimonies before alleged, that the very Shores or Ports of the Neighbor-Princes beyond-Sea, are Bounds of the Sea-Territorie of the British Empire to the Southward and Eastward; but that in the open and vast Ocean of the North and West, they are to bee placed at the utmost extent of those most spacious Seas, which are possest by the English, Scots, and Irish.

It is not surprising that the appearance of "Mare clausum" caused a sensation in Europe with this statement of the British maritime possessions, backed, as it was, not only with a thorough study of the legal questions involved, but also by a mass of historical evidence the like of which had not before appeared between two covers. As between Grotius and Selden, the latter has the better argument. But he was defending a cause which was dying as he wrote. The era of sweeping claims to the sea was on the wane. Grotius had the good fortune to voice what was becoming the best feeling of the time. It remains true, however, that the basic principles maintained by Selden, apart from his extreme claims, more nearly approximate the principles of modern international law touching territorial waters, than do those advanced by Grotius.

Sir Matthew Hale gave the weight of his name to the cause in his important treatise, "De Jure Maris." [1]

The sea is either that which lies within the body of a county or without. That arm or branch of the sea which lies within the *fauces terrae*, where a man may reasonably discerne between shore and shore, is or at least may be within the body of a county. . . .

This definition is significant, in the light of subsequent fishery disputes. Hale continues: [2]

The part of the sea which lies not within the body of a county, is called the main sea or ocean.

[1] Reprinted in *History of the Foreshore*, p. 370. "Hale's completed work, as edited by Hargrave, is here reprinted. The editor has not been able to discover the original MS." Hale lived 1609–1676. He was Lord Chief Justice under Charles II.

[2] *Ibid.*, p. 376.

The narrow sea, adjoining to the coast of England, is part of the waste and demesnes and dominions of the king of England, whether it lies within the body of any county or not.

He cites Selden. The sea outside of a county would come, according to Sir Edward Coke, within the admiralty jurisdiction. It is possible, also, that a portion of a bay may lie within this jurisdiction. Sir Matthew Hale, however, seems to think it more likely that, if one shore is discernible from the other, the county has jurisdiction. The *fauces terrae* are said to enclose not, territorial waters, but waters which are, or at least may be, within the jurisdiction of a county. The territorial waters are such because they are adjacent to the coast, whether they lie within the body of a county or not. In the case of a foreign fisherman, fishing within the *fauces terrae*, and accused of violating a fishery regulation, the question would be, not, whether he was amenable to English law, but, in what court he should appear. To resume:

In this sea the king of England hath a double right, viz., a right of jurisdiction which he ordinarily exerciseth by his admiral, and a right of propriety or ownership. The latter is that which I shall meddle with.

The evidence of this ownership is of the usual sort. He refers again to Selden. The right of fishing in the sea belongs to the Crown. The "common people" have nevertheless a right to fish there, provided that there is no particular exclusive right to bar them.[1] The king may grant such a right in the high sea.[2]

He follows Digges in holding that the Crown is the proprietor of the shore and of *maritima incrementa*.[3] This *prima facie* right does not prevent a subject from acquiring true ownership in the shore through a title based on usage or custom or prescription.[4]

The last English writer who falls within this period is John Godolphin.[5] His treatise, "A View of the Admiral Jurisdiction,"[6] is not unpleasant reading for his fellow-subjects; but it could hardly cause a flutter in those chancelleries which were engaged in digesting John Selden's observations.

[1] Hale, *op. cit.*, p. 377. [2] *Ibid.*, p. 384. [3] *Ibid.*, p. 378.

[4] *Ibid.*, p. 385.

See also, p. 387 and p. 399 for summaries of the above. Also, pp. 400–401. For royal fish, pp. 412–413.

[5] He lived, 1617–1678. [6] 2d ed., London, 1685.

The World was no sooner created [says Godolphin] but man had Dominion over the Fish of the Sea, Jure Divino, which could not well be without Naval Architecture, and some skill in the Art of Navigation. . . .[1]

That the Kings of Great Britain have an undoubted Right to the Sovereignty of the Seas of Great Britain, none but a few Mare Libertines (and that for their own Interest) ever scrupled.[2]

The Dominium et Jurisdictio Maris are such Confederates, you cannot prejudice the one and not the other; And therefore to scruple that Jurisdiction, those Ancient Rights, whereby our own are conserved and secured, may not be convenient; So that to doubt whether the Established Jurisdiction of the High Admiralty of England may judge of Marine Properties, is implicitly and in effect to inferr that the Navy Royal is equipped only to enamel the Seas and take the Air, or that their Captures at Sea must evaporate. . . .[3]

Strangely enough, Godolphin quotes from the Roman lawyers without hesitation. He relies especially on Baldus. In the writings of the Post-Glossators, he could, of course, find a passage here and there which could be made to serve his purpose by the exercise of a little ingenuity.

Although Philip II, suppressed "Mare liberum," one eminent jurist secured a copy and wrote in answer a defense of the Portuguese. This jurist was Seraphinus de Freitas.[4]

He begins at the root of the problem by attacking Grotius's theory of the *ius gentium*. The division of that law into *primarium* and *secundarium* which Grotius makes was not known, he says,[5] to the ancient jurisconsults, for whom the *ius gentium* was a unity. Since there is but one author of the *ius gentium* — *ratio naturalis* — and since there is but one end — *bonum naturae humanae* — and since all men are gathered (from this point of view) into one republic, under the authority of natural reason, it follows that the *ius gentium* is *unicum*.[6]

There are to be distinguished two natures, i. e., pure nature, and corrupt nature. The condition described above occurs in the state of pure nature, *natura integra*. The various realms and peoples of the world fall within the second class, that which is the state of corrupt nature. In the first are to be found religion, obedience to parents, the education of children, and the like. In the

[1] Godolphin, *op. cit.*, p. 7. [2] *Ibid.*, p. 24. [3] *Ibid.*, p. 31.

[4] *De Justo Imperio Lusitanorum Asiatico*, Vallisoleti, 1625.

[5] *Ibid.*, p. 4.13. [6] *Ibid.*, p. 5.14.

second are found slavery and the various present-day conditions of life. Navigation falls within this class, or condition.[1]

Incognitus, however, puts navigation in the first class, that of pure nature, or, as he terms it, *primarium ius gentium*. He is relying on Vasquez when he does this. He does not himself prove that it belongs there, nor can he, for he leaves to others the task of proving the bases of his argument — a practice which is most vicious in discussion.[2]

De Freitas takes the Romanist position that the proprietorship of the sea is lodged in no one, while it is under "Caesar" for the purposes of jurisdiction and protection.[3] Grotius, of course, holds this position. But de Freitas draws different conclusions:[4]

> Hinc descendit posse Principem non solum in portu, . . . sed et transeuntibus per ipsum mare vectigal imponere.

It is for this reason that the Venetians have their ceremony of betrothing their Duke to the sea.[5]

It follows from this, also, that the Prince has the right to punish delicts committed on the sea bordering his territory.[6] While it is true, as Grotius says, that this right of protection flows from the *ius gentium* originally, yet the right belongs to him who has already assumed the burden of assuring the safety of the sea by virtue of his governance of the adjoining state.[7]

So this *ius gentium primaevum* is really the *ius naturale* incorrectly named.

Now, a thing may come under the *ius naturale* in two ways: the first, when a *lex naturalis* ordains it; the second, by permission, prohibition, or concession. The precepts of the *ius naturale* are, generally speaking, immutable. But there is a difference between them corresponding to the two ways in which a thing may come under the law, just as there is between the two divisions, pure nature, and corrupt nature. The precepts which govern the first class of things, namely, those which are ordained by a *lex naturalis*, are *necessaria veritates*, and hence never change. The

[1] De Freitas, *op. cit.*, p. 5.15–16.
[2] *Ibid.*, p. 6.21.
[3] *Ibid.*, p. 105.30.
[4] *Ibid.*, p. 105.31.
[5] *Ibid.*, p. 105.32.
[6] *Ibid.*, p. 106.33.
[7] *Ibid.*, p. 106.36.

precepts which govern the second class of things change with changing circumstances. De Freitas, then, makes these two great divisions of the law and of things under it. As he put navigation in the number of things with a corrupt nature, so now he puts it among those things which are governed by permission, prohibition and concession. He puts it there not only because of his original classification of it, but because it changes with changing circumstances. Trade or commerce is on a like footing with it. Even if it be granted that navigation and commerce are in the *primaevo naturae integrae statu*, still they are not precepts, certainly, of the *ius naturalis*, nor yet governed by them (in so far as they are immutable decrees.) [1]

The assertion of *Incognitus*, therefore, that the freedom of navigation and commerce in foreign countries appertains to the *primum ius gentium* is not sound. It is not sound because, by his phrase, he intends the state of pure nature. His thesis cannot be sustained because he is supposing a faculty of commerce in a situation in which commerce could not be practiced.[2]

Or, if he intends by his phrase a collection of immutable precepts, then also his assertion cannot be defended. He says that the Portuguese demand from the Indian princes the right to trade with them. But that is just because they do not possess the right. It is useless to demand or to give as a privilege what the *ius commune et naturale* has already conferred.[3]

Neither the immense size of the sea, nor its nature, is repugnant to jurisdiction and occupation. As to its size, it is true that the whole ocean cannot be occupied. But that is only because no people is strong enough to undertake the occupation. It does not follow from this that a part of it cannot be occupied. There is nothing in its nature to prevent it. So in Africa and Asia there are vast stretches of desert that cannot be occupied. But this is not to say that they can not legally be occupied.[4]

It is true that the writers do not agree as to the extent of the adjacent sea. Therefore, since this portion of the ocean cannot be defined under the *ius naturale*,

[1] De Freitas, *op. cit.*, p. 6.22–p. 7.
[2] *Ibid.*, p. 8.26.
[3] *Ibid.*, p. 8.27.
[4] *Ibid.*, p. 107.38.

consequens est dicamus, et Imperio ad iurisdictione prolatari posse, vel restringi ex dominantis potentia, sicut et in arida maioribus, minoribusve territorijs urbes circumscribuntur.[1]

It is important to note that the maritime jurisdiction exercised by the Emperor or protector is of the same sort as that which he exercises on the land.[2]

From what has gone before, it easily follows that a servitude may be imposed on the sea; not *privata lege*, certainly, for Ulpian has stated that to be unlawful; but, *publica lege*, since that was not prohibited expressly.[3] It follows as simply that the Prince controls the *ius piscandi*. For when Marcianus stated that approach to the seashore *piscandi causa* should not be forbidden, he did not mention the Roman people. Thus it follows that they have the right to make such a prohibition; and that the Prince has such a right.

Constat igitur ex dictis ius piscandi occupari, et donari posse a Principe.[4]

De Freitas has two observations to make at this point.

Unum, vel alterum advertendum duximus, primum maris occupationem non exqualibet navigatione, et piscatione aequiri; [5] Secundo, adverto Lusitanos maris Oceani occupationem, et Imperium non ita vendicasse, ut alijs navigationem prohibeant, aut in illo vectigalia imponant, imo et ipsi Batavi per Oceanum et per Hispanicum mare navigant in Venetias, et in alias Provincias, nusquam tamen illi, vel alij ab Hispanis prohibiti sunt, aut vectigalia pendunt, nec tale quid memoriae proditum est.[6]

Sed illud tantum clamant nostri (ut Incogniti . . .) ne navigent Batavi ad nostras conquistas, quae tanto nostrorum sanguine, et sumptu comparatae fuere, ut certo si lucrum temporale spectetur, haud tanto pretio dignae sunt. . . .[7]

---

[1] De Freitas, *op. cit.*, p. 107.40. It is of little importance that the sea cannot be occupied or possessed any more fully than the air or *aqua profluens*. Considered as elements, they certainly cannot be occupied; but, considered in relation to the places which envelope them, considered as *locis circumscripta*, they certainly can be occupied. (P. 107.42–43).

[2] *Ibid.*, p. 107.41.

[3] *Ibid.*, p. 111.1–2.

[4] *Ibid.*, p. 117.24. For although the *usus piscandi* in the sea and in public rivers is public and open to all, nevertheless, *ex iusta causa*, the Prince, or he who has power from him, can change it all and transform the *usus maris* from a public to a private right, or, in general, suspend it, or grant it to one while forbidding it to another.

It is thus with navigation in the sea, p. 118.25. What is true in regard to the princely power above, is true here also.

[5] *Ibid.*, p. 123.39.

[6] *Ibid.*, p. 123.40.

[7] *Ibid.*, p. 123.41.

This is of course in contradiction of Grotius's argument that the Portuguese have no title to the East Indies by conquest or occupation.

As to prescription, since the law (*edictum*) of prescription is prohibitive, it is of such a nature that all things placed in *commercio* and susceptible of possession, can be prescribed by us and against us, except certain things especially prohibited by law. It is only when things are placed *extra commercium* by some special prohibition of the *ius naturale* or *ius gentium* or *ius civitatis* that we cannot acquire them by prescription or by some other legitimate means.[1]

It should be noted that there is a difference between a thing being *in commercio*, and, having a right *in commercio* over a thing.[2] The first pertains to the quality of the thing which can be alienated or possessed (that is, which can be reduced to ownership); the second has regard to the quality of the person who is capable of having commerce in the thing which is *in commercio*.[3]

Now, the King of Spain, owning no temporal superior,[4] has full imperial rights. That is to say, he has the rights of protection and of jurisdiction over the sea. By these rights he sends fleets to purge the sea of pirates and other enemies.[5] He does not claim jurisdiction over the whole extent of the ocean; but his jurisdiction does extend to those provinces which have submitted to his dominion, and over the sea of which we have assumed, by our voyages and expenditures, the care and protection.[6] And so, though this navigation and protection are common to all, the contrary may be the case by the will of the people or of the Prince; for the Emperor is master of the world (that is, of the part which submits to him), and the sea is placed under his law.[7] The Prince can decide what seems just and good to him in this regard; for his power is not less than that of public law, and public law can impose a servitude on the sea.[8]

[1] De Freitas, *op. cit.*, p. 133.4.

[2] *Ibid.*, p. 133.5: "Advertendum tamen est rem esse in commercio, et habere commercium rei longe differre."

[3] *Ibid.*, p. 134.5.

[4] *Ibid.*, p. 134.9.

[5] *Ibid.*, p. 133.8.

[6] *Ibid.*, p. 134.10.

[7] *Ibid.*, p. 134.11.

[8] *Ibid.*, p. 134.11.

The conclusion of the argument (which, naturally, was ordained from the beginning) is that the Portuguese have the right[1] of navigation by first occupation, by prescription, and by immemorial usage,[2] in flat contradiction of the Grotian argument, which, it will be recalled, denied to the Portuguese the exclusive right of navigation on the grounds that it did not meet these tests.

This, then, is the Portuguese answer to "Mare liberum." It is clever, subtle, and abstract. Selden does not seem to have made use of it. It may be doubted whether it could prove to be serviceable. It was the argument of the losing side; the nations were not, as a fact, going to permit the Spanish and Portuguese to monopolize either the ocean or the Indies. If de Freitas could have massed together the huge array of facts or of alleged facts that Selden succeeded in collecting, his argument, even then, would probably have made but little impression. His claims were too extravagant. Selden's were also far-fetched; and it may be noted that in so far as he claimed for Great Britain the western and northern seas, he was futile. The sting in his argument was his claim, and the proofs of it which he presented, of British ownership of the waters flowing about the British Isles, together with the rights, and the proofs of their actual exercise, which flow from ownership.

III. Continental Defenders of Dominium Maris

All of the doctrines which have been considered since the appearance of "Mare liberum" are partisan utterances. All of the jurists who engaged in the controversy of *mare liberum* versus *mare clausum*, are united into one well-defined group by this common characteristic, that they are partisan. It matters not for this purpose whether they defended or attacked the doctrine of *dominium maris*.

During this period there were in France and Germany jurists who developed this doctrine. They did not take sides in the controversy. That is to say, they did not side with the British lawyers, and they did not defend the claims of the Spanish and the

[1] That is to say, the exclusive right.

[2] *Ibid.*, p. 144.40.

Portuguese. It would give a wrong impression to say that they advanced claims in behalf of their respective sovereigns. What they did was to enunciate the doctrine of *dominium maris*. In so far as this position could be supposed to check the claims made in behalf of the sovereigns directly concerned with the controversy, just so far did they mingle in the dispute. Their kinship is rather with those jurists on the Continent and in England who were developing the theory in question prior to 1608, than with the jurists who are grouped around the figure of Selden.

Two strong utterances come from France. They are brief and concise, and may well be reproduced together. The first one is as follows:

> . . . auiourd'huy en France, puis que la mer, les ports, et les fleuves navigables appartiennent au Roy: il s'ensuit que le droit de pesche dans la mer, ports, en esdits fleuves, appartient au Roy.
>
> . . . le Prince peut permettre la pesche a un certain endroit de la mer, et la defendre en l'autre. . . . Car le Prince a toute puissance sur les chose, qui de leur nature estoient autres fois communes, et qui a present luy appartiennent comme il a este dit ey-dessus. Ceux qui peschent dans la mer, n'y peuvent pas pescher de nuict apportans de la lumière.

This statement comes from an Advocate of the Parliament of Paris, M. Antoine Despeisses,[1] who lived, 1594–1658.

M. de Boutaric, the other jurist, is just as firm. In referring to the existence of rights of property in the sea, he says,[2]

> Le Roi l'entend ainsi pour les Riviéres navigables, et pour la Mer qui avoisine ses Etats.

It is necessary for the public interest

> que tous les Souverains . . . se sont rendus propres les Rivages de la Mer, et non seulement les Rivages, mais la Mer qui voisine leurs Côtes et leurs Terres.

There is a liberty of fishing in the sea; but

> cette liberté a même été accordé par Sa Majesté . . . c'est par l' effet de la bonté du Roi.

Either Philip II, or Charles II, would be satisfied with the possession of such rights. These passages are not arguments; they

[1] *Les Oeuvres* (sic) *de*, 3 vols. (Alyon, 1660), iii, 195.3.

[2] Francois de Boutaric, *Tracte des Droits, Seigneuriaux*, etc., Nouvelle edition, (Tolouse (sic), 1767), pp. 552–553.

are affirmations. There is lacking only a claim to a certain area of the sea.

In the Digest of Justinian, 14.2.9, the Emperor Antoninus is reported to have said,

Εγω μεν του κοσμόυ κύριος ὁ δε νομός της θαλάσσης.

The question raised by this sentence is, Was the Emperor disclaiming lordship over the sea, or was he not? Iacobus Gothofredus wrote a pamphlet to prove that he was not. Before Gothofredus, two jurists had devoted something more than a hundred words to an exegesis of this sentence. Igneus concluded that Antoninus meant to say that he was lord of the law of the sea, as well as lord of the world, although he knew he was bluffing when he said it.[1] Alciat concluded that he was claiming the *imperium maris*.[2] At rare intervals the sentence is cited to buttress an assertion that the Emperor is *dominus mundi*. Very rarely is the question of the *imperium maris* connected with it. The sentence is quite unimportant.

When Gothofredus wrote, such a question lacked whatever reality it had ever had. His pamphlet[3] is important because of his use of the two words, *imperium* and *dominium*. He writes:

> Igitur, clarum iam ex iis omnibus quae diximus, quaeque libello Eudaemonis continentur, Imperatorem, Romanum maris dominum quoque fuisse. . . . Nemo puto cuiusquam opem, ita, ut dixi, libello depocit, nisi quem supremum dominum agnoscit. . . . Ex Libello supplicis oblatione supremum quoque eius cui libellus oblatus est, ea in re, qua de supplicatur agiturque, Dominium argui.[4]

It will be recalled that the title of his pamphlet is "De Imperio Maris." He writes in another place,[5]

> Hactenus Eudaemonis libellus a nobis discussus est, et ex eo multimodis probatum Imperatorem nihilo secius Maris atque Terrae dominium fuisse.

In a third place, he uses *dominium* and *imperium* in the same sentence:[6]

[1] Ioannes Igneus, *Commentarii in aliquot Constitutiones Principum*, etc., (Lugduni et Aureliae), 1541, p. 200.689.

[2] Andrea Alciatus, *Dispunctionum*, ii, cap. v, p. 152. Alciatus lived, 1491–1550 (Stintzing, *op. cit.*, i, p. 96).

[3] *De Imperio Maris*, etc., Genevae, 1637. I. Gothofredus was the last of the great 16th century French classicists. He lived 1587–1652.

[4] *Op. cit.*, p. 24. [5] *Ibid.*, p. 26. [6] *Ibid.*, p. 58.

. . . hac quoque legem Imperatori Maris dominium seu Imperium adseri. . . .

It seems clear that Gothofredus uses both words interchangeably, as synonyms. His selection of *seu* instead of *et* or *atque* in the last passage quoted indicates that he is under the impression that they have the same meaning.

He wrote his treatise after Selden had published his work. By that time the mixing of the notions of lordship with ownership had progressed far.

Gothofredus was imbued with the love of antiquity that is characteristic of his school. He shared the faith of his school in the efficacy of the classic Roman law. It mattered little, if anything, to him that the monarch who bore the title of Roman Emperor in the opening decades of the seventeenth century was little more than a shadow of the monarch who bore that title when he asserted that he was lord of the world. He felt no sense of the ridiculous when he published his little work; or, if he did, there is no trace of it in the work itself. It is seriously written, carefully written, presenting a painstaking exegesis of the Greek, with something of that ill-temper which is engendered by controversy. But it is an anachronism in 1640.

Proprietorship of the world was an ingredient in the civilian theory of the Roman *Princeps*. One of the greatest contributions of Bartolus to political theory was his doctrine that the *civitas* of the highest type possesses full imperial power within its territory. But even as he created this doctrine, he found himself forced to maintain that the Emperor is the lord of the world, *universaliter*, and *de iure*. He found his solution by denying to the Emperor lordship of the world, *particulariter*, and *de facto*. Gothofredus thinks that there is no real opposition between *Princeps* and *Lex*, between *mundus* and *mare*.[1] The *Lex* is the instrument for governing the *respublica*. The Emperor is the governor.[2] Gothofredus merely extends the Emperor's sphere of activity to the sea. The *lex maris*, which is the *Lex Rhodia*, derives its validity from the Emperor, by whose will it is valid, and by whose will it is enforced.[3]

[1] Gothofredus, *op. cit.*, p. 33. [2] *Ibid.*, p. 34. [3] *Ibid.*, p. 36.

The development of the theory of *dominium maris* receives excellent illustration in the work of Johannes Loccenius, whose lifetime covers the first three quarters of the seventeenth century.[1] He devotes two chapters of "De Jure Maritimo" to an exposition of his doctrine.

Loccenius lays down the proposition that the sea is open to all by both natural and divine law.[2] He argues for freedom of navigation on the ground that the

> ius navigandi est innoxia facultas transfretandi ad vicinos aut remotos populos, a jure naturae, gentium, divino et civili permissa,

and because, as has been noted, the use of the sea is free to all by natural and by civil law.[3]

From a defense of the freedom of navigation, he turns to a defense of the theory of *dominium maris*. The chapter (IV) in which he expounds his doctrine, he entitles, "De Imperio Maris." It appears at once that he uses *imperium* and *dominium* interchangeably:

> At praecedenti capiti dictis obstare videtur imperium vel dominium maris, quo navigationis usus

and so forth.[4] And he proceeds to say that it is certain that by the primeval law of nature and by the condition of men, the sea is open and free to all. Then he observes,

> sed Reges, Principes, et Respublicae liberae ejus dominium vi imperii in terras suas et undas illis conjunctas paulatim ad se traxerunt.

That is, possessing the *imperium*, they have gradually acquired the *dominium*.

In this passage, *dominium* is acquired by the use of *imperium;* and *terras* and *undas conjunctas* are coupled. He finds early evidence of the practice.

> Non tamen Principes aut liberi populi habent in universum mare, sed quod eorum terrae vel territorio magis adjacet. Eo sensu accipiendum est illud, quod dici solet: Illum, qui littus possidet, sequi dominium maris.

[1] 1599–1677. A German historian and publicist who was professor of history and politics at Upsala in 1625.

[2] *Libri tres* (Holmiae), 1664, p. 163.

[3] *Ibid.*, p. 162.

[4] *Ibid.*, p. 168.

But they cannot take away the natural right of a common liberty of navigation, or hinder it at random. His thought is not entirely clear, owing to his somewhat free use of Latin; it would seem fairly certain, nevertheless, that he is endorsing the theory of the adjacent sea, and maintaining the freedom of the open sea.

He mentions the (late) controversy over *mare liberum* and *mare clausum;* but

illorum controversias nunc fere quiescentes (non?) resuscitabo,

especially since many of the contradictory opinions expressed are capable of being brought into agreement.[1] This is surely true, he thinks, of the distinction between

imperium maris universale et particulare ejusve modum [rightly considered]. Dominium maris universum et summum nulli hominum, sed soli Domino dominorum competere.[1]

Sed mare particulare, ut vocant, vel singulare imperio Regis, Principis aut Reipublicae subesse potest, quatenus est in ejus ditionis.

Of course, this was the whole point. According to the doctrines made vocal by Selden, British jurisdiction stopped at the coast of France. As to the maritime jurisdiction of Spain, no one was quite sure whether there was a limit in this world. Loccenius at any rate limited the exercise of this jurisdiction in regard to its powers; freedom of navigation must not be prevented or hindered.

He notes that the Scandinavian kings have from time immemorial exercised maritime *imperium* in the ocean and in the Baltic sea, again,

quatenus intra ditiones eorum fluit, vel littora alluit. Etenim ipsa natura videtur hoc jus illis ab initio attribuisse. . . .[2] [And then he speaks][3] de dominio vero et imperio maris Balthici, quod ad immemoriali tempore possident Reges Sueciae et Daniae . . . [while maintaining his] discrimen inter imperium maris universale et particulare [at the same time].[4]

Loccenius rejects the theory that maritime *imperium* grew out of the necessity of protecting the adjacent sea from the pirates. On the contrary, this *imperium* confers an obligation on the state possessing it to suppress piracy. The passage is worth reproducing in full:[5]

[1] Loccenius, *op. cit.*, p. 169.
[2] *Ibid.*, p. 171.
[3] *Ibid.*, p. 172.
[4] *Ibid.*, p. 173.
[5] *Ibid.*, p. 178.

Quamvis enim facile demus, eos, qui imperium particulare maris habent, navibus praesidarius in illo dispositis posse et debere mare tueri, praedonibus purgare, atque eos, ut decet, plectere; tutamque transeuntibus navigationem praestare: quo nomine etiam vectigal pendi, non iniquum est; hoc tamen non est reciprocum, ut, qui mare aut flumen protegit, piratas tollit: statim habeat maris aut fluminis dominium.

The use of *dominium* may be noted.

Quippe protectio et jus pacificandi, ut vocant, non dat dominium, sed solam liberationem et defensionem contra vim piratarum continet.

The power of *protectio* and *jurisdictio* — more strictly, it should be two powers — this composite power, which is temporary, must be distinguished from *proprietas maris*. This is a surprising distinction for him to make. A victorious enemy can hold the *imperium maris;* but the *imperium* is lost if fortune changes, or if it is restored to the original holder by the terms of peace. But *dominium* — he uses this word, and not, *proprietas* — is by its nature perpetual. *Dominium* is used here in its classic and proper meaning, that of property, and is used interchangeably with *proprietas*. These two are contrasted with *imperium*, the power of jurisdiction and protection. Finally, the source of this power to punish pirates and to protect navigation is the *jus commune*, which all free peoples have.[1]

Loccenius turns now to the subject of jurisdiction. He who has jurisdiction in a territory or district bordering on the sea is deemed to have jurisdiction in the sea also, over as much as can be traversed in a two days' journey.[2] He notes the disagreement

[1] Loccenius, p. 179. "Accedit, quod protectio et jurisdictio, quae aliquanfacto do deusurpari, et quae temporaria esse potest, a proprietate maris distinguenda est. Potest item hostis classe potentior, et victor, imperium maris tenere; sed idem fortuna vertente amittere, vel pace facta priori domino restituere; quod obvia passim exempla docent. Dominium autem ex sua natura perpetuum est. Sed et classes praesidium navigantium disponere, atque piratas punire, non ex proprio, sed communi jure descendit, quod etiam aliae liberae gentes habere possunt. Sic Hollandi aliquando purgarunt mare praedonibus, cujus rei signum *Scopae* malo impositae praeferebant; non tamen inde sibi proprietatem maris vindicarunt." The following paragraph may be added: "Illud interim largiendum est, inter gentes vicinas ita convenire posse, ut capti in maris hac vel illa parte, hujus aut illius reipublicae judicio sistantur, atque ad commoditatem distinguendae jurisdictionis fines describantur. Quod ipsos quidem hanc sibi legem dicentes, non alios obligat; neque locum alicujus proprium facit, sed jus in personas contrahentium constituit."

[2] *Ibid.*, p. 179. He does not cite his authority.

prevalent among the writers as to the area of the sea covered by this jurisdiction. He mentions the sixty-mile limit of Bodinus, and Gentilis' advocacy of the hundred-mile limit. At any rate, he adds, each one has jurisdiction over his own shores. But he says *dominium*, instead of *jurisdictio*. He adds,

Nimirum ut unicuique juxta sua littora competat dominium:

it is possible that he means *dominium*. Then he proceeds,

extra ea, quatenus classe locum occupavit, vel quousque ejus territorium juxta mare porrigitur.

If this means anything at all, it means that the state has *dominium* beyond its shores as far as its fleet can operate effectively. The whole sentence reads,

Nimirum ut unicuique juxta sua littora competat dominium; extra ea, quatenus classe locum occupavit, vel quousque ejus territorium juxta mare porrigitur. [1]

A few observations on the problem as to where a person accused of an offense committed at sea shall be tried, closes this part of Loccenius' theory on *imperium maris*.[2]

This theory may be summed up as follows: monarchs and republics have extended their *dominium* on land and sea. This is the *dominium vi imperii*. He who possesses the shore possesses also the *dominium maris*. This *dominium*, however, is confined to *mare particulare*, that is, to the territorial waters, or, perhaps, to the adjacent sea. *Mare universale*, the high seas, remains free to all. The maritime area covered by the *dominium* of the monarch or republic is limited to that over which he exercises jurisdiction. This in turn is described as being so much as can be covered in a two days' sail, or, so much as can be protected by the fleet. It will be perceived that the principle behind this latter estimate

[1] Loccenius, *op. cit.*, p. 181.

[2] *Ibid.*, p. 181. "Communiter tamen delictum in mari particulari perpetratum in illa civitate vel republica puniri solet, ad cujus jurisdictionem mare spectat, cujusque portui locus ille maris propinquior est. Sed si crimen in mari inter duas urbes aequaliter distantes commissum sit, ejus cognitio ad utramque per concursum jurisdictionis pertinebit: quia delictum commissum est in confinio, quod est commune utriusque civitatis. Si vero eadem pars maris ad plures pertineat, illi omnes poterunt cognoscere; ita tamen ut sit praeventioni locus. Praevenire autem dicitur, qui delinquentem cepit in mari; licet alius judex prius eum citarit."

is that of protection of the waters by the neighboring state. The former estimate is more nearly arbitrary. Although, up to this point, Loccenius has used *imperium* and *dominium* in a manner to convey the impression that he regards them as meaning much the same thing, he now distinguishes between them. He begins his distinction by using the words *protectio* and *jurisdictio;* but he abandons them almost at once for the word *imperium.*[1] In like manner, he begins with the word *proprietas*, and drops it immediately for *dominium. Imperium*, then, is to be distinguished from *dominium.* And the distinction is this, that the former is temporary and the latter permanent. *Imperium* is temporary because it is obtained by force and may be extinguished either by a superior force or by agreement. *Dominium* is permanent because that quality is inherent in its nature. Finally, the right to protect navigation is a common right, and not *ex proprio.*

It is difficult to arrive at a clear understanding of what Loccenius means. According to his differentiation between *imperium* and *dominium*, the former can hardly be translated, "sovereignty." Furthermore, as he himself points out, any victorious fleet can exercise, for it possesses, this *imperium.* It should be recalled that Loccenius is writing in the seventeenth century, and not in the middle age. For him, the *imperium* is marked chiefly by the power to give protection and to exercise jurisdiction. And — this is important — it does not depend for its use upon the ownership of the area over which it is put into effect. It depends solely upon the physical mastery of the area in question. He can hold this position at a time when it would be entirely correct to translate *imperium* by "sovereignty." As for *dominium*, he makes *proprietas* synonymous with it. He takes as a matter of course the existence of property rights in the sea. Those rights are, apparently, permanent, even if the surface is controlled by an enemy. The whole tenor of his exposition suggests the word, "sovereignty," for *dominium.* This suggestion is increasingly powerful when the king or republic is thought of as being in undisturbed possession of the territorial waters, that is, when his *imperium* is not extinguished.

[1] See note 2 on the preceding page.

In regard to this possible meaning of the word, it may be recalled that in the feudal law, and certainly in feudal practice, the notions of sovereignty and property are intermingled. All land was held immediately or ultimately from the king (or, the Emperor); he was, in strictness, a territorial monarch, the first landowner of the realm, and the lord of the inhabitants, his vassals. When feudalism broke up, the king emerged as an absolute monarch, outside, as it were, of the state; he was set over against the state, the irresponsible ruler of his people. There were no gradations between them. Feudalism had provided such a system, but it had disappeared, leaving the king at the top and the people at the bottom. The king remained as a territorial sovereign. Feudalism, however, left behind it some traces of its system and influenced profoundly the young and vague conception of sovereignty as it is known to modern theory. One such mark of its influence is the making of lordship dependent upon ownership of the soil. If ownership of the sea is postulated, then it is in accord with this idea to postulate sovereignty of the sea also. Loccenius seems to be suffering from this confusion of ideas. It is interesting to note that Grotius distinguishes between property and sovereignty.[1]

The differentiation of *imperium* and *dominium* may be an effort to separate sovereignty from territory. If Loccenius was making any such attempt, it seems that he was too much under the influence of the feudal conception, and too little of a clear thinker, to be able to succeed.

There are a few remaining points to be noticed. Although the sea and public rivers are open, he says,[2] to the common use of many people by the *ius gentium* (it is not clear whether he is inferentially excluding some people), nevertheless the local magistrates may prescribe the mode in which this right of use is to be exercised. *Certi termini navigationis* may be defined by convention or treaty, which binds only the parties concluding it.[3] The

[1] *De Jure Belli ac Pacis, libri tres*, transl. by William Whewell, 3 vols. (Cambridge, 1853), II, iii, iv.

[2] *Op. cit.*, p. 182.

[3] "Illa tamen definitio imperium maris non absolutum reddit; ita ut aliorum

lord has no obligation to adopt towards any merchants or foreigners any given policy. What favors they receive are given them *cum gratia*, through trade agreements, or from the law of common humanity. But foreigners ought to have security of person and property and a right of access to certain ports.[1] This idea is found in Selden. His chapter closes with some observations on the nature of the salutes to be exacted from foreign vessels in the coastal waters of another power.[2]

Stypmann and Conring are two German jurists who distinguish between *imperium and dominium*, and who defend the right of *dominium* in the waters adjacent to a state. Each of them has left a tract in which he states his doctrine on the subject.

populorum, ad quos illa pacta nihil pertinent, libertatem navigandi plane tollat, aut eos obligat," p. 182.

[1] "Sed nec domini in suas terras et mare ad quosvis mercatores et peregrinos suscipiendos inviti iure gentium cogi possunt; sed id facient bona cum gratia, vel ex indultu, commerciorum foedere, vel communi humanitatis lege. Modo peregrini ad licitos portus accedant, ibique quod debent vectigal solvant; nec se indignos, humana consuetudine, et justis amicisque commerciis reddant; nec vetitia aut illicita inferant aut ob justum securitatis propriae metum transitu prohibeantur vel detineantur." Loccenius, *op. cit.*, pp. 182–183.

[2] *Ibid.*, p. 190. "Quamvis mos vetus sit, in accursu Regiarum aut liberae Reipublicae navium, aut arcis regiae, demittere aplustre aut summum velum . . . aut tormentorum explosione naves tales obvias salutare; tamen hodie plerumque fit, et haud dubie apud majores, es iisdem causis, vel respectu domini in subjecto mari, quod navigatur; vel honoris causa: ubi vel non alteruti, vel neutri maris est dominium. quod (*sic*) aliquando fraudi fuit transeuntibus navibus. . . . Hodie ejusmodi incommodi vitandi causa, talis salutatio paucis solum tormentis exoneratis, et solenni ac usitato singulis Regibus ac Rebuspublicis explosionis signo fieri solet. Ista vero salutatio si studio, vel contemtu transeuntium omitatur, infesto tormentorum ictu vindicatur. Cum ignorantibus tamen exteris et amicis non ex rigore agi solet. . . . Si hac supremi veli demissione et tormentorum in transitu exoneratione, inter Reges, Principes ac Respublicas non satis conveniri possit, sub certo pacti modo illud dirimi ac determinari solet." He mentions a treaty of peace between the Kings of Sweden and Denmark, 1645; another, between the King of Great Britain and the "Belgian Confederation," in 1660; and one between the Kings of Great Britain and France, in 1669.

A problem arises when one king sends his representative to another who is on terms of friendship with him. If the ship carrying his representative meets a royal vessel belonging to the king to whom he is sending his agent, and the vessel is lying at anchor, should the visiting ship strike the topsail? On the one hand, the ship at anchor is royal, *i. e.*, the king's ship, and it is in its own waters. It demands that the salute be given. On the other hand, the Legatus represents the king whose emissary he is. To fire a salute, or to strike the flag, or to lower the sails before the

Stypmann approaches the problem from commerce as a starting-point. *Commercii*, he says,[1] *vero seu duo sunt genera*, namely, that which is carried on between distant peoples, and that which is carried on between citizens or subjects of the same state. The former kind of commerce outranks the latter in his esteem.

> Honestior autem est mercatura maritima terrestri, quia multa multis impertit, et ideo secundum ipsam naturam necessaria. Quae enim emeris, ut vendas, Juris gentium est. Cum igitur commercandi libertas sit ex jure gentium, quod naturalem causam sub se habet, tolli non potest, et si deberet omnium gentium consensus opus esset.

In general, Stypmann exalts maritime countries at the expense of "terrestrial" ones. To maritime countries, navigation is essential; the right of free or unrestricted navigation is essential. Ships, which carry sea-borne commerce, bring wealth and power. Inland countries, lacking a coastline, have not the same resources for expansion. They are not, however, dependent upon the sea. Maritime countries, on the other hand, are. This dependence is, in his mind, sufficient reason why commerce should be free from restrictions.

There is another reason. The first use which was made of the sea was for navigation.[2] Without a doubt the private individual has equal rights with the prince, at sea. The fact of this equality of standing is the reason why the sea is said to be common.[3]

It is clear that Stypmann does not question the freedom of *mare altum*. His position on territorial waters is as follows:

other ship is to commit an indignity against the honor of his king. Loccenius feels that the proprieties are observed by a mutual salute, p. 193. There still remains the question, Who will salute first? Or the difficulty of arranging a simultaneous salute. But he does not attempt to remove these problems.

It will have been observed that he couples *Respublica* with *Rex* or *Princeps* throughout this passage, and in others in this chapter. This use furnishes an interesting illustration of the late mediaeval or early renaissance ideas on sovereignty. It will be remembered that at this time the great states emerged from feudalism as absolute monarchies. This period has been called (by Figgis) the Age of Despots. The sovereign was identified with the state in both its internal and external relations. As the Republic had no sovereign, sovereignty had to be attributed to it. It was necessary to rank the republican state as a sovereign.

[1] Franciscus Stypmannus, *Tractatus de Jure Maritimo*, bound with Selden's *Mare clausum*, *op. cit.* (Wratislavae, 1751), i, c. 1.21, p. 195.

[2] *Ibid.*, I. c. 3.9, p. 206.

[3] *Ibid.*, I, c. 3.13.

Quoad maria particularia distinguendum est, quod alii plenum in iis jus, seu dominium habent, alii minus plenum, id est, tantum nudum usum. Dominium illud vel suo quis jure habet, vel alieno. Suo jure habent, qui mare primitus occuparunt, vel devicto hoste in ejus locum successerunt, vel alio modo principalis jure nituntur. Ex eo ipso enim quod privatum factum duos dominos in solidum habere nequit. Effectus est, . . . quod non solum libere navigare, piscari etc., in mari possunt, sed etiam aliis modum praescribere, quousque navigent vel piscentur, punire deliquentes in mari, jubere, prohibere navigationem si res postulat, imo omnes actus dominii exercere, quos quivis privatus in re propria. . . . Minus plenum jus seu nudium usum qulibet privatus habet in maribus occupatis. Hoc enim quod in maris occupationem tacite genus humanum consenserunt, innoxius usus qui in navigando consistit, reservatus praesumitur. Hic tamen usus ex variis causis restringi, imo exteri plane ab eo arceri possunt.[1]

The rights inherent or appertaining to his theory of *dominium* are not different from those which have been noticed. In one respect Stypmann is more liberal that the usual statements of writers of the *mare clausum* school would indicate them to be: he states explicitly that the right of innocent passage through territorial waters is presumed to remain to foreigners after the occupation of those waters. This right may of course be restricted in the interests of the state.

The method of acquiring ownership of these waters is simple. They may be appropriated by the first comer, either peaceably, or by force of arms. An essential element in this occupation is the settlement of the occupier on the land the shores of which are washed by the waters which have been appropriated. This, however, goes without saying, for the ruler of a maritime state is presumed to have occupied the waters off his coast.

His theory of the origin of the divisibility of the sea is little more than a statement that it is divisible. The unknown and vast extent of the ocean preserved it from division at the time that the land was divided.[2] Private ownership resulted from a corruption of an originally pure nature.[3] But, while the sea has remained free — and this condition is permanent — particular parts of it may be occupied; and, after they have been occupied, they may be divided.[4] Both necessity and utility urge this occupation

[1] Stypmann, *op. cit.*, I, c. 3.14.

[2] *Ibid.*, I, c. 4.13, p. 209.

[3] *Ibid.*, I. c. 4.1–11, p. 208.

[4] *Ibid.*, I, c. 5.1–2, p. 215.

upon princes and peoples.[1] Title by prescription is, of course, valid.

Stypmann buttresses his views with an appeal to history, beginning with that monarch who so suddenly became prominent, King Minos of Crete, and running down to his own time.

Hermann Conring, the celebrated German jurist, distinguishes between *imperium* and *dominium* in a manner singularly concise and lucid. The passage in question occurs in his "Exercitatio de Dominio Maris." It is worth reproducing, because it marks a thorough-going separation from the *imperium-dominium* school:[2]

> Differt dominium ab imperio quia dominium est in res et bona, imperium vero in personas. Sic pater imperat liberis et dominus servis . . . rerum autem acquisitio vocatur dominium . . . in quo nulla mentio fit imperii. Deinde Imperans in Republica omnia imperio possidet, singula vero a privatis dominio possidentur.
>
> Differt dominium a proprietate non in se sed subtilitate juris. Nam proprietas et dominium, qua jus significant, et si in propria acceptione sumuntur, recte dicuntur synonima.

Conring defines *dominium maris* as follows:[3]

> Est . . . Dominium Maris jus Majestati competens partem aliquam maris tam quoad proprietatem quam quoad imperium sibi vindicandi, omnesque alios ab ejus occupatione arcendi, jure naturali aut gentium acquisitum.

The usual objections urged by the opponents of *dominium maris* are disposed of rapidly, one after another. He first answers the objection that the sea cannot be reduced to ownership because all things were originally held in common, and the further objection that all things are unstable and temporary in character and therefore cannot be owned.[4] How can this instability hinder ownership, he asks. This characteristic of things was ordained by God in order to make their assimilation by men possible. Man himself has but a short life and one full of vicissitudes. There is no necessity for *dominium stabilitas*. He does not treat of the objection based on an original community of ownership.

[1] Stypmann, *op. cit.*, I, c. 5.15, p. 216. He recurs to this idea on p. 219.86. Freedom of navigation, "nisi prohibitione interveniente," p. 216.

[2] The tract is bound with Selden's *Mare clausum*, *op. cit.* (Wratislavae, 1751). Conring lived 1606–1681. (Stintzing, ii, p. 165 and p. 167.) IV, i, p. 276.

[3] *Ibid.*, VII, p. 278.

[4] *Ibid.*, XII, p. 280.

Again, they say, The sea flows and reflows. But what has this to do with *dominium?* So do rivers; but they may become the objects of private property.

He next considers the objection that the sea is so vast that no limits can be placed to it; hence it cannot be bounded in any part. Further, it suffices (they say) for the use of all men as it is. But this capacity for universal use, this ability to satisfy the needs of all men, does not prevent the acquisition of property rights in parts of it. Indeed, this characteristic facilitates it. For if the sea is so vast that it can be used by all men, what is to hinder someone from occupying a part of it without doing injury to some one else? What are the shores, but limits to the sea — call them by what name one will? Nature herself set them. Both shores and islands are suitable means for indicating the limits of the maritime jurisdiction of a state.[1]

His opponents say that the sea has never been occupied, but has always remained in *libero suo statu*. He will not concede this. But even if it were so, he adds, it would not affect his thesis.

Nam a non esse ad non posse esse non valet consequentia.

To say, this man is not a doctor, therefore he cannot become a doctor, is absurd. In the same way, to say, the sea is not occupied, therefore it cannot be occupied, is inconsequent. The conclusion does not follow.[2]

They urge vehemently that occupation impedes the freedom of commerce and travel. These are natural liberties; to hinder them (they say) is inequitable and a *causa belli*. Then according to this reasoning, Conring replies, cities must not become the objects of private property. Public roads must not be included among those things which are susceptible of being owned as private property. Those who make the above assertions of the sea must make them also of roads and cities. As a matter of fact, innocent passage is granted to travelers; nor are rights of ownership jeopardized thereby.[3]

This much in reply to the usual objections urged against *dominium maris*. There remain the ancient jurisconsults. It is true

[1] Conring, *op. cit.*, XIII, p. 280. [2] *Ibid.*, XV, p. 281. [3] *Ibid.*, XVI, p. 281.

that the classic Romanists deny the *dominium maris*. But the conditions under which they spoke no longer exist. Since their day population has increased. The amount of navigation has increased. These new conditions have made necessary alterations in that *ius gentium* which they expounded, in order to make it fit for application to the modern world.[1]

Conring did a valuable service by his realistic treatment of the problem. He stands unappalled before the law of nature and the rights of man, that formidable body of immutable laws which formed a sacred deposit once for all delivered to the lawyers. He finds that the law of nature, and the rights of man, considered separately, contain no obstacle to a just adaptation of states and peoples to the conditions of life in which they find themselves placed.

The Government of the United Provinces found its adaptation to modern conditions facilitated by the naval victories of Admiral Tromp. This enlightened state of mind received expression at the hands of the Dutch lawyer, Martin Schoock, who wrote a little book advocating a greater Navy.[2]

Imperium maris, he believes, had its origin in naval supremacy. Great naval armaments are created in order to give security to the country possessing them; but once created, they give *imperium maris*. He would no doubt admit that security may be obtained in most cases by a seapower something less than overwhelming; but he would add that perfect security, which, after all is said, is most desirable, comes only to that country which possesses a dominant Navy.

This *imperium*, then, rests upon powerful fleets, is temporary in nature, and is directed towards the preservation of the security of the state and of its citizens or subjects.

Non debet vero hoc ita cum multis intelligi, quasi vastus Oceanus, in quo nulli limites definiri possunt, dominii capax sit; sed quod quidam armis praevalentes aut in eo imperium affectarint, aut in mari Mediterraneo, quod neutiquam cum ipso Oceano componi potest, reipsa quoque imperium illud exercuerint magis, alio prohibendo illius maris usu, quem reipsa possederint.[2]

[1] Conring, *op. cit.*, XX, *et seq.*, p. 284.

[2] M. Schoockius, *Imperium Maritimum* (Amstelodami, 1654), p. 13.

The *imperium* which he describes in this passage would seem to have much the same practical results that *dominium* gives.

In the first seven chapters of his work, Schoock gives an outline of the history of *imperium maris* from the earliest time to the present. It appears that the ancient world was familiar with the idea and with the practice, and that modern nations have profited by the experience of the past. A chapter each is given to France, England, and Spain. Then follow in order the Portuguese, the Danes, the Swedes, the Venetians, the Genoese, and the Knights of Rhodes. There are some chapters giving a history of Dutch naval prowess, and a chapter each on the Dutch East India Company and the Dutch West India Company.

At the end, Schoock makes his plea for a greater Navy — to be directed especially against English sea power. An appendix contains a eulogie of Admiral Tromp.

IV. Summary

The evidence produced in the foregoing pages points to the conclusion that the somewhat uncritical praise which has been given occasionally to Grotius's essay on the freedom of the sea is not altogether warranted. The freedom of the high seas was not disputed by the advocates of a state's ownership of its territorial waters, with the possible exception of Selden. And even he conceded that, in practice, freedom of trade and of navigation should not be violated. His point that there is nothing in the *nature* of the sea to prevent its appropriation is sound. That the sea has not in fact been appropriated by the Powers is due to reasons of an entirely practical character. The only two countries which attempted to put into practice their claims to a monopoly of the western highways of traffic found that their case fell of its own weight. The fiats of the *ius gentium*, of the *ius naturale*, and of the *ius civile* simply had nothing to do with it. The reason why Spain and Portugal failed to make good their claim was this, that it was unworkable. At the other extreme lay the claims to absolute rights in territorial waters. Here, the weight of opinion is overwhelmingly in favor of the thesis that a state has the rights of ownership in the sea adjacent to its coasts. Grotius's position on the matter is ambiguous. He separated gulfs, bays and inlets from the main sea; but he failed to clothe the state with tangible rights in these waters. He failed also to distinguish between that strip of coastal waters which had become known as the adjacent sea, and the main body of the sea. In his later work on the law of war and peace he modified his position somewhat on this latter question, but he failed there also to make any concession which would seem to countenance the existence of property rights in the sea. So far as can be gathered from his cautious statements on the whole subject, he seemed to think that the rights of the state in the waters in question extended only to the maintenance and enforcement of a certain jurisdiction over these waters, and to the protection of navigation and fishing therein. It may be said with some certainty that this is the view of "Mare liberum." When it is said that Selden and his colleagues were quick to see that Grotius had attacked the British claims in "Mare liberum," it should be remembered that it is his position on the adjacent sea which constituted the attack, and not his position on the high seas. For the Continental lawyers, also, who were not parties to the British controversy, the question concerned the adjacent sea only. Outside of Holland, the Grotian position found no support. Legal theory pronounced against the community of ownership, against a common proprietorship, of the littoral sea. The British claims, and, to a less degree, the Scandinavian claims, were extravagant to the point where they encroached upon the high sea. When Grotius denounced such pretensions, he spoke to the mark. But he denounced them for the wrong reason. This question is essentially different from the former one. That is to say, that the question, how far out to sea territorial waters extend, is essentially different from the question, whether there can be territorial waters. Grotius, in denouncing the pretensions referred to, denounced them on the ground that there could be no territorial waters. . . . The real problem was, to restrict territorial waters within reasonable bounds. And here, oddly enough, Grotius pointed the way.

The problem, how to restrict the limits of territorial waters within reasonable, that is, within workable, bounds, was a problem for diplomacy rather than for law. The boundary must be restricted sufficiently to remove territorial waters from the sphere of international rivalry, and to safeguard ocean traffic; within the scope of this restriction there might be a lack of uniformity as to the limits of the territorial waters of any particular state.[1] Grotius performed an important service by suggesting that territorial waters — he called this portion of the sea, *proximum mare* — might be limited to so much as could be defended from the shore.

The theory of *dominium maris* holds that the rights of a state in its territorial waters are those of an owner over his property. The bare statement of the theory shows the need of an immediate qualification. Stypmann indicated the nature of the qualification required when he reserved the right of innocent passage for foreigners through such waters. For this property resembles at this point the property of a private individual, which is affected with a public interest under municipal law, although, in the latter case, the will of the state may prevail over the will of the private owner, whereas the control of a state over its territorial waters is absolute. Nevertheless, the existence of this public interest serves to guide the state in the exercise of its jurisdiction over its waters. The unqualified theory of *dominium maris* holds that the rights of a state over its territorial waters are those of a sovereign over his property. Stypmann perceived that the necessities of international intercourse must limit the exercise of those rights.

The Continental defenders of the theory do not seem to have attempted to use it as a weapon for combating the pretensions of either Spain and Portugal, or of Great Britain. Nor do they seem to have been interested in the immediate furtherance of any particular nationalistic ambitions. This detached position was favorable to unbiased thought, as may be easily perceived. It was pointed out in the discussion of the origin of the dispute over the rights of a state in the sea adjacent to its coasts, in the preceding chapter, that the fundamental conflict of opinion was over the extent of the ownership of the sea, rather than over the rights of ownership of a state in its territorial waters. It was further noted

[1] The history of the evolution of the three-mile limit is ably recounted by Fulton in his book, *The Sovereignty of the Sea.*

that, although this was the issue which had provoked the difference of opinion which found expression in the controversy between the advocates of a *mare liberum* and a *mare clausum*, this issue had been befogged by the divergent aspirations of the countries chiefly concerned. The British controversialists replied to a tract which was primarily concerned with attacking the claims made to the high seas by Spain and Portugal as if it had been an attack on British claims, whereas the British claims were not, essentially, the same as those of Spain and Portugal; while Grotius and his supporters made their arguments broad enough to comprehend the British claims, as if both sets of claims rested upon the same premises, the same bases, whereas in fact they did not. The point at which both sets of claims met and overlapped, or, in other words, the ground which was common to Spain and Portugal on the one hand, and to Great Britain on the other, was vaguely sensed by the parties to the controversy; but it was not clearly perceived, much less defined. The British defended at great length what Grotius had not expressly — and, perhaps, not implicitly, for, as has been remarked, he is ambiguous on the point — denied, that is, the existence of *some* territorial waters. They perceived that he would deprive them of property rights in their coastal fisheries. And they defended their title to those rights by claiming a large part of the sea adjacent to the British Isles, including the whole of the British Channel. If they had done only this; if Selden had written his book to prove that the English kings had always owned the sea for a distance of five hundred, or fourteen miles offshore, then the issue would have been fairly clear. But they did not do this. They assumed that the existence of property rights in the sea must be demonstrated. They undertook to prove that the British sovereign possessed the title to the sea *for some distance offshore* by proving that he possessed a title to the sea. The very existence of property rights was thus called into question. The result was that the true issue was lost sight of, and the controversy raged around the new one. Yet the true issue remained to cloud thought and to warp judgments.

It was the more easy to argue over the existence of territorial waters because a theory covering them had yet to be constructed.

The work had been proceeding swiftly in the world of affairs; a theory was bound soon to be formulated. The controversy had this merit, that it forced a definition. But the controversialists were debarred by the exigencies of the dispute from performing this service. This is the point at which the Continental defenders of *dominium maris* come in. Aloof from the controversy, with no policies to defend, they were admirably placed for a study of the problem. The controversy had precipitated elements which had hitherto been in solution. The European jurists (and particularly, the German jurists) studied the product and constructed their formulas. Boundaries to *mare adiacens* had already been proposed; they had been in existence, as propositions, since the age of Bartolus. The jurists left this problem to be settled by diplomacy. They concerned themselves with the nature of the rights of a sovereign in this sea. They arrived at the theory of *dominium maris*.

They arrived at this theory by two methods of reasoning. The first method involved an interchangeable use of *imperium* and *dominium*, a merging of the meaning of the one with the meaning of the other, so that the two became practically synonymous terms. The other method involved a separation of *imperium* and *dominium*, and was essentially realistic in its nature. Of the use of the first method, the work of Loccenius is perhaps the best illustration. Of the use of the second, Conring offers a first-rate example.

CHAPTER IX

THE CASE FOR THE VENETIANS

From the beginning of their rise as a maritime power, the claims of the Venetians to the Adriatic Sea, claims which they not only asserted, but enforced, had constituted a problem for the jurists. So long as the Venetians enjoyed naval supremacy, they did not trouble to defend the legality of their position; they were content with exacting obedience to it. But with the decline of their sea power in and after the sixteenth century, they found it necessary to resort to the pen.

Antonius Peregrinus has left a full statement of the Venetian position in his work, "De Privilegiis,"[1] in the eighth chapter, *De Aquis*, under the heading, *De Mari*. After giving a conventional definition of the sea,[2] he observes that its waters are divided. There is the Ocean, which encircles the earth; and there are particular seas which flow from it, and which bear the names of the kingdoms the shores of which they wash, such as, for example, the German Sea, and the British Sea.

In the sea, *imperium* and jurisdiction belongs[3] to the dominant Prince. According to the written law, the sea, as regards *proprietas*, is *nullius;* as to use, it is common to all. As to jurisdiction, it is under the reigning Prince. Because the sea is *nullius in bonis* by natural law, it and its shores as well are open to occupation. The liberty of the Venetians is founded on this freedom of the sea, because the state is built in the sea, on the islands in the sea, and on the shores of the sea. Consequently, from its birth it has been free, with its own laws and its own jurisdiction, and its own governmental machinery.

The Prince of Venice[4] thus recognizes no superior in the temporalities, within his dominions. When the power of the Roman Empire disappeared in the Adriatic, under the attacks of the

[1] Venetiis, 1604. Peregrinus died in 1616 (Hommel, *op. cit.*, p. 338).
[2] P. 387. [3] He uses the singular. [4] He uses this title.

Barbarians, the imperial authority was extinguished, and the sea deprived of one who had exercised jurisdiction over it. The Venetians, by their own valor, substituted their own authority, wresting the sea from the Barbarians.[1] *Inveterata consuetudo* has confirmed the Venetians in the free possession of the Adriatic; a fact which is recognized by the jurisconsults.

Peregrinus now proceeds to prove that the Venetians possess the *dominium* of the Adriatic. There is jurisdiction *in mari*, he observes, just as there is *in terra*.

> Inveterata autem, et immemorialis praescriptio, seu Consuetudo vim veri tituli habet. [It is truly said that] Venetos habere mare distinctum.[2]

Moreover, the jurists infer that that which is found in the territory and district of the Prince of Venice is under Venetian law, and that those who judge on the sea judge also in the territory and district of Venice.

The sea is thus treated as being within the territory of Venice. Because this is the fact, the Prince has control over navigation, over the laying of customs, over the confiscation of goods. He possesses the sea who has jurisdiction and *imperium* in the sea. Furthermore, although it is permitted by the *ius gentium* to build on the shore and in the sea, all buildings, and the persons constructing them and using them, are under the jurisdiction of the Prince.

The question arises, whether princes who possess the sea *per inveterata tempora* acquire a property right in it. The answer is affirmative.

> [The Dukes of Venice] per inveteratam consuetudinem praescripserunt, et acquierunt sibi proprietatem Maris Adriatici.[3]

[1] Peregrinus, *op. cit.*, p. 389.9. "Tantum aut abest, quod caeteri Principes id facere tunc possent, quod omnes potius ad Venetorum pietatem et auxilium oculos, et animos intenderent, et ad eos recurrerent, ut Mare ipsum a tanta Barbarorum feritate, vastitate, et servitute, tutum, et liberum redderent; quod cum longissimi temporis spatio ab eisdem, non solum infinita propemodum auri, et argenti impensa, sed innumerabilium civium quoque; suorum sanguinis effusione, ac eorundem magna pietate, et virtute, factum fuerit, defensum, et in dies hactenus nostros tutatum a Piratis, et incursoribus, merito, belli, ac gentium iure, in eorum dominium, superioritatem, Iurisdictionem, et protectionem, translatum, ac redactum esse dici debet, et firmiter tenendum. . . ."

[2] *Ibid.*, p. 389.12.

[3] *Ibid.*, p. 391.23.

In general, the sea is a district of the adjacent state.[1] This, of course, was the doctrine of Baldus.

Although Peregrinus holds that the Prince possesses the ownership of the sea, he does not give him the full rights of a proprietor. The use of the shore is common to all the subjects of the Prince. They may not be forbidden to approach the sea for the purpose of fishing, and in order to tend their nets. There is also freedom of building, providing that no harm is done thereby to the public welfare.[2] Thus Peregrinus guards the liberty of the subject.

It goes without saying that the Prince has full and complete jurisdiction over his ports and harbors.

Peregrinus devotes some attention to rights of fishery.

> Regula est iuris scripti: Piscationes in mari, portubus, et fluminibus publicis iure permissas esse, et pisces inde capti, efficiuntur capientum.[3]

Fishing before the private house of another person is permitted. *Praesides* and the lesser lords cannot prohibit the use of sea fisheries, or the use of those in harbors and public rivers.[4] Whether the Prince can do so is a disputed question. It is doubtful that he has the authority to do so, because in these waters the right of fishery is common to all. Peregrinus, however, is not clear on the subject. He inclines to the view that the Prince possesses no *ius prohibendi* over the sea; but ports and public rivers are the property of the Prince,[5] and this fact furnishes some ground for hesitation. Peregrinus does not commit himself.

Whatever the rights of the Prince may be in this regard, he does possess the right to grant fisheries to individuals. Peregrinus says that *piscationum redditus de regalibus esse.*[6] It follows that fisheries may be granted in certain parts of the sea either by a contract or by privilege.

The subject may, however, himself acquire exclusive rights to a fishery without the intervention of the Prince. An "inveterate" and immemorial custom of fishing in one place gives to the person following it a prescriptive right to exclude others from

[1] Peregrinus, *op. cit.*, p. 391.24. [2] *Ibid.*, p. 392.26.

[3] *Ibid.*, p. 392.34. The "ius piscandi omnibus commune est" (393.37).

[4] *Ibid.*, p. 393.35.

[5] *Ibid.*, p. 392.32. Is "autem Princeps, cuius est portus, indicere potest subeuntibus portum vectigalia, et gabellas." [6] *Ibid.*, p. 393.37.

enjoying the fishery in question, provided that these others have acquiesced in his assumption of the right to exclude them.

Peregrinus is not at all sure of himself in the statement of his doctrine on this point.[1] The fundamental question here is,[2] whether *proprietas* in those rights which are common to all by the *ius gentium* can be acquired by an individual by prescription against the Prince, the republic,[3] and the common use of all, even though such prescription be from time immemorial. He, Peregrinus, does not answer the question. He cites six authorities for the affirmative, against one for the negative, and then proceeds with his argument on the basis of an affirmative answer. The law seems to be that an uninterrupted and exclusive exercise of the *ius piscandi*, if it conforms to the usual laws of prescription, leads to the same result for the user as if it, that is, the *ius piscandi* in question, had been given to him by a grant, concession, or privilege from the Prince.

Pacius, writing after the question of the territoriality of the sea or of any part of it had come to the fore in legal theory, treats the claims of the Venetians from another point of view.[4] The question as he puts it [5] is, Is the Republic of Venice lord of the Adriatic Sea, and, if so, by what right, and to what extent.

[1] Peregrinus, *op. cit.*, p. 393.39–41. "Sed utrum ius piscandi in his (aquis) praescribi possit, quaestio est notabilis. Primo tamen advertendum est, quod sine possessione nulla currit praescriptio.

"Secundo, quod possessio iuris piscandi, ut acquiratur, non sufficit, quem per se, et auctores suos in aliqua parte maris, aut fluminis, seu portus piscasse per plurimos annos, sed ulterius requiritur, quod alios piscari volentes prohibuerit, et illi acquieverint prohibitioni, hoc enim modo, et non alio, in iuribus incorporalibus acquiritur possessio.

"Tertio advertendum est: nam quaesita possessione, clarum est, possidenti duos contingere notabiles effectus: Primus est, ut turbantem eum in sua possessione possit interdictis possessorijs, vel etiam iniuriarum compescere. . . . Secundus est, ut etiam possit de facto piscari volentem impune prohibere, et propria auctoritate pro tuitione suae possessionis repellere."

[2] *Ibid.*, p. 394.42.

[3] Peregrinus uses this word.

[4] Iulius Pacius, *Disceptatio de Dominio Maris Hadriatici pro Venetis*. To be found in Joach. Hagemeier, *De Imperio Maris variorum dissertiones*, Francofurti ad Moenum, 1663.

[5] "An Serenissima Respublica Veneta sit domina maris Hadriatici, et ex quo jure, et in quantum. . . ." P. 11.

The influence of the method of appealing to historical records for a justification of the claims to be defended is apparent in his work.

This question must not be decided by the Roman *ius civile*, because the Republic is not subject to the Roman Empire. Nor is it bound by the Roman laws, except in so far as it has adopted them of its own free will because of their excellence. The question must not be decided, either, by an appeal to Venetian law, because, although the Venetians live under this law, it does not bind foreign republics or "provinces." There remains, then, the *ius gentium*, according to which the question must be decided,

> quod naturali ratione apud omnes gentes valet . . . et ut singularum rerum dominia, ita etiam regna, et imperia distinxit.[1]

Pacius cites a number of doctors, headed by Bartolus, who answer in the affirmative the question he has put.

> Omnes Doctores [he remarks] qui usque ad haec tempora scripserunt, uno ore testantur, Dominos Venetos esse hujus maris dominos.[2]

The testimony of the historians is found to be in harmony with that of the doctors. This testimony is confirmed by the actual fact that the Venetians have been in control of the Adriatic for many years.

What is the legal justification for the claims of the Venetians?

> [On this point,] Doctores vulgo putant, eam id praescripsisse spatio temporis, cujus initii memoria non extat. . . . Cum hac autem praescriptione dicunt concurrere tacitam concessionem principis, et ita, acquiri simul praescriptione et privilegio.[3]

Pacius notes a certain confusion among the doctors as to whether prescription or custom is the basis of this title. Nor are they quite clear on the relation of custom (*consuetudo*) to prescription. As for himself, he feels that the Venetians may justly rest their title on both prescription and custom.[4]

Pacius sums up his argument in the following words: [5]

> Imperii igitur in mare acquisitio secundum Doctores referri potest ad praescriptionem respectu Imperatoris, cui aufertur, et ad consuetudinem respectu navigantium per mare. Item ad privilegium, quia haec praescriptio, cum sit tanti temporis, cujus initii memoria non extat, vim habet tacitae concessionis Caesareae et privilegij. Ergo in summa Doctorum communissima sententia est. Illustrissimos Dominos Venetos habere imperium maris Had-

[1] Pacius, *op. cit.*, p. 19. II.
[2] *Ibid.*, p. 11. I.
[3] *Ibid.*, p. 14.
[4] *Ibid.*, p. 16.
[5] *Ibid.*, p. 16.

riatici, illudque praescripsisse longissimo tempore, cujus initii non est memoria: quae praescriptio dici etiam potest consuetudo, vel diverso respectu, vel late sumpto praescriptionis vocabulo: et vim habet privilegii.

The doctors, he notes again, do not make exact inquiries into the mode of this form of acquisition. Therefore one says, *ex consuetudine*, another, *ex concessionis principis*, another still, *ex privilegio et concessione Caesarea, vel usurpatione, vel pro frequente usu.* But it must be repeated that the rights of the Venetians flow from the *ius gentium*, and not *ex jure Romano*, except in so far as the precepts of the *ius gentium* are contained therein.

And he concludes,[1]

Hoc posito, dico Serenissimam Rempublicam Venetam esse dominam maris Hadriatici per ejus occupationem. Probatur hoc fieri posse, quia mare cum sit nullius, naturali ratione, proinde jure gentium conceditur occupanti, ut cetera, quae communia cicuntur.

Now, having shown that the *dominium maris*[2] pertains to the Venetian Republic, it remains to show in what ways this *dominium* manifests itself. This is the third point in Pacius's demonstration. He finds that the exercise of the rights of *dominium* takes five forms. These are as follows:[3]

1. The Dukes make the sea secure; this security is obtained, in particular, by the suppression of piracy.
2. They protect their own subjects.
3. They punish offenders apprehended at sea under the same laws that are applied to offenders caught within their dominions.
4. They can prohibit navigation.
5. They can levy tribute and taxes on navigation.

Venice was, of course, the one country for which almost any good lawyer could make out an excellent case. The Venetians had enjoyed supremacy in the Adriatic throughout the middle age. Their claims had been acquiesced in very generally, both by statesmen and jurists. In saying that the Venetians had been in control of the Adriatic "for many years," Pacius was understating the facts. It is not clear that Pacius is urging a right of property in the sea, although he does expressly do so in one place

[1] Pacius, *op. cit.*, p. 17.

[2] The substitution of *dominium* for *imperium* is perhaps noteworthy.

[3] *Ibid.*, pp. 20–21.

in his argument. It seems reasonable to conclude, nevertheless, that he regards the *imperium* for which he is contending as a species, at the least, of ownership. This conclusion is strengthened by his use of the word *dominium*. And if his argument is placed in the light of the history of Venice in the Adriatic, there can be little doubt that he regarded that republic as the proprietress of that sea.[1]

[1] Bound with the 1635 English edition of Selden's *Mare Clausum* is a tract entitled *Dominium Maris*, or, *The Dominion of the Sea*. It purports to be a translation from the Italian of an argument between the representatives of the Republic of Venice and the Emperor Ferdinand, in which the former succeeded in demonstrating, if not to the satisfaction of their opponents, at least to the point of winning their case, that the Republic possessed a right of property in the Adriatic. The tract is dated London, 1652.

The (unknown) translator says in his preface: "I chancing som years past to bee at Venice, upon consideration of the premisses, did labor with a great desire, to know the grounds of that title, whereupon the Venetians founded their Dominion of the Sea; and after much search, even to the despair of obteining of it, I hapned upon this ensuing argument, conteining a Plea or Dispute, betwixt the Austrians and Venetians, touching the Dominion of the Adriatick Sea, not fictitious or devised onely to color the caus, but faithfully transcribed from out the publick Registers of that Citie, which I offer herewith to the Reader in English." (The pages of the preface are unnumbered; the page containing this quotation should be numbered 5.)

Commissioners representing the "Republick" and the Emperor met in Friuli in 1563 to settle all outstanding differences. The chief complaint on the imperial side was that subjects of the Emperor were not allowed to navigate freely on the Adriatic. The Venetians forced their ships to put in at Venice, and forced them to pay customs there. These acts constituted violations of the freedom of navigation; or, if not, then they were in violation of the terms of certain Capitularies in force between the Duke of Venice and the Emperor Ferdinand. (P. 4; pp. 6–7.)

During the course of the arguments on both sides, one of the Venetian Commissioners found occasion to defend the claims of the Republic to the Adriatic. The translator uses the word dominion, to express the word *dominium*. "To say that the sea is common and free to all," observed the Commissioner, "is only to say that the sea cannot be appropriated by a private person. It is to say that a private person cannot monopolize the use of the sea. It does not mean that the sea cannot be under the protection of a Prince. It does not preserve the sea from being subject to the laws of such a Prince. The sea, in just the same way as the land, is subject to bee divided amongst men, and appropriated to Cities and Potentates. . . ." (Pp. 14–15.) He calls in the testimony of writers and of history to substantiate his position, to prove that the Venetians have possessed the Adriatic with full rights of ownership from time out of mind. As the Emperor has the right to levy customs on land, so the Venetians have a similar right to levy customs at sea; for their dominion is on the sea, rather than on the land.

"The Imperialists after they had conferred together, took a resolution not to persevere in the demand of Justice, and the Baron with Suorz said openly, that the Republick was Patron of the Gulf, and might impose what Customs they thought fitting; and that they thought so in their consciences: but therewithal they were of the opinion, that for honestie sake . . . it should be done with the least incommoditie of the subjects" concerned. "The other three said, that it was now no time, either to approve or to disapprove the Dominion of the Sea," but to find a *modus vivendi*. (Pp. 36–37.)

BIBLIOGRAPHY

BIBLIOGRAPHY

I. Sources[1]

Abdy and Walker, *Commentaries of Gaius and Rules of Ulpian*. Cambridge, 1874.

——, *Institutes of Gaius*. Cambridge, 1874.

——, *Institutes of Justinian*. Cambridge, 1878.

Accursius, *Institutionum Iuris Civilis . . . cum Accursiana Interpretatione*, etc. Lugduni, 1542.

Afflictis, Matthaeus de, *Sanctiones, et Constitutiones novissima Praelectio*, 2 vols. Venetiis, 1562.

——, *Commentarius super tres Libros Feudorum* (Francofurti, 1598?). The title-page is missing.

*Alciatus, Andrea, *In Pandectarum seu Digestorum Iuris Civilis . . . Commentaria*, etc., 3 vols. Basileae, 1582.

——, *Dispunctionum*. Basileae, 1523.

Almeyda, Dominicus H. de, *Analysis exellentiarum in Jure Numeri quinarii. Accesserunt nonnullae Allegationes super variis Juris Quaestionibus*. Conimbricae, 1726.

Alteserra, A. D., *Brevis et Euncleata Expositio in Institutionum Iustiniani*. Tolosea, 1664.

*Althusius, Johan., *Dicaeologicae, libri tres*. Francofurti, 1618.

Alvarottus, Iacobus, *De Feudis*. Francofurti, 1570.

*Amaya, Franciscus, *Commentarii in Codicis Imperatoris Iustiniani*. Lugduni, 1639.

Ambrosius, S(anctus), *Hexameri Libros Sex*. Edited by R. O. Gilbert. Lipsiae, 1840.

——, *De Officiis Clericorum, libros tres*. *Ibid*., 1839.

Amicangelus, Iosus, *Quaestiones Feudales*. Neapoli, 1653. Contains his *Tractatus de Regalibus Officiis*.

*Angelus, A., *Institutionum Iustiniani Libros Commentarii*. Venetiis, 1558.

Ansaldis, Ansaldus de, *De Commercio et Mercatura Discursus legales*. Romae, 1689.

[1] The names of those jurisconsults who take the classical position in regard to the legal status of the sea are marked with an asterisk.

Arumaeus, D., *Discussionem Academicorum de Iure Publice*, 5 vols. Jenae, 1621.

*Aymus, Baptista, *De Alluvionum Iure universo*, 3 vols. Bononiae, 1580.

*Azevedus, Alphonsus de, *Commentariorum Iuris Civilis in Hispaniae Regias Constitutiones*, new ed. Duaci, 1612.

*Azo, *Summa Azonis*, etc. Venetiis, 1610.

Balbus, Ioan. Franciscus, *De Praescriptionibus*, in the *Tractatus illustrium in utraque tum Pontifici, tum Caesarei Iuris Facultate Iurisconsultorum*, etc., 17 vols. Venetiis, 1584, vol. xvii.

*Balduinus, Franciscus, *Commentarii in Libros quatuor Institutionum Iuris Civilis*. Pariis, 1554.

Baldus (Ubaldi), *Opera*, Lugduni, 1585. Bound in ten folios. *In Usus Feudorum Commentaria*. Lugduni, 1585. *Opera*. Venetiis, 1586. Bound in ten folios. *Praelectiones in quatuor Institutionum Libros*. Venetiis, 1586.

Barbatus, Horatius, *De Divisione Fructuum*. Neapoli, 1638.

Bartolus (de Saxaferrato), *Opera*. Basileae, 1529. Bound in five folio volumes.

——, *Opera*. Venetiis, 1602. Bound in five folio volumes.

——, *Tyberiadis Tractatus de Fluminibus*. Bononiae, 1576.

Bitschius, Caspar, *Commentarius in Consuetudines Feudorum*. Edited by J. M. Bitschius. Argentorati, 1673.

Bodin, I., *Les Six Livres de la République*. Paris, 1576.

Bodinus, Ioan., *De Republica, libri sex*. Francofurti, 1622.

Bonus, Benedictus, *De Censibus*, in the *Tractatus illustrium*, q.v., vol. vi. Pars I.

*Borcholten, Ioan., *Ad Instituta Iustiniani Commentaria*, new ed. Lugduni, 1653.

Borellus, C., *De Magistratuum Edictio Tractatus*. Venetiis, 1620.

Boretius, *Capitularia Regum Francorum*, in the *Monumenta Germaniae Historica*, Legum Sectio II. i. Hannoverae, 1883.

Borough(s), Sir John, *Sovereignty of the British Seas*. Edited by T. C. Wade. Edinburgh, 1920.

Bossius, Regidius, *Tractatus varii*. Venetiis, 1570.

Boutaric, François de, *Traité des Droits Seigneuriaux et des Matières Feodales*, new ed. Tolouse (sic), 1767.

Brachylogus, etc. Edited by D. H. C. Senckenberg, Francofurti et Lipsiae, 1743.

*Bracton, Henricus de, *De Legibus et Consuetudinibus Angliae.* Edited by Sir Travers Twiss, 6 vols. London, 1878–83.

*Brant, Sebastianus, *Titulorum omnium Iuris.* Lugduni, 1560.

Breslau, *Die Urkunden Konrads II*, in the *M.G.H.*, q.v., *Conradi II. Diplomata*, tom. iv. Hannover und Leipzig, 1909.

**Britton.* Translated and edited by F. M. Nichols, 2 vols. Oxford, 1865.

*Broeus, Fran., *Expositiones in Imperatoris Iustiniani Institutionum.* Lutetiae Parisiorum, 1622.

Brunnemannus, Joh., *Commentarius in Codicem Justinianeum*, 2 vols. Lugduni, 1715.

——, *Commentarius in quinquaginta Libros Pandectarum.* Edited by Samuel Stryk. 'Coloniae Allobrogum, 1752.

Brussius, Alex., *Principia Juris Feudalis.* Edinburgi, 1713.

*Buccaferreus, Hier., *Responsorum.* Bononiae, 1645.

Bursatus, Fran., *Conciliorum*, 4 vols. Francofurti, 1594.

*Caballus, Petrus, *Resolutionum criminalium.* Venetiis, 1644. Contains his *Tractatus de omni Genere Homicidii.*

Caepolla, Bartholomaeus, *Opera omnia.* Lugduni, 1578.

——, *Tractatus de Servitutibus*, 4th ed. Coloniae Agrippinae, 1660.

——, *De Servitutibus rusticorum Praediorum*, in the *Tractatus illustrium* q.v., vol. vi. Pars II.

Calcagninus, Carolus L., *Opus de Variatione ultimae Voluntatis*, 3 vols. Romae, 1747.

Callis, Robert, *Reading of, on the Statute of Sewers, 23 Hen. VIII. c. 5*, 4th ed., by W. J. Broderip. London, 1824.

*Calvinus, Ioh., *Lexicon iuridicum Iuris Caesarei.* Genevae, 1670.

*Cancerius, J., *Variarum Resolutionum Iuris*, etc. Barcinone, 1608.

Caponus, Iulius, *Controversiarum forensium.* Coloniae Allobrogum, 1732.

*Castro, Alphonso de, *De Potestate poenalis*, quoted (in part) by Grotius, *Mare liberum*, etc., q.v.

*Castro, Paul de, *In Digesta*, 6 vols. Lugduni, 1553.

Coke, Sir Edward; Thomas, J. H., *Systematic Arrangement of Lord Coke's First Institute of the Laws of England*, 3 vols. Philadelphia, 1836.

——, *Fourth Part of the Institutes of the Lawes of England*, 4th ed. London, 1669.

Connanus, F., *Commentariorum Iuris Civilis.* Basileae, 1562.

Conrat, M., *Breviarum Alaricianum*, etc. Leipzig, 1903.

Conring, Hermann, *Exercitatio de Dominio Maris*, bound with Seldeni, Joh., *Mare clausum*, etc. Wratislaviae, 1751.

Constitutiones et Acta publica Imperatorum et Regum, in the *M.G.H.*, q.v., Legum Sectio IV. viii, Pars prior. Hannoverae et Lipsiae, 1910.

Conversanus, M., *Commentaria super Ritu Regni Siciliae*, etc. Panormi, 1614.

*Cormanus, F., *Commentariorum Iuris Civilis*. Basileae, 1562.

*Cormerius, Thoma, *Henrici IIII. . . . Codex Iuris Civilis Romani*. Lugduni, 1602.

Corpus Iuris Civilis, Commentariis Accursii, et multorum insuper Doctorum, etc., 5 vols. Pariis, 1559.

Corpus Iuris Civilis, 2 vols. Edited by D. Gothofredus. Amsterodami, 1663.

Corpus Iuris Civilis, 2 parts, ster. ed., 5th impression. Edited by Fratres Kriegelii and A. E. Hermann. Lipsiae, 1875.

Corpus Iuris Civilis, 3 vols., ster. ed., 15th impression. Edited by Fratres Kriegelii, A. E. Hermann, and D. E. Osenbruegen. Lipsiae, 1875.

Corpus Iuris Civilis, 3 vols. Edited by Krueger, Mommsen, Schoell, and Kroll. Berlin, 1904–08.

Corvinus, Ioh. F., *Digesta per Aphorismos*, etc. Amsterodami, 1642.

——, *Ius Feudale*, 3d ed. Amsterodami, 1580.

Cragius, Thomus, *Jus Feudale*, 3d ed. Edinburgi, 1732.

*Cujacius, Jacobus, *Opera omnia*, 10 vols. Neapoli, 1758.

*Curtius, Rochus, *Enarrationes*. Lugduni, 1550.

Danaeus, Lambertus, *Aphorismi Politici et Militares*, etc. Lugduni Batavorum, 1639.

*Daoyz, Stephanus, *Juris Civilis Summa*, etc., 2 vols. Mediolani, 1742.

Decianus, Tiberius, *Responsorum*, 3 vols. Venetiis, 1579.

Despeisses, Antoine, *Les Oevures de*, 3 vols. Alyon, 1660.

Digges, Thomas, *Proofs of the Queen's Interest in Lands Left by the Sea and the Salt Shores thereof*. Lansdowne MSS. No. 100, art. 6, Brit. Mus. Reprinted in Moore, S. A., *History . . . of the Foreshore*, q.v.

*Donellus, Hugo, *Commentarii de Iure Civili*, 6th ed., 16 vols. Norimbergae, 1827.

*Duarenus, Franciscus, *In Lib. iv. Cod. et tertiam Partem Digest. Commentarii*, 2 vols. Allobrogum, 1608.

*Dupleix, Scipio, *In Institutionum Iustiniani Imperatoris*. Pariis, 1635.

*Everhardus, Nicolas, *Consilia sive Responsa.* Antverpiae, 1643.
*Faber, Ioannes, *In Institutiones Commentarii.* Lugduni, 1557.
Firmanus, Ioan. Bert., *Repertorium*, 4 vols. Basilieae, 1573.
**Fleta, seu Commentarius Juris Anglicani*, with Seldenus, Joan., *Ad Fletam, Dissertatio historica*, 2d ed. Londoni, 1685.
Forsterus, Valentinus, *De Historica Iuris Romani, libri tres.* Helmaestadii, 1610. Contains his *De Iurisdictione Romana.*
Fortescue, Sir John, *De Laudibus Legum Angliae . . . translated into English illustrated with the notes of Mr. Selden*, etc., 2d ed. In the Savoy, 1741.
——, *Governance of England.* Edited by Charles Plummer. Oxford, 1885.
*Frantzkius, Georgius, *In iv. Libros Institutionum Juris Civilis Justiniani . . . Commentarius.* Argentorati, 1653.
Freitas, Seraphinus de, *De Justo Imperio Lusitanorum Asiatico.* Vallisolati, 1625.
Garsia, Ioan., *De Expensis et Molierationibus*, in the *Tractatus illustrium*, q.v., vol. xvii.
Gentilis, Albericus, *Hispanicae Advocationis, libri duo*, 2d ed. Amstelhedami, 1661.
Godolphin, John. *A View of the Admiral Jurisdiction*, 2d ed. London, 1685.
Gothofredus, Iacobus, *De Imperio Maris*, etc. Genevae, 1637.
*Graswinckel, Theod., *Stricturae ad Censuram Joannis a Felden ad Libros Hugonis Grotii De Iure Belli ac Pacis.* Amstelaedami, 1654.
Gregorius, Petrus, *Syntagma Iuris universi, atque Legum pene omnium Gentium*, 2 vols. Lugduni, 1587.
*Grotius, Hugo, *Mare liberum*, etc. Translated by R. Van D. Magoffin, as, *The Freedom of the Seas*, etc. New York, 1916.
——, *De Iure Belli ac Pacis, libri tres*, with an abridged translation by William Whewell, 3 vols. Cambridge, 1853.
Gruterus, Ianus, *Florilegij magni, seu Polyanthtae*, 2 vols. Venetiis, 1625.
Gudelinus, Petrus, *Opera omnia.* Antverpiae, 1685.
Hale, Sir Matthew, *A Narrative Legall and Historicall Touching the Customes*, Hargrave MS. No. 98. Reprinted in Moore, S. A., *History . . . of the Foreshore*, q.v.
——, *De Jure Maris*, Hargrave MS. No. 97; and Addit. No. 30228 Brit. Mus. Reprinted, Moore, S. A., *op. cit.*

Heimbach, D. C. G. E., *Basilicorum Libri LX* . . . 5 vols. Lipsiae, 1836–50.

Hervé, *Théorie des Matières feodales et censuelles*, 8 vols. Paris, 1785–88.

Igneus, Ioannes, *Commentarii in aliquot Constitutiones Principum.* Lugduni et Aureliae, 1541.

Institutiones Iuris Civilis. Venetiis, 1578.

Isernia, Andrea de, *In Usus Feudorum Commentaria.* Lugduni, 1579.

Klockius, Caspar, *Tractatus Juridico-Politico-Polemico-Historicus de Aerario, libri duo.* Norimbergae, 1671.

Krueger, Paul, *Codex Iustinianus.* Berolini, 1877.

——: *Ulpiani Liber Singularis Regularum; Pauli Libri quinque Sententiarum*, etc. Berolini, 1878.

Krueger and Mommsen, *Theodosiani Libri XVI*, etc., 2 vols. Berolini, 1905.

Lehmann, Karl, *Das Langobardische Lehnrecht.* Göttingen, 1898.

Lenel, O., *Das Edictum perpetuum*, 2d ed. Leipzig, 1907.

Leunclavius, Ioan., *LX. Liborum, Basilikon*, etc. Basileae, 1575.

——, *Iuris Graeco-Romani.* Francofurti, 1596.

Limpius, Pompeius, *Repetitionum in variis Iuris Civilis Leges*, 8 vols. Venetiis, 1608.

Loccenius, Johannes, *De Jure maritimo, Libri tres.* Holmiae, 1664. Bound and paged with his *Seuciae Regni Jus maritimum.* Holmiae, 1674.

Maitland, F. W., *Selected Passages from Bracton and Azo.* London, 1895.

Malynes, Gerard, *Consuetudo vel, Lex Mercatoria.* London, 1656.

*Matthaeus, Antonius, *Commentariis ad Institutiones.* Trajecti ad Rhenum, 1672.

Medici, Sebastianus, *De Venatione, Piscatione, et Aucapio*, in the *Tractatus illustrium*, q.v., vol. xvii.

Menochius, Iacobus, *Consiliorum sive Responsorum*, 4 vols. Francofurti, 1628.

Mornacius, Antonius, *Observationes in viginti quatuor priores Libros Digestorum*, new ed., 2 vols. Lutetiae Parisiorum, 1721.

Mühlbacher, *Die Urkunden Pippins, Karlomanns und Karls des Grossen*, in the *M. G. H.*, q.v., *Diplomatum Karolinorum; Pippini, Carlomanni, et Caroli Magni Diplomata.* Hannover, 1906.

Muirhead, John, *Institutes of Gaius and Rules of Ulpian.* Edinburgh, 1880.

*Mynsingerus, Ioach., *Apotelesma*, etc. Venetiis, 1602.
Natta, Marciant, *Consiliorum sive Responsorum*, 2 vols. Venetiis, 1584.
*Negusantius, Hadrianus, *Sylva Responsorum et Practicarum Disputationum.* Venetiis, 1619.
*Nicasius, *Super Institutionibus.* Lipsiae, 1541.
Pacianus, Fulvius, *Consilia.* Augustae Vindelicorum, 1605.
Pacius, Iulius, *Analysis ad Instituta.* Lugduni Batavorum, 1649.
——, *Disceptatio de Dominio Maris Hadriatici pro Venetis*, in Hagemeier, Joach., *De Imperio Maris variorum Dissertationes.* Francofurti ad Moenum, 1663.
Pasquier, d'Etienne, *L'Interpretation des Institutes de Justinien.* Paris, 1847.
Peregrinus, Antonius, *De Privilegiis.* Venetiis, 1604.
*Perezius, Antonius, *Iuris Civilis Antecessoris Institutiones imperiales.* Vesaliae, 1670.
*Perneder, Andreas, *Institutiones*, etc. Ingolstadt, 1573.
Picardus, Antonius, *Commentariorum in quatuor Institutionum . . . Libros*, 3d ed., 2 vols. Salmananticae, 1618.
Plowden, Edmund, *The Argument of, in Sir John Constable's Case*, Hargrave MS. No. 15, fo. 95d. Reprinted in Moore, S. A., *History . . . of the Foreshore*, q.v.
Pontanus, J. I., *Discussiones historicae. Quibus Mare clausum Johanni Seldeni propius Inspicitur Expenditurque.* Bound with Seldeni, J., *Mare clausum.* Wratislaviae, 1751.
Ponte, I. Franciscus de, *De Potestate Proregis, Tractatus.* Neapoli, 1611.
*Porcus, Christopher, *Super Institutionibus.* Lugduni, 1540. This volume contains Faber on the *Institutes.*
Post, Edward, *Gaii Institutionum Iuris Civilis Commentarii quatuor*, 3d ed. Oxford, 1890.
*Pothier, A. G., *Pandectae Justiniae*, etc., 5 vols., 4th ed. Paris, 1818.
Rebuffus, Iacobus, *Lectura super tribus ultimis Libris Codicis.* Augustae Taurinorum, 1591.
Rosenthal, Henricus a, *Tractatus et Synopsis totius Juris Feudalis.* Taurini, 1616.
*Ruinus, Carolus, *Consiliorum seu Responsorum*, 5 vols. Venetiis, 1591.
Sandars, T. E., *Institutes of Justinian.* London, 1853.

Schneidewinus, Ioan., *In quatuor Institutionum imperialum D. Iustiniani Libros Commentarii.* Argentorati, 1586. (In the Venice edition of 1615, the author's name appears as Oinotomus, Io.)

Schoockius, Martinus, *Imperium maritimum.* Amstelodami (sic), 1654.

Schurpft, Hieronymus, *Consiliorum seu Responsorum Iuris.* Francofurti ad Moenum, 1575.

Schwalm, *Constitutiones et Acta publica Imperatorum et Regum,* in the *M.G.H.*, q.v., two volumes: Legum Sectio II. iv, i, and *ibid.*, IV. iii. Hannoverae et Lipsiae, 1904–06.

*Scurus, Io. Baptista, *In Iustiniani . . . Institutiones.* Perusiae, 1621.

Selden, John, *Mare clausum; The Right and Dominion of the Sea,* etc. Translated by J. H., *Gent.* London, 1663.

Seldenus, Ioannes, *Mare clausum, seu Dominio Maris, libri duo.* Londoni, 1635. Bound with an English translation by Marchamont Nedham. London, 1652.

Senckenberg, H. C. E. von, *Ius Feudorum Langobardicum,* in his *Corpus Iuris feudalis Germanici,* etc. Edited by D. L. F. Eisenhart. Halle, 1772.

*Soacius, Thaddaeus, *Commentaria in quatuor Institutionum . . . Libros.* Venetiis, 1600.

Sola, Antonius, *Commentaria ad Decreta antiqua, ac nova, novasque Constitutiones.* Augustae Taurinorum, 1607.

Solorzanus, Ioannes, *De Indiarum Iure.* Lugduni, 1672.

Stypmannus, Io. Franciscus, *Scriptorum de Iure nautico et maritimo Fasciculus.* Halae Magdeburgicae, 1740.

——, *Tractatus de Iure maritimo,* bound with Seldenus, Ioan., *Mare Clausam.* Wratislaviae, 1751.

*Suarez, Rodericus, *Opera omnia,* 2 vols. Antverpiae, 1618.

Surdus, Ioan. Petrus, *Consiliorum sive Responsorum,* 4 vols. Venetiis, 1615.

T., L., *Collection de Jurisprudence sur les Matières Feodales et les Droits Seigneuriaux,* new ed., 2 vols. Avignon, 1773.

Tabor, Joh. Otto, *Tractatuum Opus,* 2 vols. Lipsiae, 1688.

Telfy, I. B., *Corpus Iuris Attici,* etc. Pestini et Lipsiae, 1868.

*Theophilus, *Institutionum Libri IV.* Edited by Carolus Annibal Fabrotus, 2d ed. Pariis, 1679.

*Treutlerus, Hieronymus, and Schöpsius, Andrea, *Consiliorum sive Responsum.* Francofurti, 1625.

Tuschus, Dominicus, *Practicarum Conclusionum Iuris in omni Foro frequentiorum,* 8 vols. Romae. 1606.

Die Urkunden Heinrichs II und Arduius, in the *M. G. H.*, q.v., *Heinrici et Arduii Diplomata*, tom. IIII. Hannover, 1900–03.

Die Urkunden Otto des II, in the *M. G. H.*, q.v., *Ottonis II et III. Diplomata*, tom. II. i. Hannover, 1888–93.

Die Urkunden Otto des III, *ibid.*, tom. II. ii.

*Vasquius, Fernandus, *Controversiarum Illustrium, libri tres*. Venetiis, 1564.

Vinnius, Arnoldus, *In quatuor Libros Institutionum . . . Commentarius*. Edited by Heineccius. Lugduni Batavorum, 1726.

Weiland, *Constitutiones et Acta publica Imperatorum et Regum*, in the *M. G. H.*, q.v., Legum Sectio IV. vi, Partis prioris Fasciculus I. Hannoverae et Lipsiae, 1914.

Welwood, William, *An Abridgement of all the Sea Lawes*. London, 1636.

——, *De Dominio Maris Iuribusque ad Dominium praecipue Spectantibus Assertio brevis et methodica*. Cosmopoli, 1615. (Quoted by Fulton, T. W., *Sovereignty of the Sea*, q.v.)

*Wesenbecius, Matthaeus, *Institutionum . . . Iustiniani*. Basileae, 1572.

*Zasius, Udalricus, *Opera omnia Commentaria*, 2 vols. Francofurti, 1590.

Zeumer, *Leges Visigothorum*, in the *M. G. H.*, q.v., Legum Sectio I. Hannoverae et Lipsiae, 1902.

*Zobel, Christoff, *Sachsenspiegel*. Leipzig, 1595.

*Zoesius, Henr., *Commentarius ad Digestorum*, 2 vols. Lovanii, 1656.

——, *Commentarius Digestorum seu Pandectarum*, Edited by Valerius Andreas and C. D. H. A. Proingo, 4th ed. Brussels, 1718.

II. Secondary Works

Abdy, J. T., *Feudalism: Its Rise, Progress, and Consequences*. London, 1890.

Aristotle, *Oeconomica*. Translated by E. S. Forster. Oxford, 1920.

——, *Politics*. Translated by William Ellis. New York, 1919.

Austin, John, *Lectures on Jurisprudence*, 3d ed., by Robert Campbell, 2 vols. London, 1869.

Beauchet, L., *Histoire de Droit Privé de la République Athènienne*, 4 vols. Paris, 1897.

Böckh, A., *Die Staatshaltung der Athener*, 2d ed., 4 vols. Berlin, 1851.

Bonjean, Georges, *Explication méthodique des Institutes de Justinien*, 2 vols. Paris, 1878–80.

Buckland, W. W., *Text-Book of Roman Law from Augustus to Justinian.* Cambridge, 1921.

Carlyle, R. W. and A. J., *History of Mediaeval Political Theory in the West*, 4 vols. New York, 1903–22.

Cicero, *De Officiis.*

——, *Pro Sex. Roscius Amerino.*

Dapper, D'O., *Description exacte des Isles de l'Archipel, traduite du flamand.* Amsterdam, 1703.

Figgis, C. N., *Bartolus and the Development of European Political Ideas*, Royal Historical Society, *Transactions*, xix, 156. *See* also, *Divine Right of Kings*, 2d ed., Cambridge, 1914, Appendix, for this paper.

Fulton, T. W., *Sovereignty of the Sea.* Edinburgh and London, 1911.

Gierke, Otto, *Das Deutsche Genossenschaftsrecht*, 4 vols. Berlin, 1881.

——, *Political Theories of the Middle Age.* Translated by F. W. Maitland, with an Introduction. Cambridge, 1922.

d'Halicarnasse, D. (or, Halicarnassensis, D.), *Opera*, 5 vols. Edited by Io. Iac. Reiske. Lipsiae, 1774–77.

Hommelius, C. F., *Litteratura Iuris*, 2d ed. Lipsiae, 1779.

Hunter, W. A., *Systematic and Historical Exposition of Roman Law in the Order of a Code.* London, 1876.

Lacroix, M. L., *Isles de la Grèce.* Paris, 1881.

Landsberg, E., *Die Glosse der Accursius.* Leipzig, 1883.

Lipenius, Martinus, *Bibliotheca realis iuridica*, etc. Edited by Gottlob Augustus Ienichen. Lipsiae, 1736.

Livy, *Historia.*

Maitland, Frederic W., *Constitutional History of England.* Cambridge, 1908.

Maynz, Charles, *Cours de Droit Romain*, 4th ed., 3 vols. Bruxelles, 1876.

Moore, Stuart A., *History and Law of the Foreshore*, 3d ed. London, 1888.

Nys, Ernest, *Le Droit Romain, Le Droit des Gens, et Le Collège des Docteurs en Droit Civil.* Bruxelles, 1910.

——, *Les Origines du Droit International.* Bruxelles et Paris, 1894.

Ortolan, Eugene, *Explication Historique des Instituts de l'Empereur Justinien*, 8th ed., 3 vols. Paris, 1870.

Ovid, *Metamorphoseon.*

Plautus, *Rudens.*

Plutarch, *Lives*, Dryden's Translation, revised by A. H. Clough, 5 vols. London, 1859.

Polybius, *The Histories*. Translated by W. R. Paton, 6 vols. London and New York, 1922.

Savigny, F. C., von, *Geschichte des Römischen Rechts im Mittelalter*, 2d ed., 6 vols. Heidelberg, 1834–51.

Seneca, *De Beneficiis*.

Stintzing, R., *Geschichte der Deutschen Rechtswissenschaft*, 2 vols. München und Leipzig, 1880–84; completed by Landsberg, E., a third volume, divided into 3, 3.1, 3.2. Text, and 3.2. Notes, 1896–1910.

Strabo, *Geography*, 3 vols. Translated by H. C. Hamilton and William Falconer. London, 1857.

Thézard, L., *Répétitions Ecrites sur le Droit Romain*, 2d ed. Paris, 1873.

Woolf, C. N. S., *Bartolus of Sassoferrato*. Cambridge, 1913.

A General Survey of . . . Continental Legal History, by various European Authors, vol. 1 of *Continental Legal History Series*. Edited by the Association of American Law Schools. Boston, 1912.

Bei Fragen zur Produktsicherheit wenden Sie sich bitte an:
If you have any questions regarding product safety,
please contact:

Walter de Gruyter GmbH
Genthiner Straße 13
10785 Berlin
productsafety@degruyterbrill.com